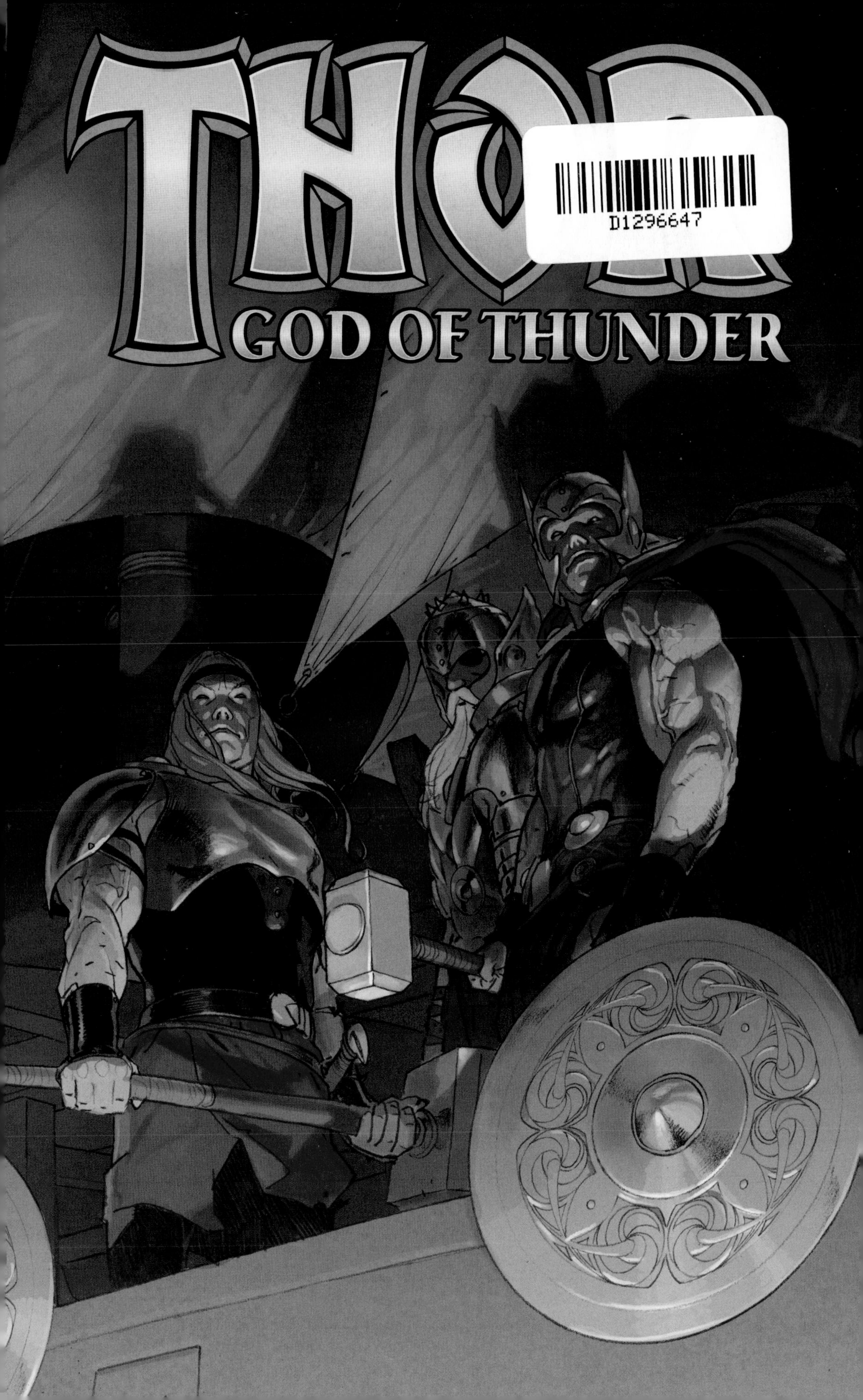
THOR
GOD OF THUNDER

Collection Editor: **Jennifer Grünwald**

Assistant Editor: **Sarah Brunstad**

Associate Managing Editor: **Alex Starbuck**

Editor, Special Projects: **Mark D. Beazley**

Senior Editor, Special Projects: **Jeff Youngquist**

SVP Print, Sales & Marketing: **David Gabriel**

Book Design: **Jeff Powell**

Editor in Chief: **Axel Alonso**

Chief Creative Officer: **Joe Quesada**

Publisher: **Dan Buckley**

Executive Producer: **Alan Fine**

THOR: GOD OF THUNDER VOL. 2 — GODBOMB. Contains material originally published in magazine form as THOR: GOD OF THUNDER #6-11. First printing 2014. ISBN# 978-0-7851-6698-6. Published by MARVEL WORLDWIDE, INC., a subsidiary of MARVEL ENTERTAINMENT, LLC. OFFICE OF PUBLICATION: 135 West 50th Street, New York, NY 10020. Copyright © 2013 and 2014 Marvel Characters, Inc. All rights reserved. All characters featured in this issue and the distinctive names and likenesses thereof, and all related indicia are trademarks of Marvel Characters, Inc. No similarity between any of the names, characters, persons, and/or institutions in this magazine with those of any living or dead person or institution is intended, and any such similarity which may exist is purely coincidental. **Printed in the U.S.A.** ALAN FINE, EVP - Office of the President, Marvel Worldwide, Inc. and EVP & CMO Marvel Characters B.V.; DAN BUCKLEY, Publisher & President - Print, Animation & Digital Divisions; JOE QUESADA, Chief Creative Officer; TOM BREVOORT, SVP of Publishing; DAVID BOGART, SVP of Operations & Procurement, Publishing; C.B. CEBULSKI, SVP of Creator & Content Development; DAVID GABRIEL, SVP Print, Sales & Marketing; JIM O'KEEFE, VP of Operations & Logistics; DAN CARR, Executive Director of Publishing Technology; SUSAN CRESPI, Editorial Operations Manager; ALEX MORALES, Publishing Operations Manager; STAN LEE, Chairman Emeritus. For information regarding advertising in Marvel Comics or on Marvel.com, please contact Niza Disla, Director of Marvel Partnerships, at ndisla@marvel.com. For Marvel subscription inquiries, please call 800-217-9158. **Manufactured between 4/18/2014 and 5/26/2014 by R.R. DONNELLEY, INC., SALEM, VA, USA.**

10 9 8 7 6 5 4 3 2 1

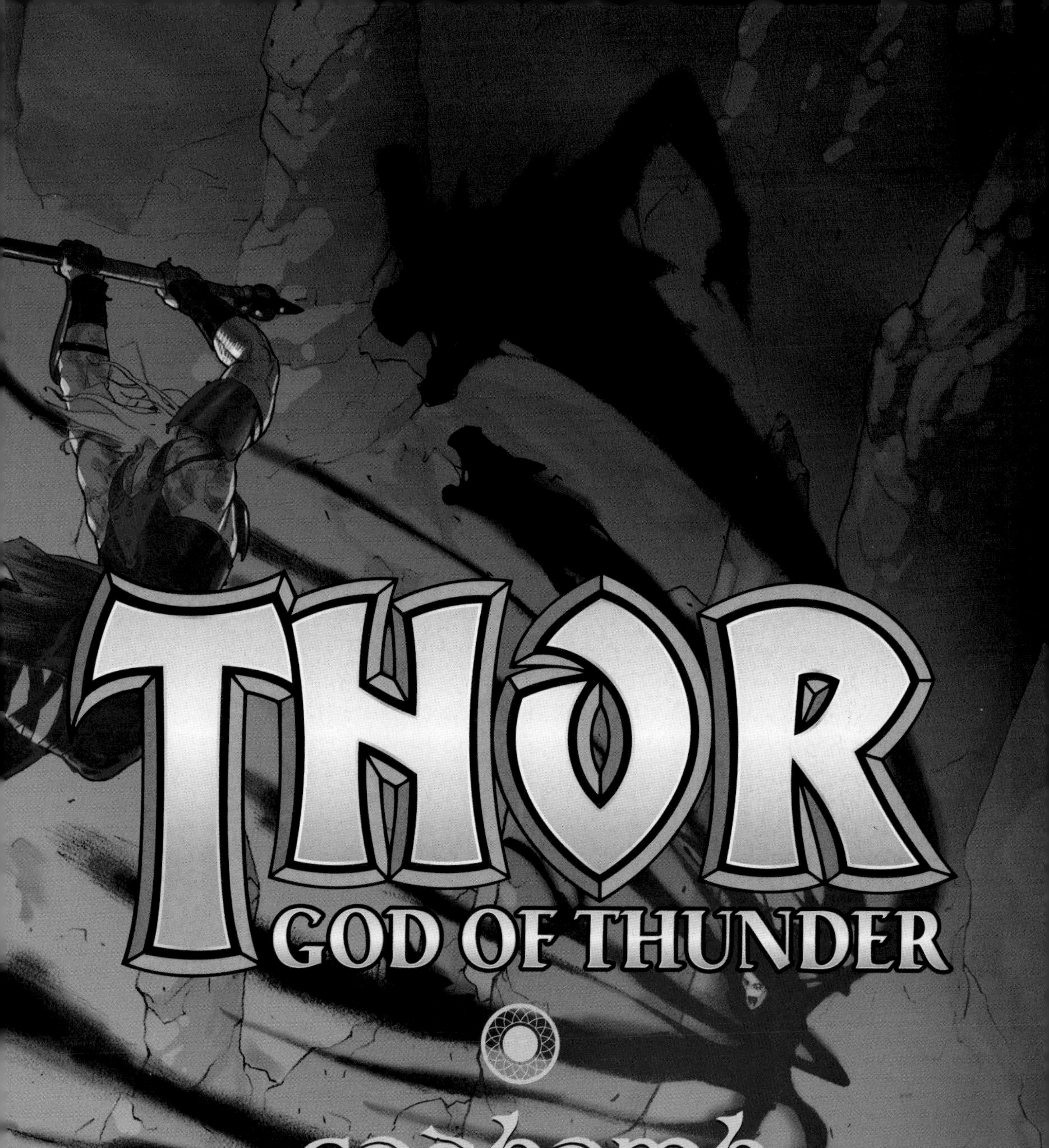

THOR
GOD OF THUNDER
GODBOMB

WRITER
JASON AARON

ARTIST, #7-11
ESAD RIBIC

PENCILER, #6
BUTCH GUICE

INKER, #6
TOM PALMER

COLOR ARTIST
IVE SVORCINA

LETTERER
VC'S JOE SABINO

COVER ART
ESAD RIBIC

ASSISTANT EDITOR
JAKE THOMAS

EDITOR
LAUREN SANKOVITCH

PREVIOUSLY

In a crusade spanning millennia, a creature known
only as Gorr the God Butcher has vowed to kill
all deities across the cosmos. After numerous
encounters with Thor over the centuries, the God
Butcher has finally revealed the horrific endgame to
his mad quest.

But who is this strange being of deadly reckoning?

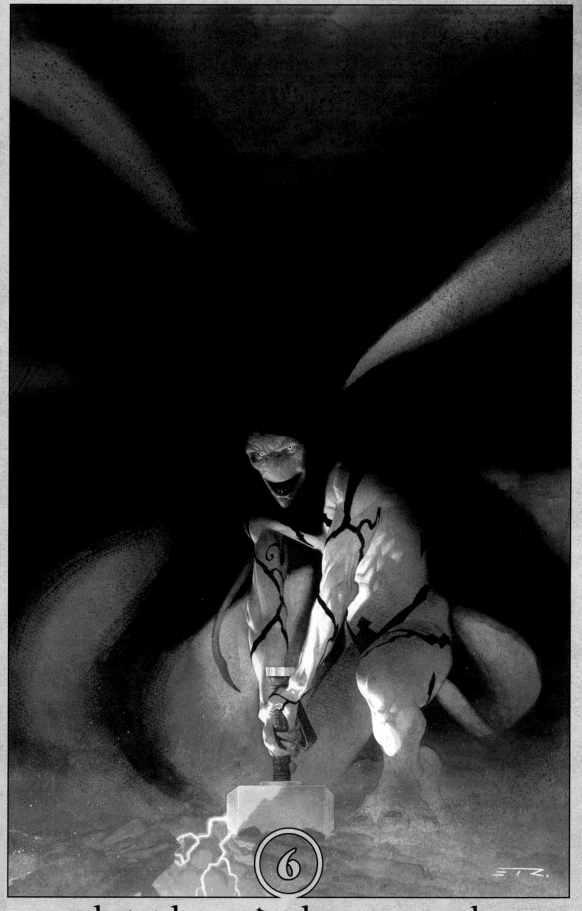

WHAT THE GODS HAVE WROUGHT

3000 Years Ago, A Planet Without A Name.

I'M *HUNGRY*, MOMMA.

I KNOW, MY LOVE. THAT'S WHY WE'RE HERE.

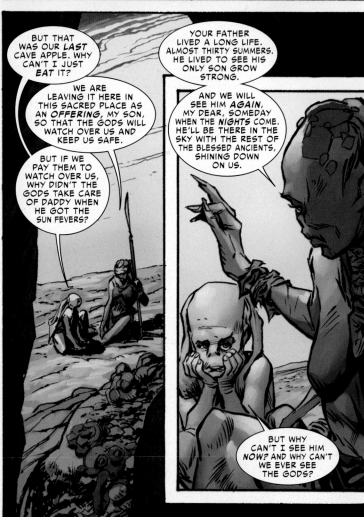

BUT THAT WAS OUR *LAST* CAVE APPLE. WHY CAN'T I JUST *EAT* IT?

WE ARE LEAVING IT HERE IN THIS SACRED PLACE AS AN *OFFERING*, MY SON, SO THAT THE GODS WILL WATCH OVER US AND KEEP US SAFE.

BUT IF WE PAY THEM TO WATCH OVER US, WHY DIDN'T THE GODS TAKE CARE OF DADDY WHEN HE GOT THE SUN FEVERS?

YOUR FATHER LIVED A LONG LIFE. ALMOST THIRTY SUMMERS. HE LIVED TO SEE HIS ONLY SON GROW STRONG.

AND WE WILL SEE HIM *AGAIN*, MY DEAR, SOMEDAY WHEN THE *NIGHTS* COME. HE'LL BE THERE IN THE SKY WITH THE REST OF THE BLESSED ANCIENTS, SHINING DOWN ON US.

BUT WHY CAN'T I SEE HIM *NOW?* AND WHY CAN'T WE EVER SEE THE GODS?

YOU WILL SEE THEM SOMEDAY, ALL AROUND YOU, ONCE YOU TRULY BELIEVE.

I DO, MOMMA.

I THINK I DO.

ALWAYS HONOR THE GODS, MY SON, AND THEY WILL SHOWER YOU WITH *BLESSINGS*, AS THEY HAVE ME. *YOU* ARE MY GREATEST BLESSING. MY *DARLING* LITTLE BOY.

MY BELOVED *GORR.*

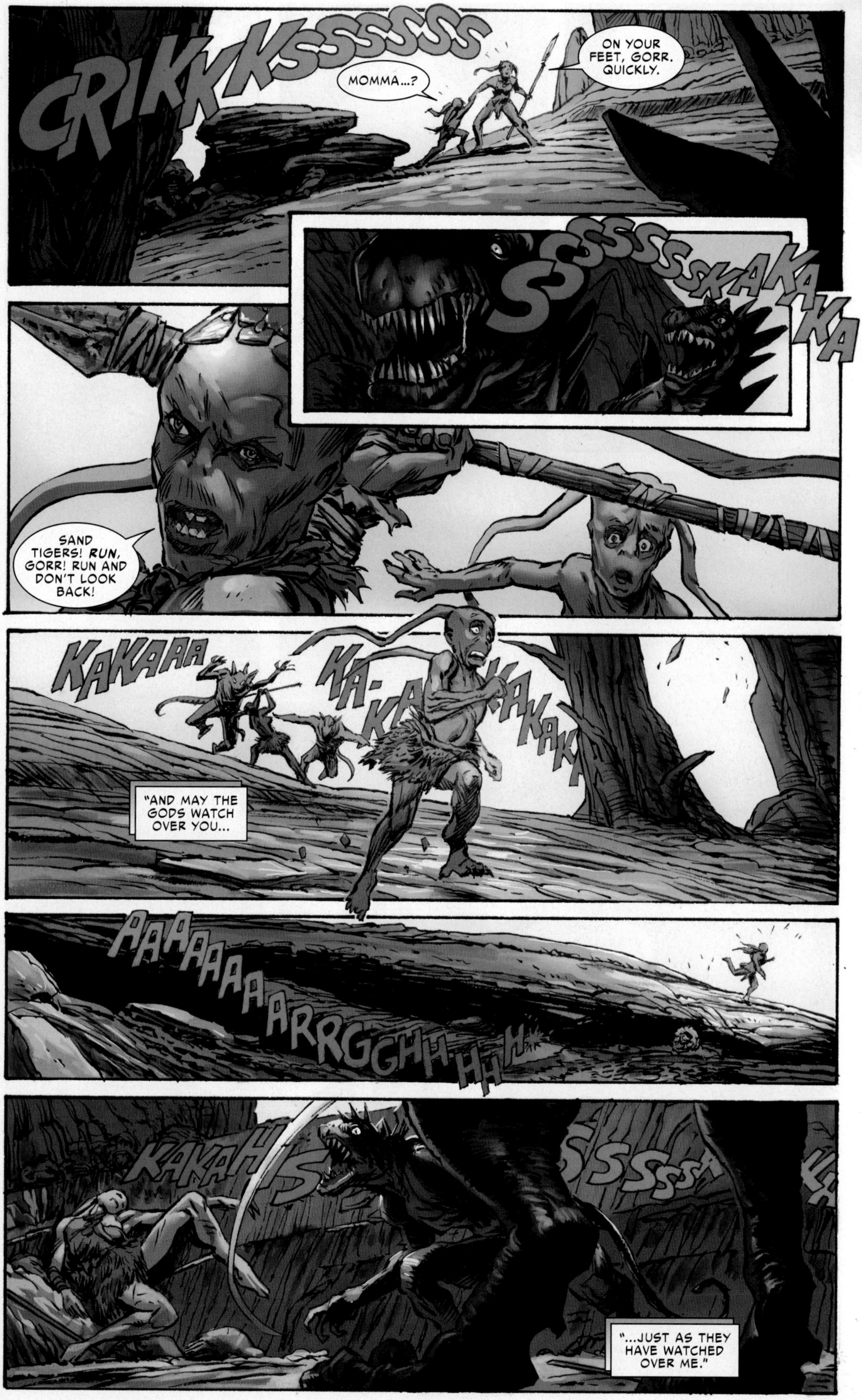
CRIKKKSSSSSSS
MOMMA...?
ON YOUR FEET, GORR. QUICKLY.
SSSSSSSKAKAKAKA
SAND TIGERS! RUN, GORR! RUN AND DON'T LOOK BACK!
KAKAAA
KA-KA-KAKAKAKA
"AND MAY THE GODS WATCH OVER YOU...
AAAAAAAAARRGGHHHHH
KAKAH
SSSSSS
"...JUST AS THEY HAVE WATCHED OVER ME."

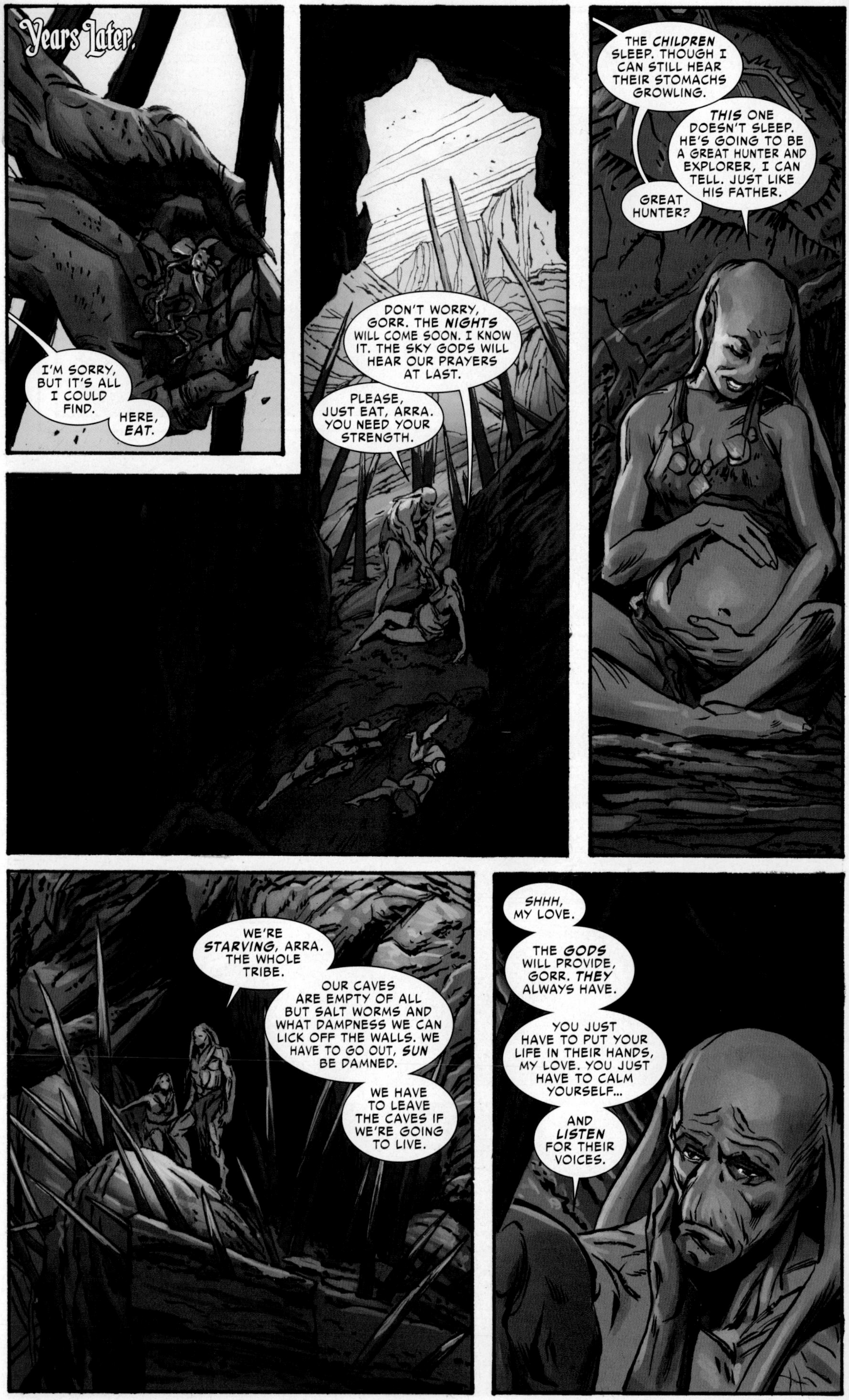
Years Later.
I'M SORRY, BUT IT'S ALL I COULD FIND.
HERE, EAT.
DON'T WORRY, GORR. THE NIGHTS WILL COME SOON. I KNOW IT. THE SKY GODS WILL HEAR OUR PRAYERS AT LAST.
PLEASE, JUST EAT, ARRA. YOU NEED YOUR STRENGTH.
THE CHILDREN SLEEP. THOUGH I CAN STILL HEAR THEIR STOMACHS GROWLING.
THIS ONE DOESN'T SLEEP. HE'S GOING TO BE A GREAT HUNTER AND EXPLORER, I CAN TELL. JUST LIKE HIS FATHER.
GREAT HUNTER?
WE'RE STARVING, ARRA. THE WHOLE TRIBE.
OUR CAVES ARE EMPTY OF ALL BUT SALT WORMS AND WHAT DAMPNESS WE CAN LICK OFF THE WALLS. WE HAVE TO GO OUT, SUN BE DAMNED.
WE HAVE TO LEAVE THE CAVES IF WE'RE GOING TO LIVE.
SHHH, MY LOVE.
THE GODS WILL PROVIDE, GORR. THEY ALWAYS HAVE.
YOU JUST HAVE TO PUT YOUR LIFE IN THEIR HANDS, MY LOVE. YOU JUST HAVE TO CALM YOURSELF...
AND LISTEN FOR THEIR VOICES.

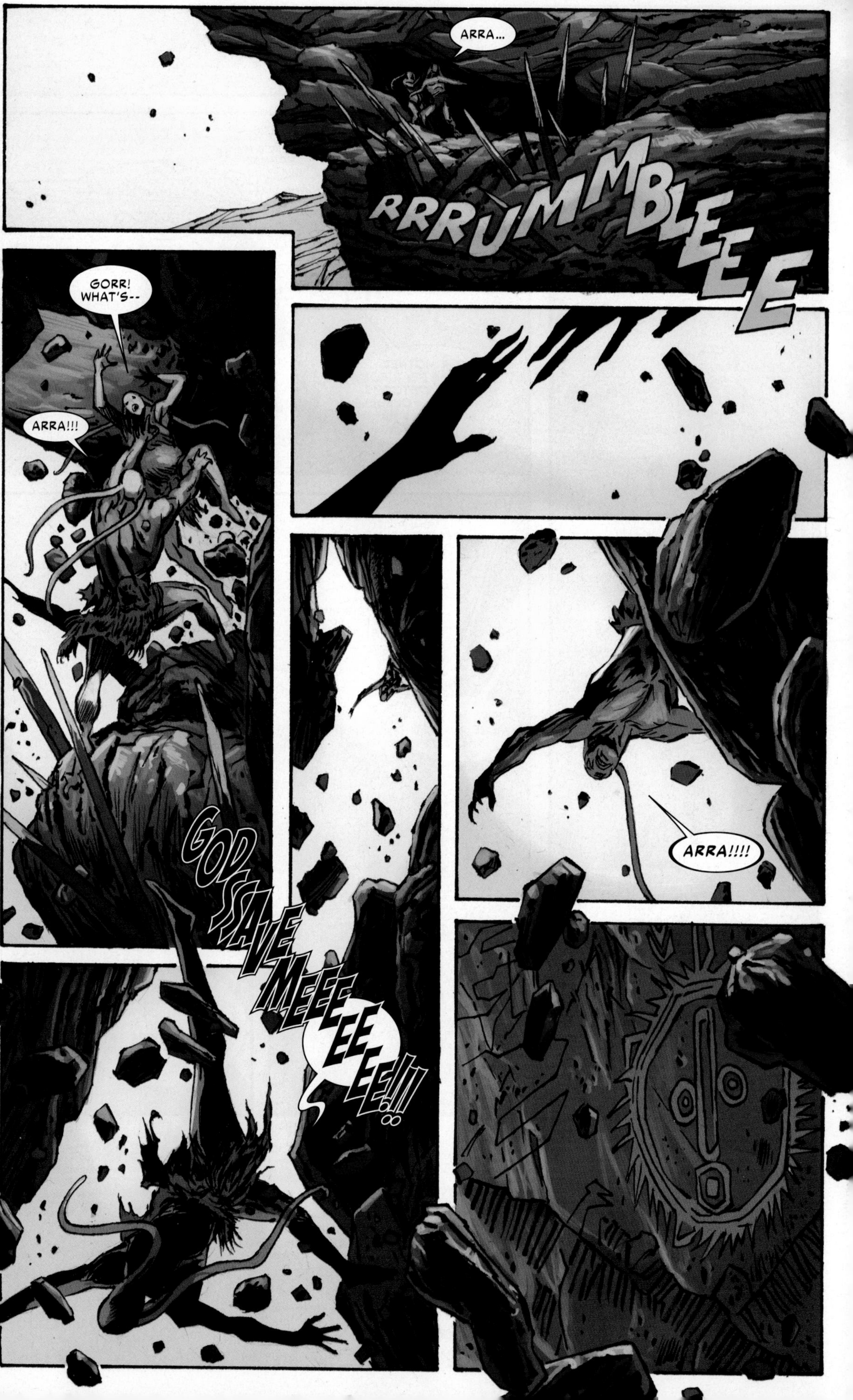
ARRA...
RRRUMMMBLEEEE
GORR! WHAT'S--
ARRA!!!
ARRA!!!!
GODSSAVEMEEEEEEEE!!!

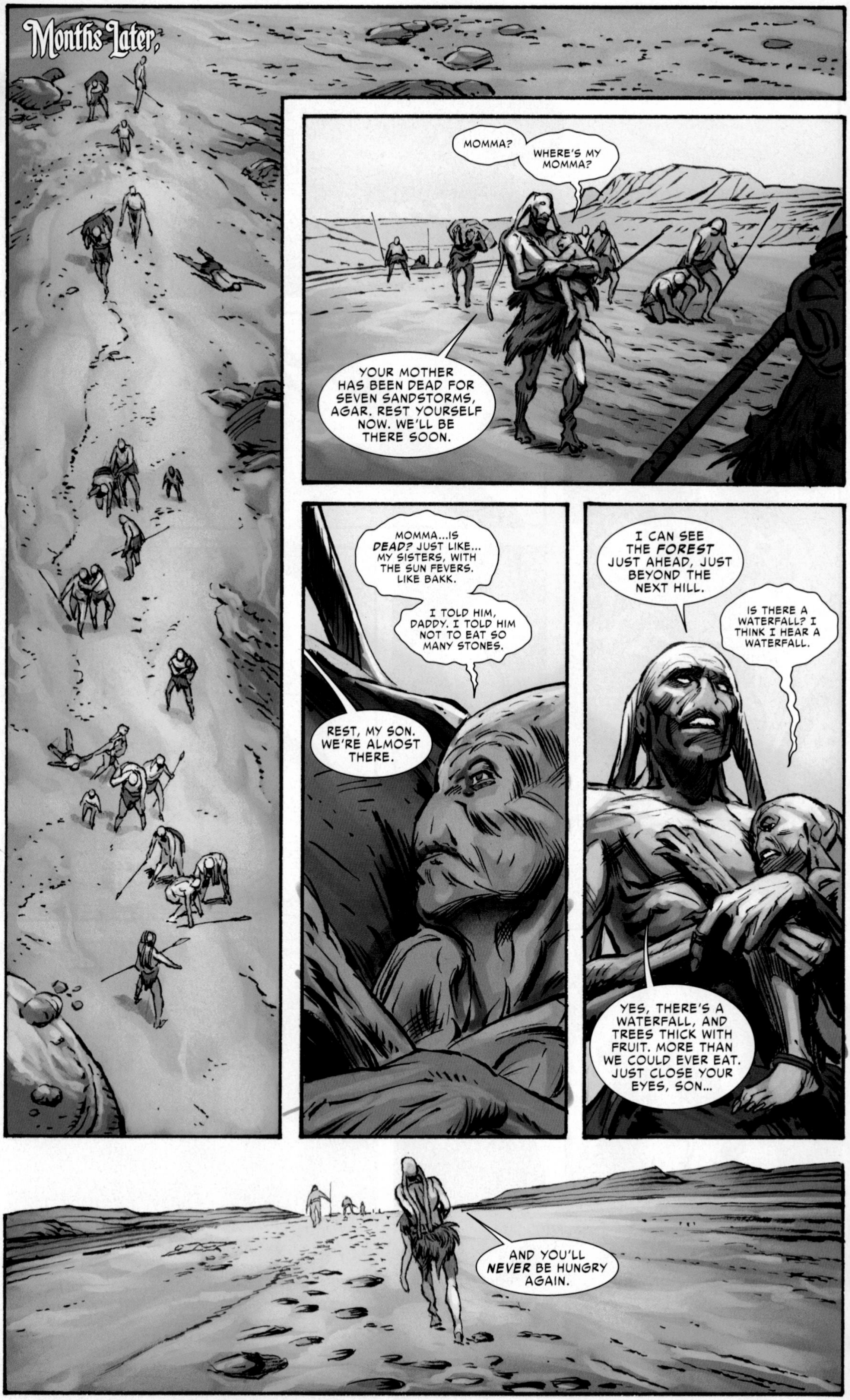
Months Later,
MOMMA?
WHERE'S MY MOMMA?
YOUR MOTHER HAS BEEN DEAD FOR SEVEN SANDSTORMS, AGAR. REST YOURSELF NOW. WE'LL BE THERE SOON.
MOMMA...IS DEAD? JUST LIKE... MY SISTERS, WITH THE SUN FEVERS. LIKE BAKK.
I TOLD HIM, DADDY. I TOLD HIM NOT TO EAT SO MANY STONES.
REST, MY SON. WE'RE ALMOST THERE.
I CAN SEE THE FOREST JUST AHEAD, JUST BEYOND THE NEXT HILL.
IS THERE A WATERFALL? I THINK I HEAR A WATERFALL.
YES, THERE'S A WATERFALL, AND TREES THICK WITH FRUIT. MORE THAN WE COULD EVER EAT. JUST CLOSE YOUR EYES, SON...
AND YOU'LL NEVER BE HUNGRY AGAIN.

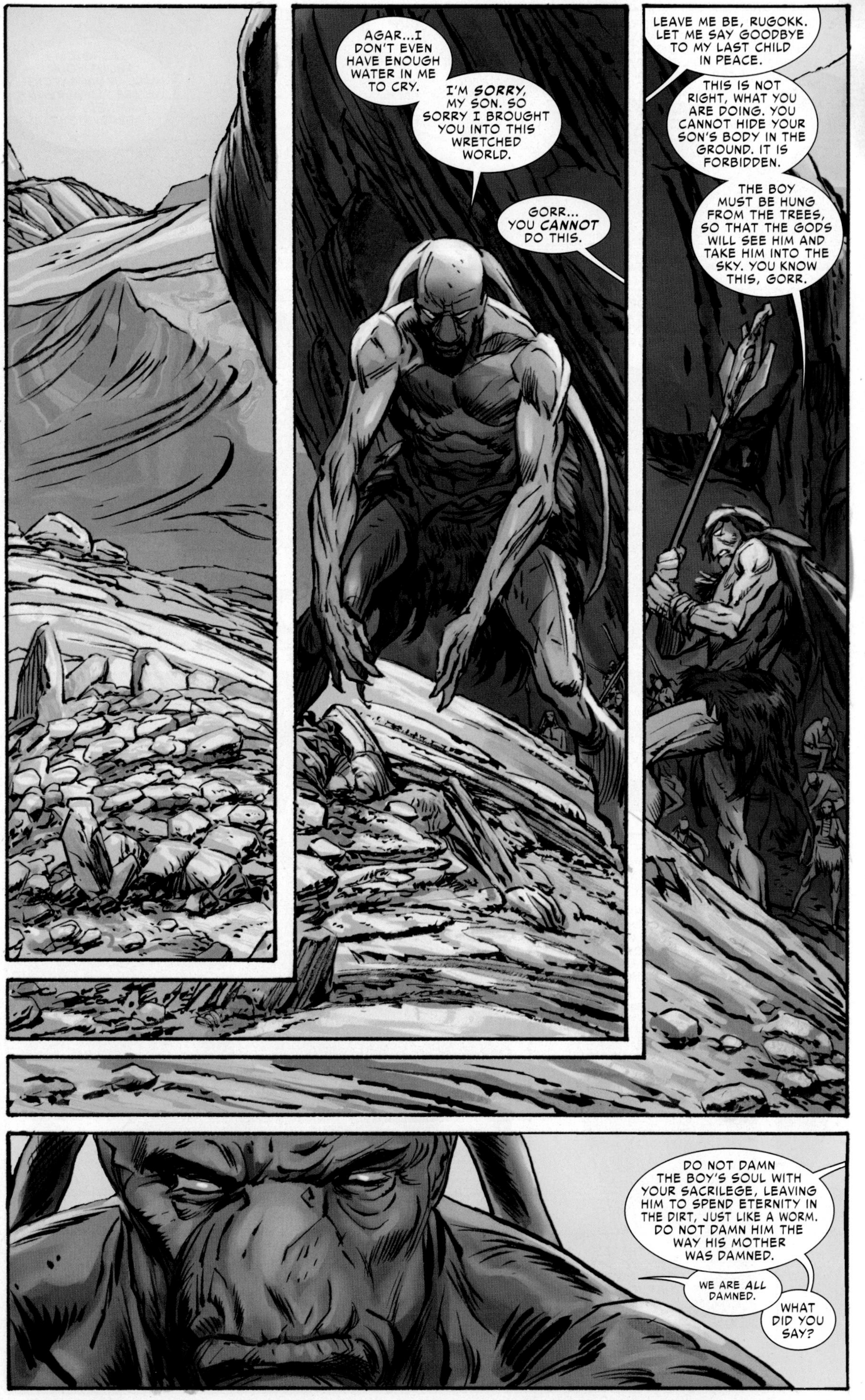

AGAR...I DON'T EVEN HAVE ENOUGH WATER IN ME TO CRY.
I'M SORRY, MY SON. SO SORRY I BROUGHT YOU INTO THIS WRETCHED WORLD.
GORR... YOU CANNOT DO THIS.
LEAVE ME BE, RUGOKK. LET ME SAY GOODBYE TO MY LAST CHILD IN PEACE.
THIS IS NOT RIGHT, WHAT YOU ARE DOING. YOU CANNOT HIDE YOUR SON'S BODY IN THE GROUND. IT IS FORBIDDEN.
THE BOY MUST BE HUNG FROM THE TREES, SO THAT THE GODS WILL SEE HIM AND TAKE HIM INTO THE SKY. YOU KNOW THIS, GORR.
DO NOT DAMN THE BOY'S SOUL WITH YOUR SACRILEGE, LEAVING HIM TO SPEND ETERNITY IN THE DIRT, JUST LIKE A WORM. DO NOT DAMN HIM THE WAY HIS MOTHER WAS DAMNED.
WE ARE ALL DAMNED.
WHAT DID YOU SAY?

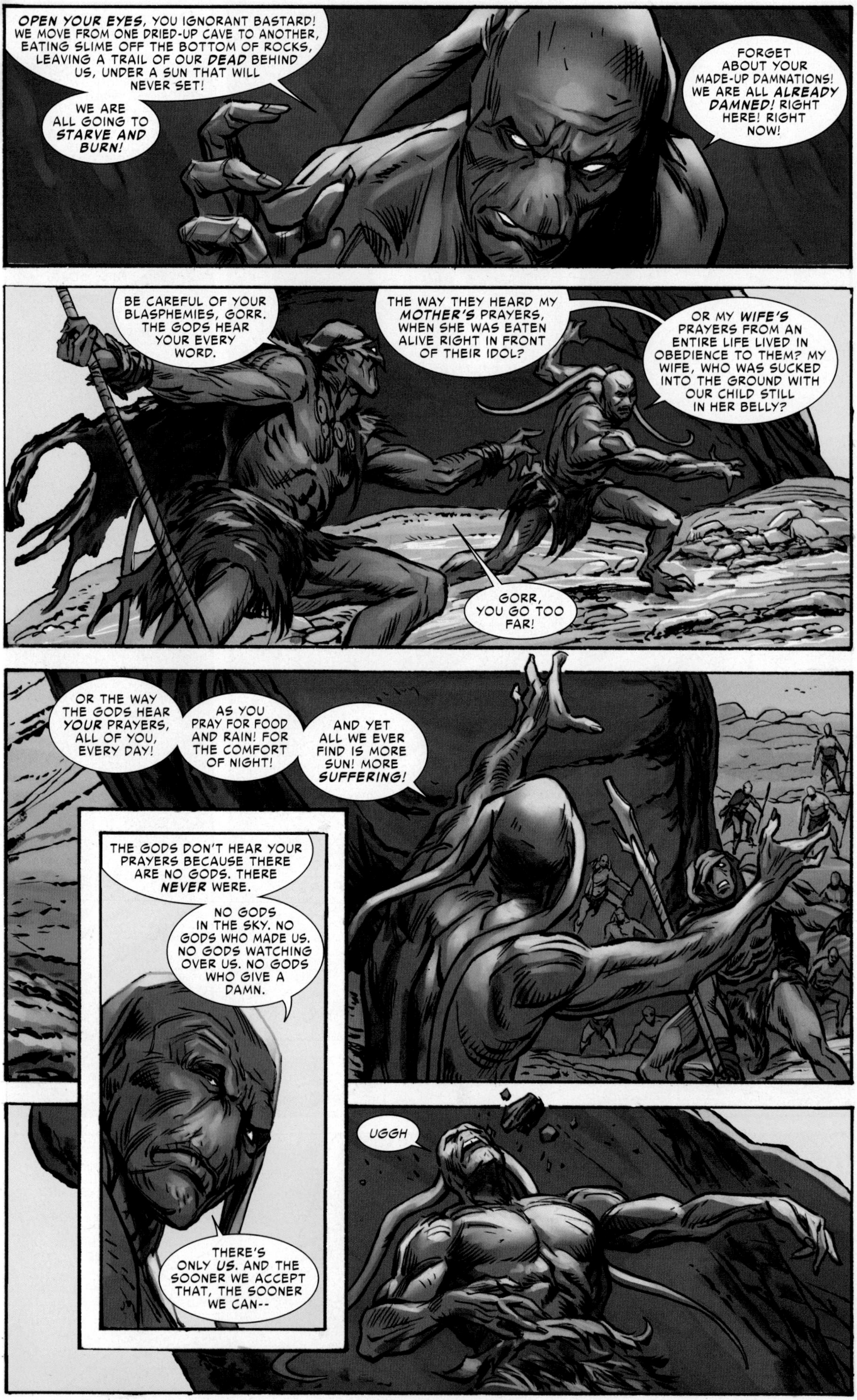
OPEN YOUR EYES, YOU IGNORANT BASTARD! WE MOVE FROM ONE DRIED-UP CAVE TO ANOTHER, EATING SLIME OFF THE BOTTOM OF ROCKS, LEAVING A TRAIL OF OUR DEAD BEHIND US, UNDER A SUN THAT WILL NEVER SET!
WE ARE ALL GOING TO STARVE AND BURN!
FORGET ABOUT YOUR MADE-UP DAMNATIONS! WE ARE ALL ALREADY DAMNED! RIGHT HERE! RIGHT NOW!
BE CAREFUL OF YOUR BLASPHEMIES, GORR. THE GODS HEAR YOUR EVERY WORD.
THE WAY THEY HEARD MY MOTHER'S PRAYERS, WHEN SHE WAS EATEN ALIVE RIGHT IN FRONT OF THEIR IDOL?
OR MY WIFE'S PRAYERS FROM AN ENTIRE LIFE LIVED IN OBEDIENCE TO THEM? MY WIFE, WHO WAS SUCKED INTO THE GROUND WITH OUR CHILD STILL IN HER BELLY?
GORR, YOU GO TOO FAR!
OR THE WAY THE GODS HEAR YOUR PRAYERS, ALL OF YOU, EVERY DAY!
AS YOU PRAY FOR FOOD AND RAIN! FOR THE COMFORT OF NIGHT!
AND YET ALL WE EVER FIND IS MORE SUN! MORE SUFFERING!
THE GODS DON'T HEAR YOUR PRAYERS BECAUSE THERE ARE NO GODS. THERE NEVER WERE.
NO GODS IN THE SKY. NO GODS WHO MADE US. NO GODS WATCHING OVER US. NO GODS WHO GIVE A DAMN.
THERE'S ONLY US. AND THE SOONER WE ACCEPT THAT, THE SOONER WE CAN--
UGGH

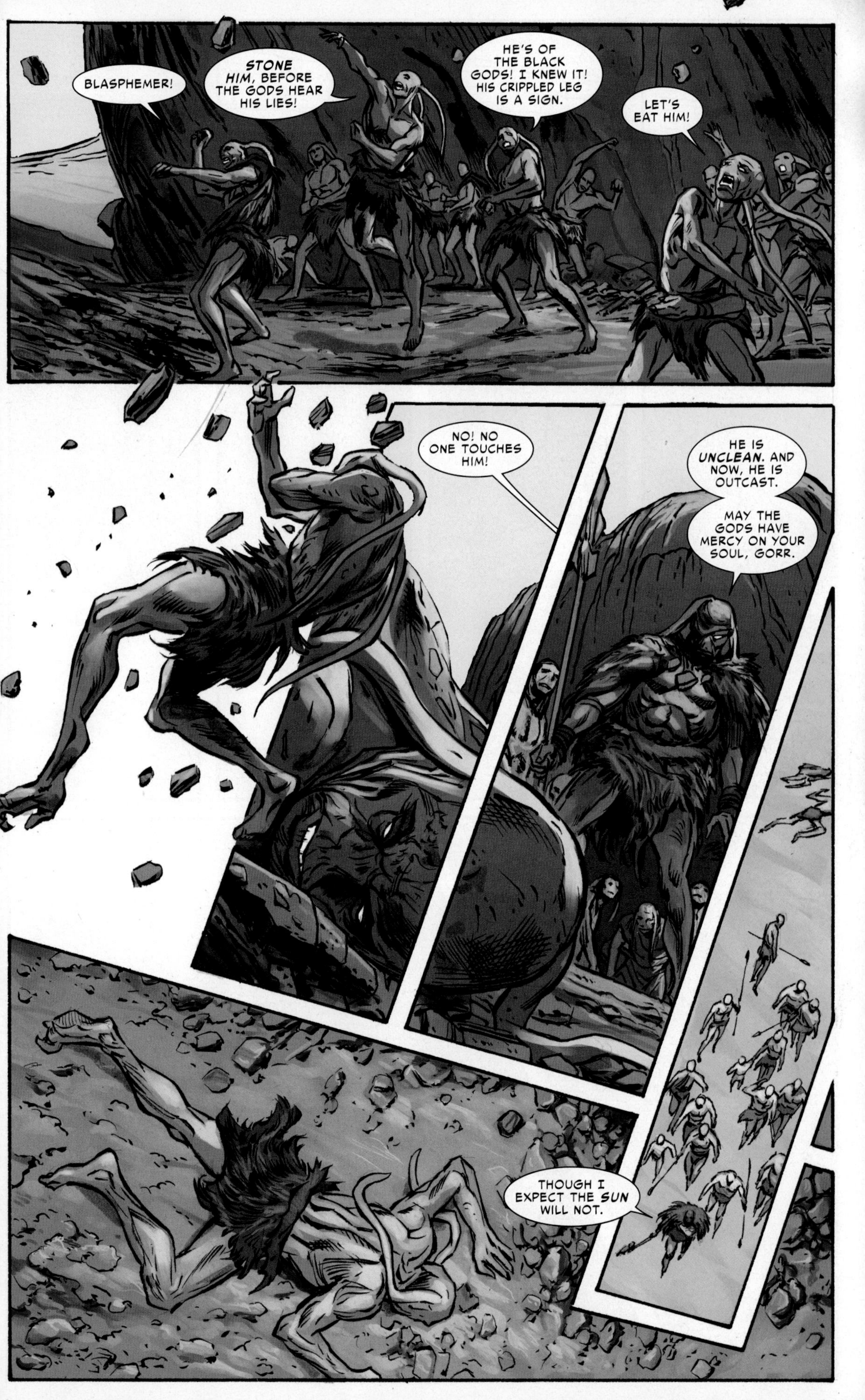
BLASPHEMER!
STONE HIM, BEFORE THE GODS HEAR HIS LIES!
HE'S OF THE BLACK GODS! I KNEW IT! HIS CRIPPLED LEG IS A SIGN.
LET'S EAT HIM!
NO! NO ONE TOUCHES HIM!
HE IS UNCLEAN. AND NOW, HE IS OUTCAST.
MAY THE GODS HAVE MERCY ON YOUR SOUL, GORR.
THOUGH I EXPECT THE SUN WILL NOT.

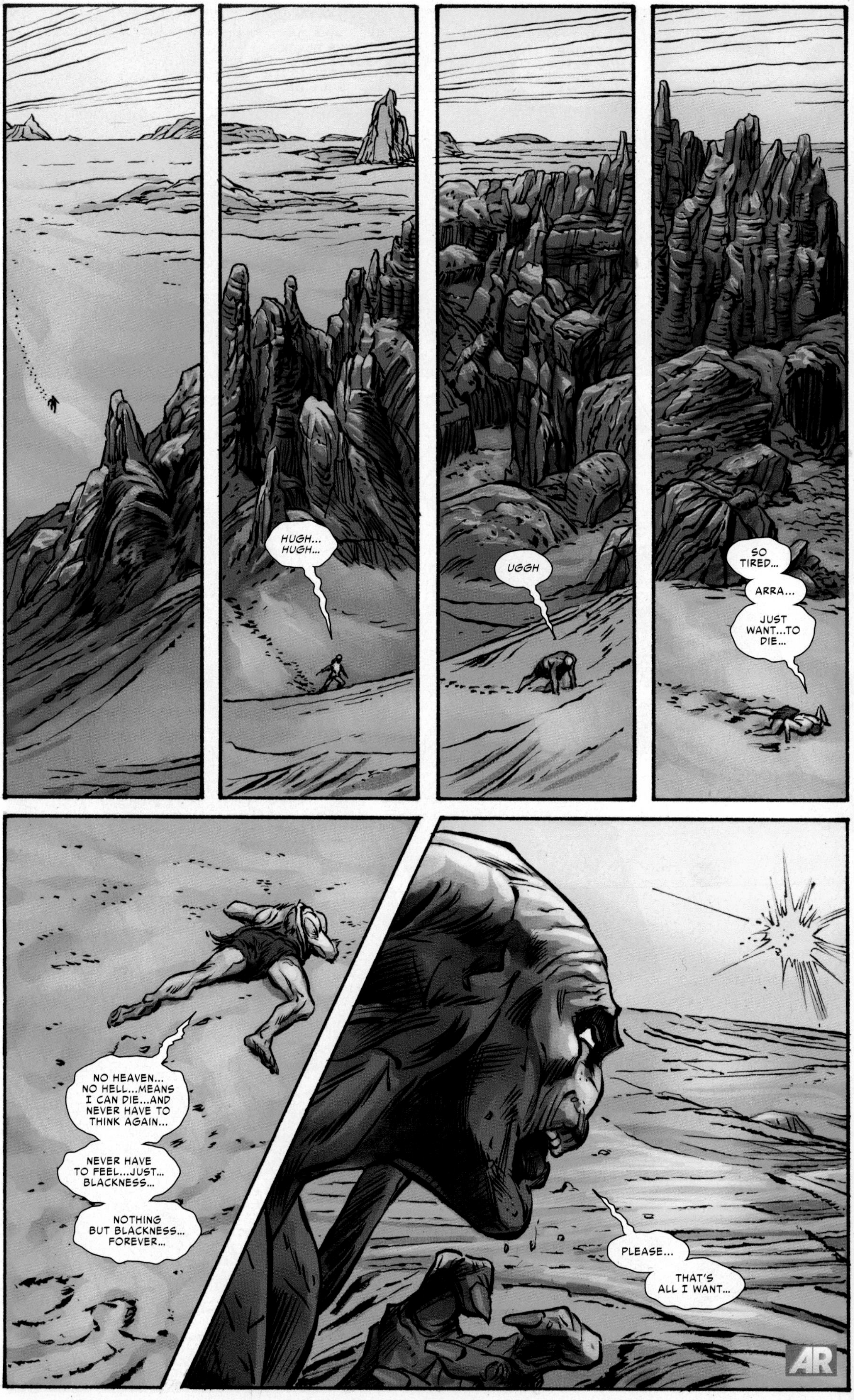
HUGH... HUGH...
UGGH
SO TIRED...
ARRA...
JUST WANT...TO DIE...
NO HEAVEN... NO HELL...MEANS I CAN DIE...AND NEVER HAVE TO THINK AGAIN...
NEVER HAVE TO FEEL...JUST... BLACKNESS...
NOTHING BUT BLACKNESS... FOREVER...
PLEASE...
THAT'S ALL I WANT...

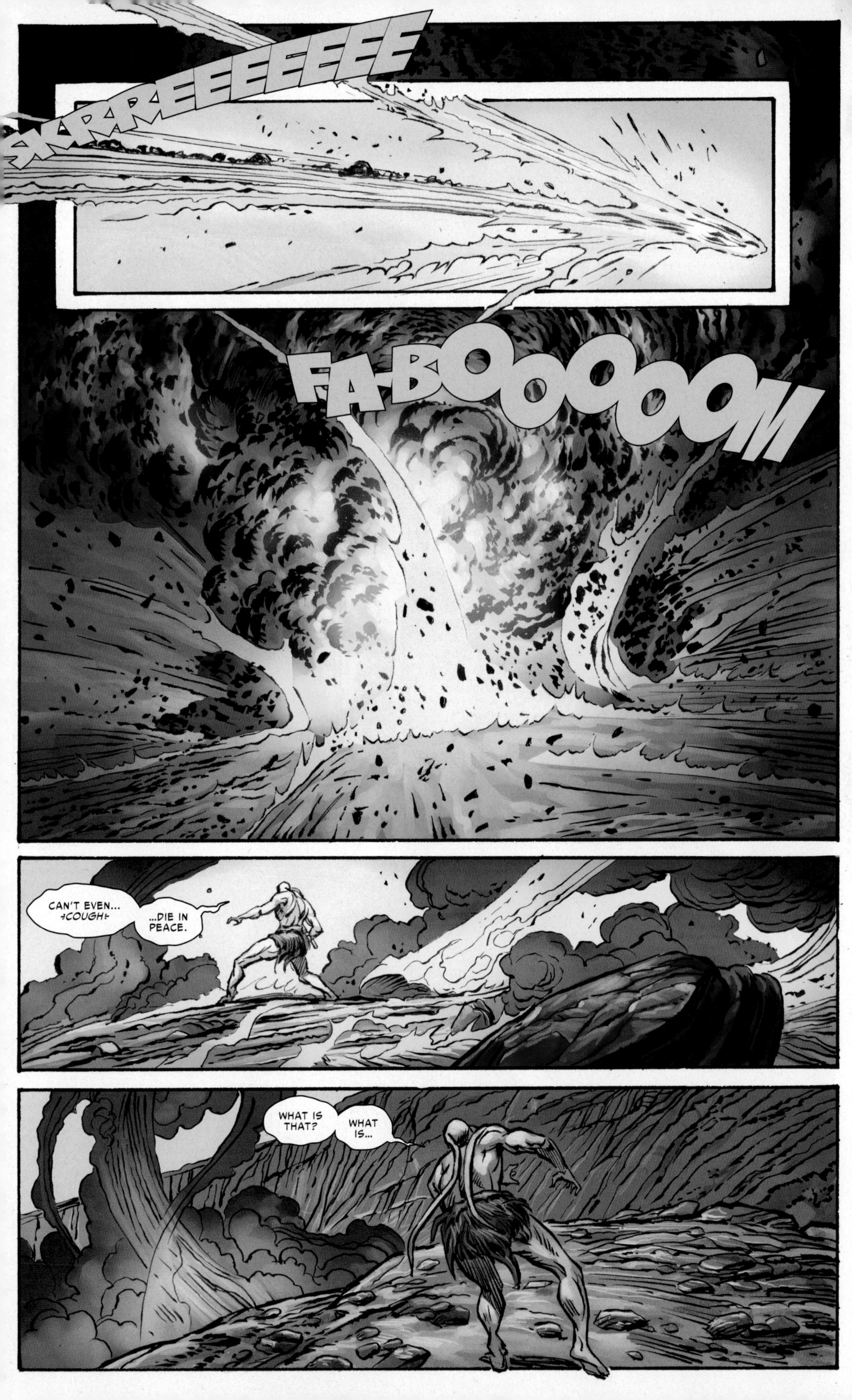
SKRREEEEEEEE
FA-BOOOOOOM
CAN'T EVEN... -COUGH-
...DIE IN PEACE.
WHAT IS THAT?
WHAT IS...

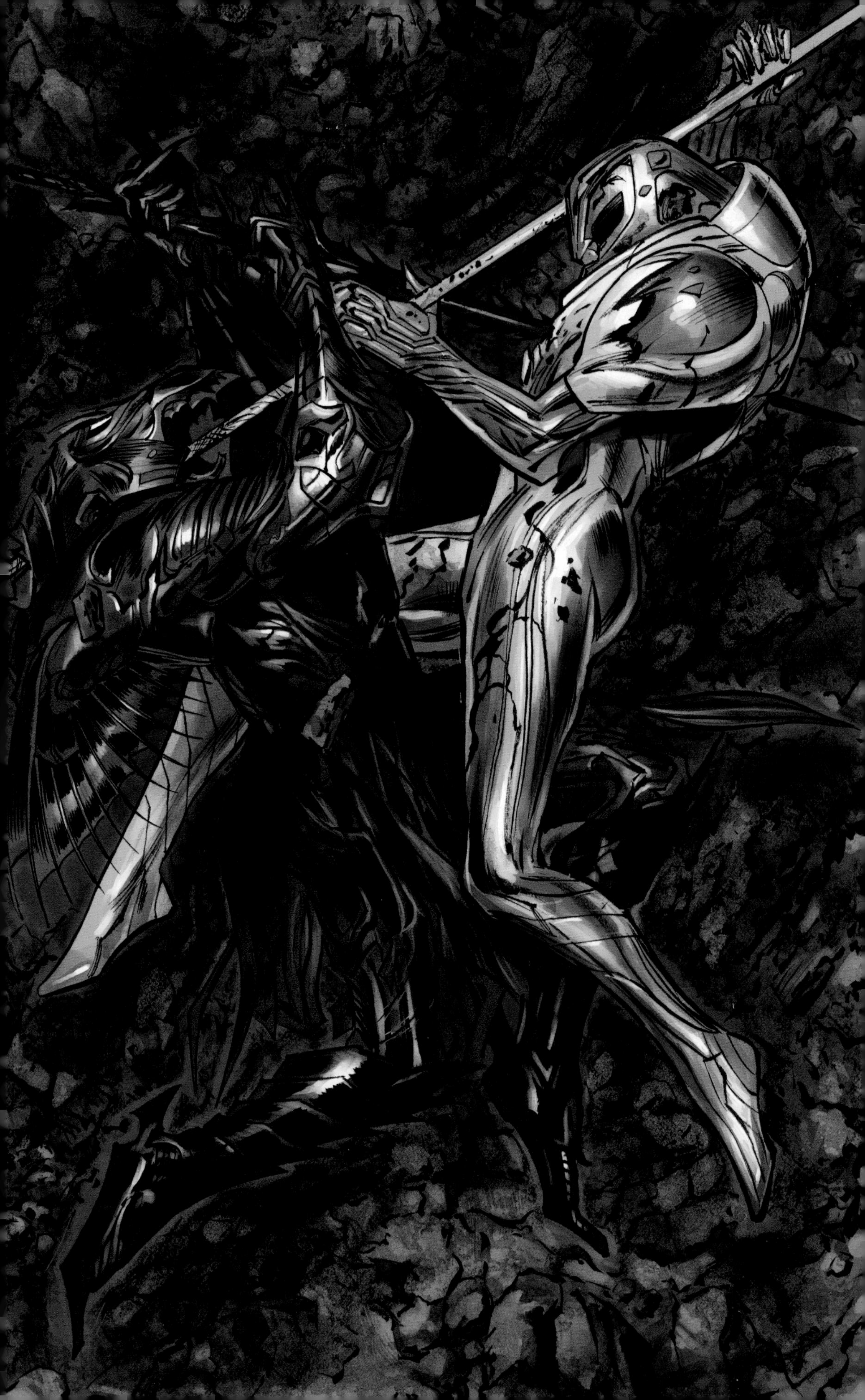

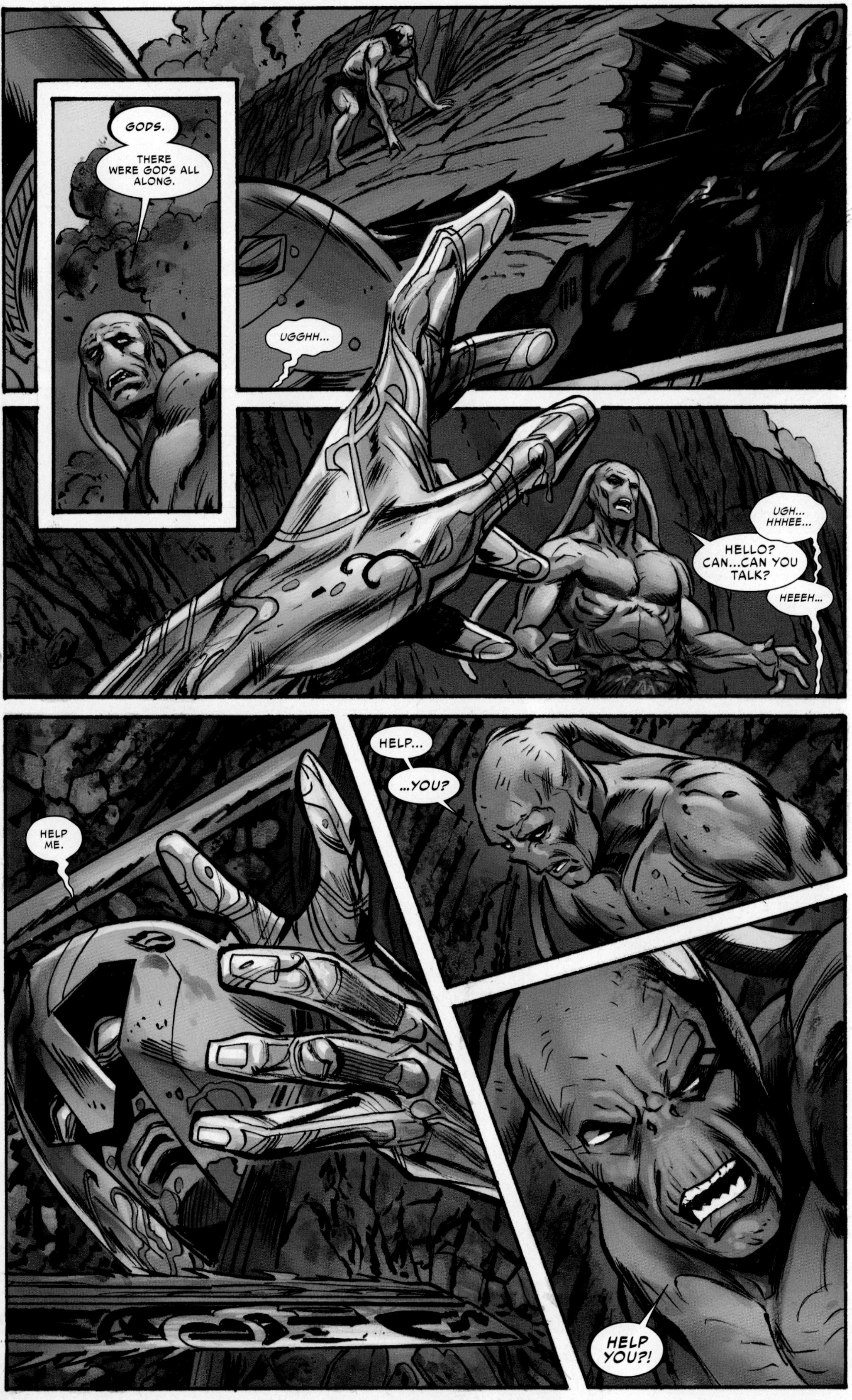
GODS.
THERE WERE GODS ALL ALONG.
UGGHH...
UGH... HHHEE...
HELLO? CAN...CAN YOU TALK?
HEEEH...
HELP ME.
HELP...
...YOU?
HELP YOU?!

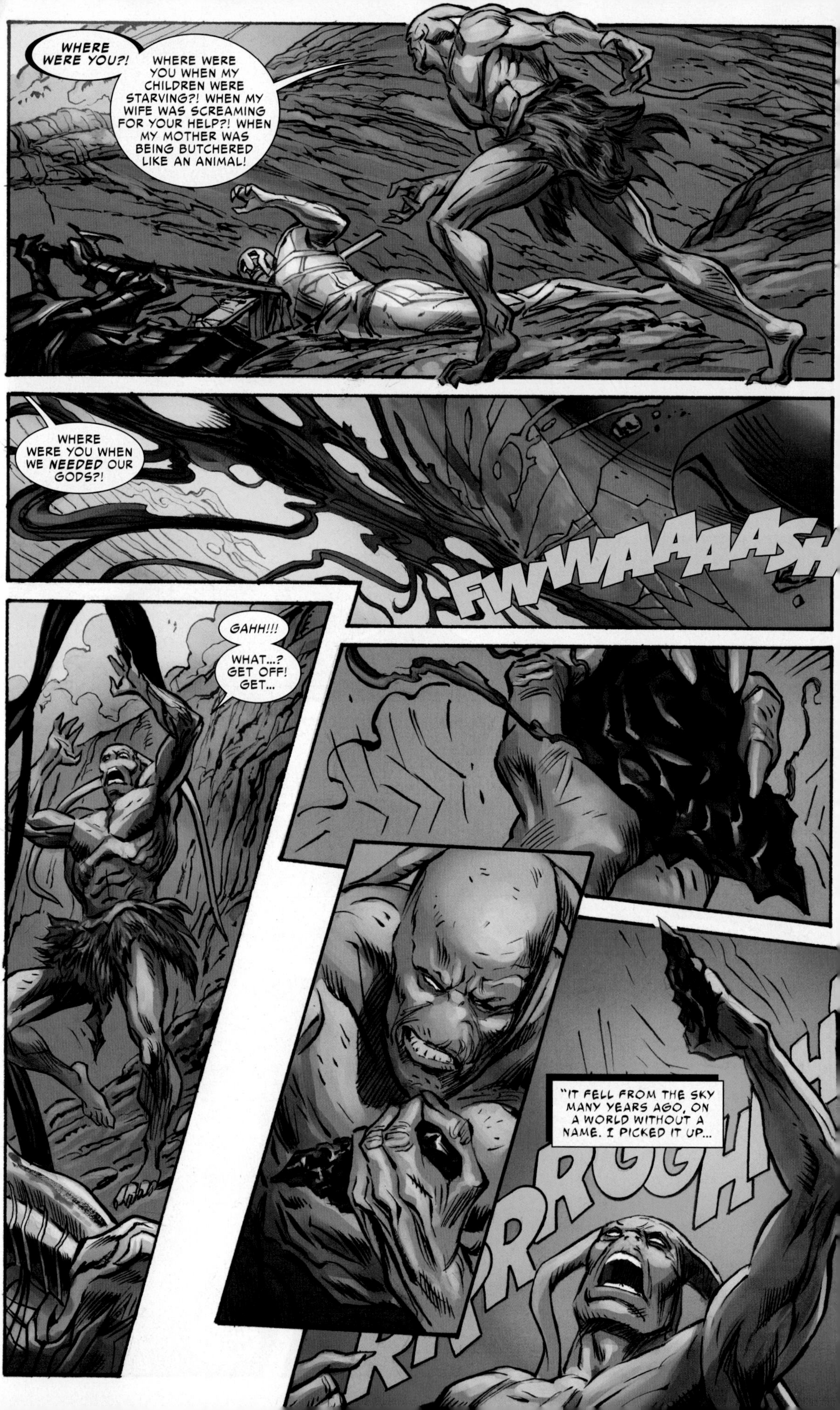

WHERE WERE YOU?!
WHERE WERE YOU WHEN MY CHILDREN WERE STARVING?! WHEN MY WIFE WAS SCREAMING FOR YOUR HELP?! WHEN MY MOTHER WAS BEING BUTCHERED LIKE AN ANIMAL!
WHERE WERE YOU WHEN WE NEEDED OUR GODS?!
FWWAAAASH
GAHH!!!
WHAT...? GET OFF! GET...
"IT FELL FROM THE SKY MANY YEARS AGO, ON A WORLD WITHOUT A NAME. I PICKED IT UP...
RRRGGH

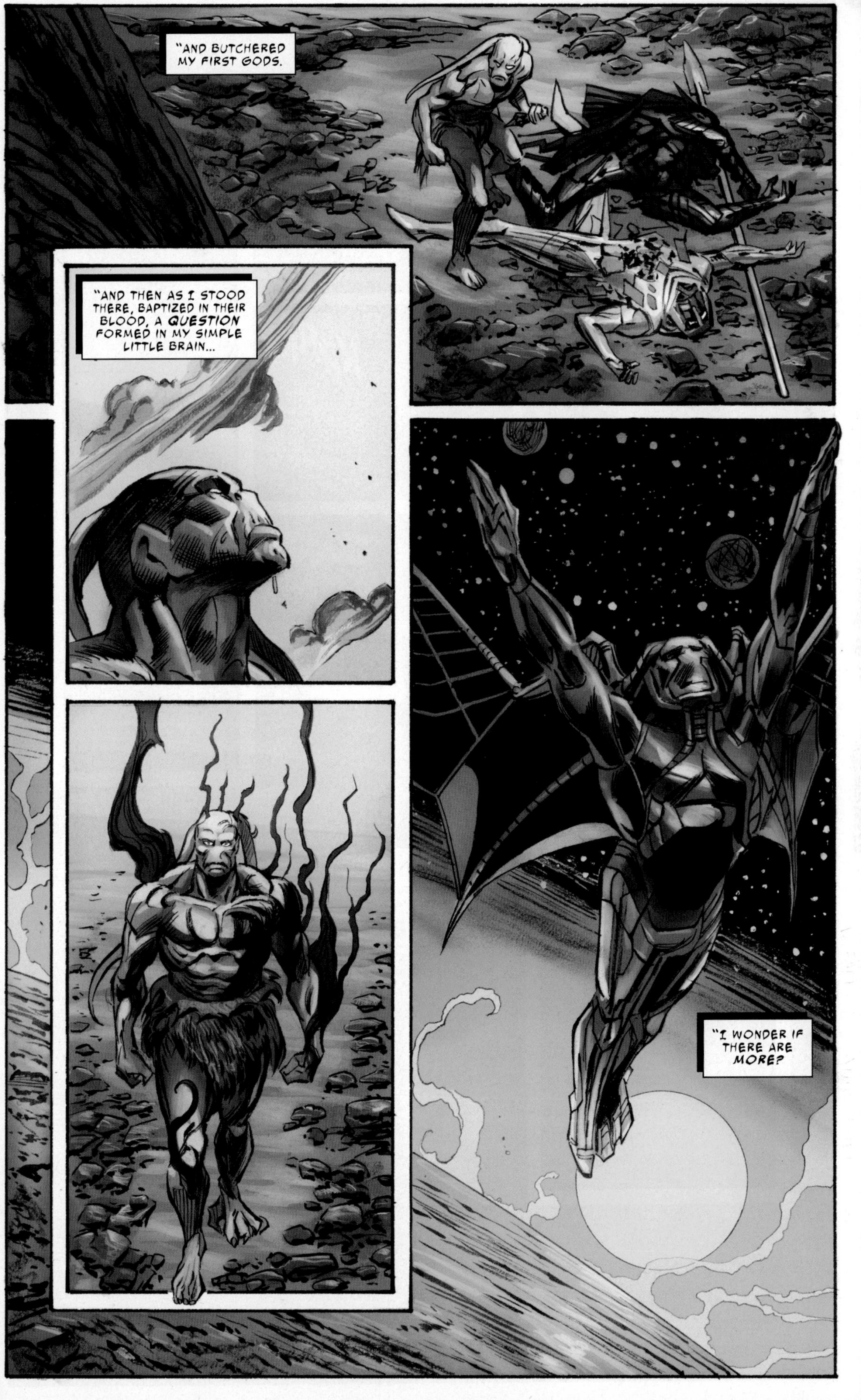
"AND BUTCHERED MY FIRST GODS.
"AND THEN AS I STOOD THERE, BAPTIZED IN THEIR BLOOD, A QUESTION FORMED IN MY SIMPLE LITTLE BRAIN...
"I WONDER IF THERE ARE MORE?

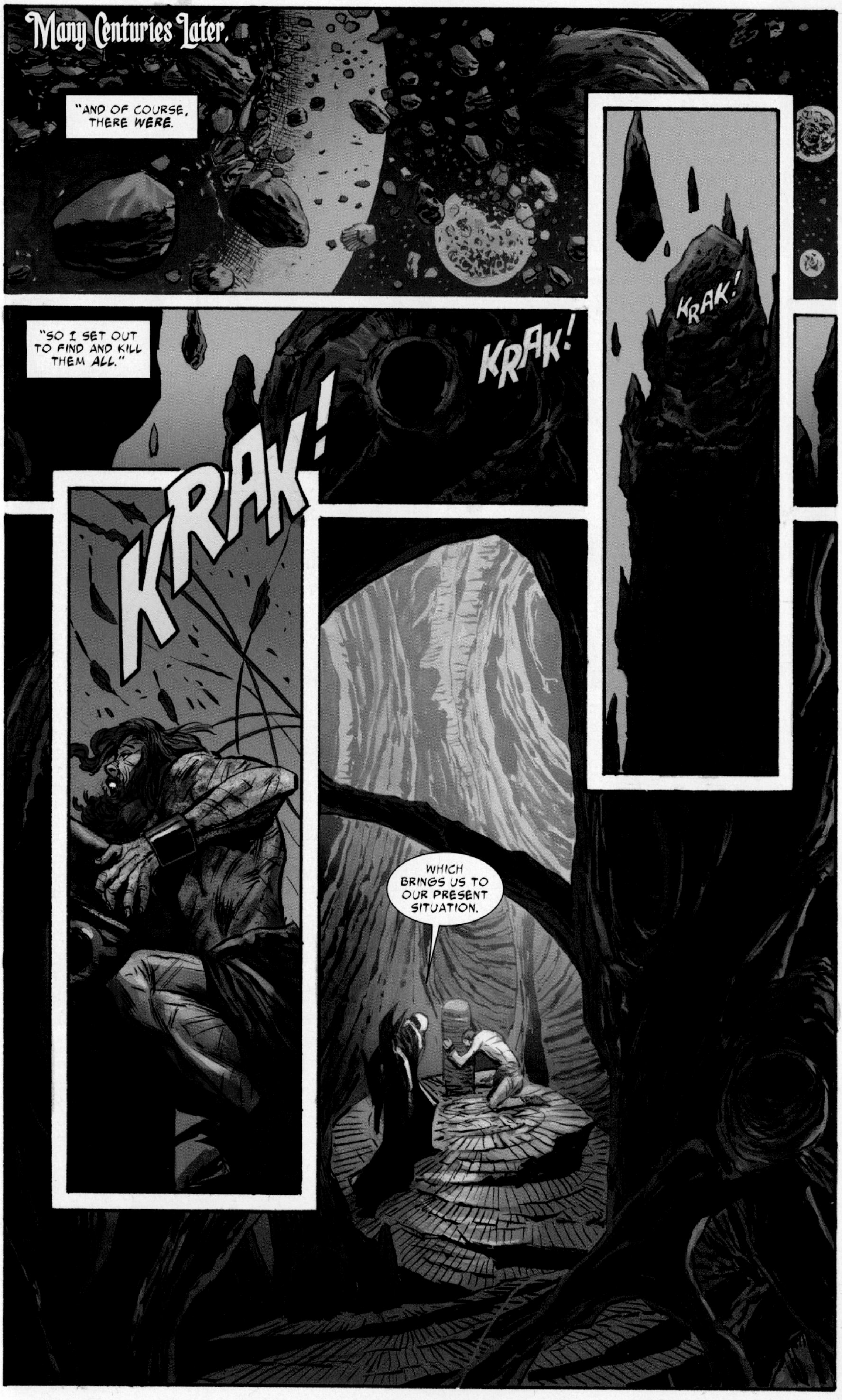
Many Centuries Later.
"AND OF COURSE, THERE WERE.
"SO I SET OUT TO FIND AND KILL THEM ALL."
KRAK!
KRAK!
KRAK!
KRAK!
WHICH BRINGS US TO OUR PRESENT SITUATION.

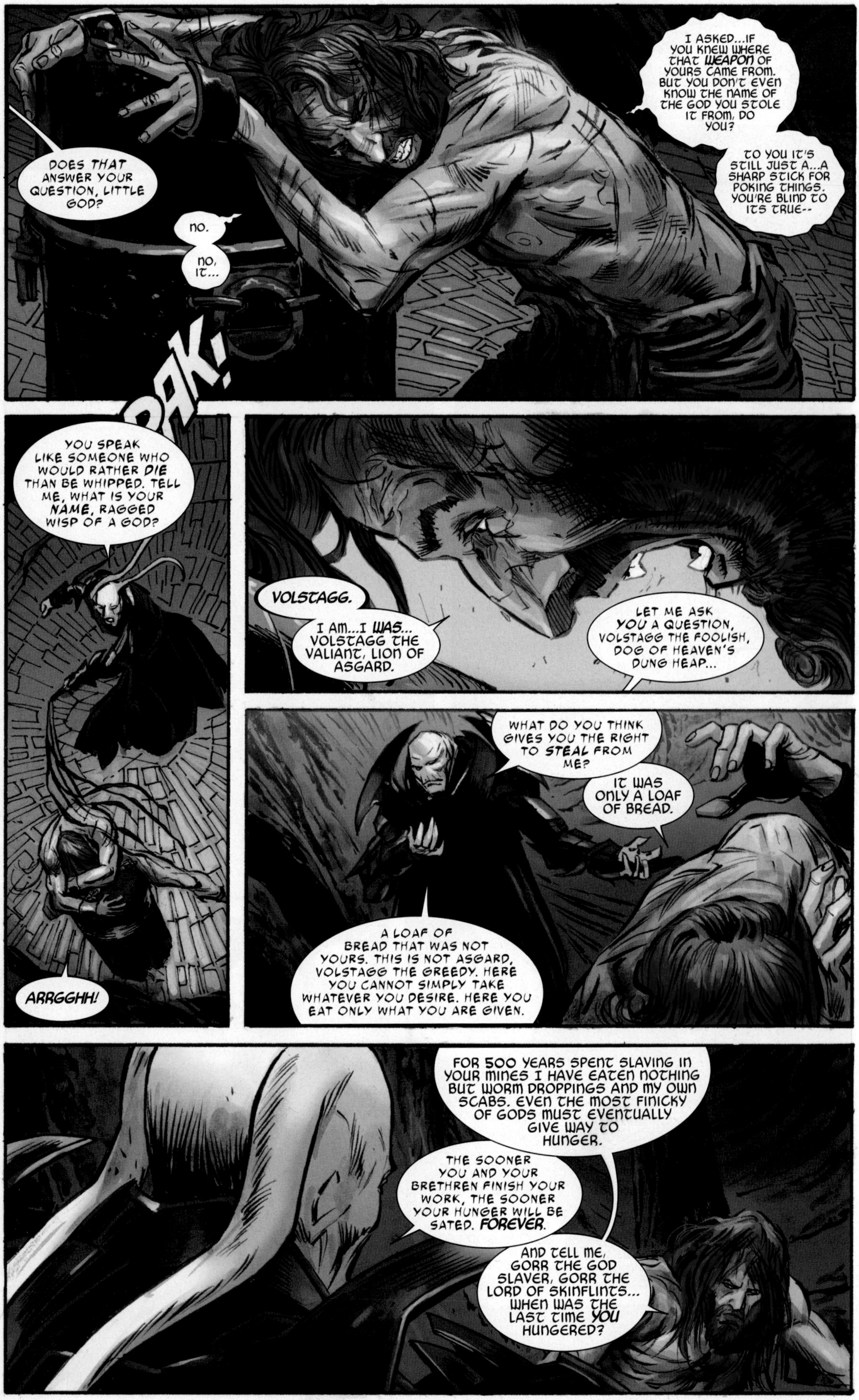

I ASKED...IF YOU KNEW WHERE THAT WEAPON OF YOURS CAME FROM. BUT YOU DON'T EVEN KNOW THE NAME OF THE GOD YOU STOLE IT FROM, DO YOU?
TO YOU IT'S STILL JUST A...A SHARP STICK FOR POKING THINGS. YOU'RE BLIND TO ITS TRUE--
DOES THAT ANSWER YOUR QUESTION, LITTLE GOD?
NO.
NO, IT...
PAK!
YOU SPEAK LIKE SOMEONE WHO WOULD RATHER DIE THAN BE WHIPPED. TELL ME, WHAT IS YOUR NAME, RAGGED WISP OF A GOD?
ARRGGHH!
VOLSTAGG.
I AM...I WAS... VOLSTAGG THE VALIANT, LION OF ASGARD.
LET ME ASK YOU A QUESTION, VOLSTAGG THE FOOLISH, DOG OF HEAVEN'S DUNG HEAP...
WHAT DO YOU THINK GIVES YOU THE RIGHT TO STEAL FROM ME?
IT WAS ONLY A LOAF OF BREAD.
A LOAF OF BREAD THAT WAS NOT YOURS. THIS IS NOT ASGARD, VOLSTAGG THE GREEDY. HERE YOU CANNOT SIMPLY TAKE WHATEVER YOU DESIRE. HERE YOU EAT ONLY WHAT YOU ARE GIVEN.
FOR 500 YEARS SPENT SLAVING IN YOUR MINES I HAVE EATEN NOTHING BUT WORM DROPPINGS AND MY OWN SCABS. EVEN THE MOST FINICKY OF GODS MUST EVENTUALLY GIVE WAY TO HUNGER.
THE SOONER YOU AND YOUR BRETHREN FINISH YOUR WORK, THE SOONER YOUR HUNGER WILL BE SATED. FOREVER.
AND TELL ME, GORR THE GOD SLAYER, GORR THE LORD OF SKINFLINTS... WHEN WAS THE LAST TIME YOU HUNGERED?

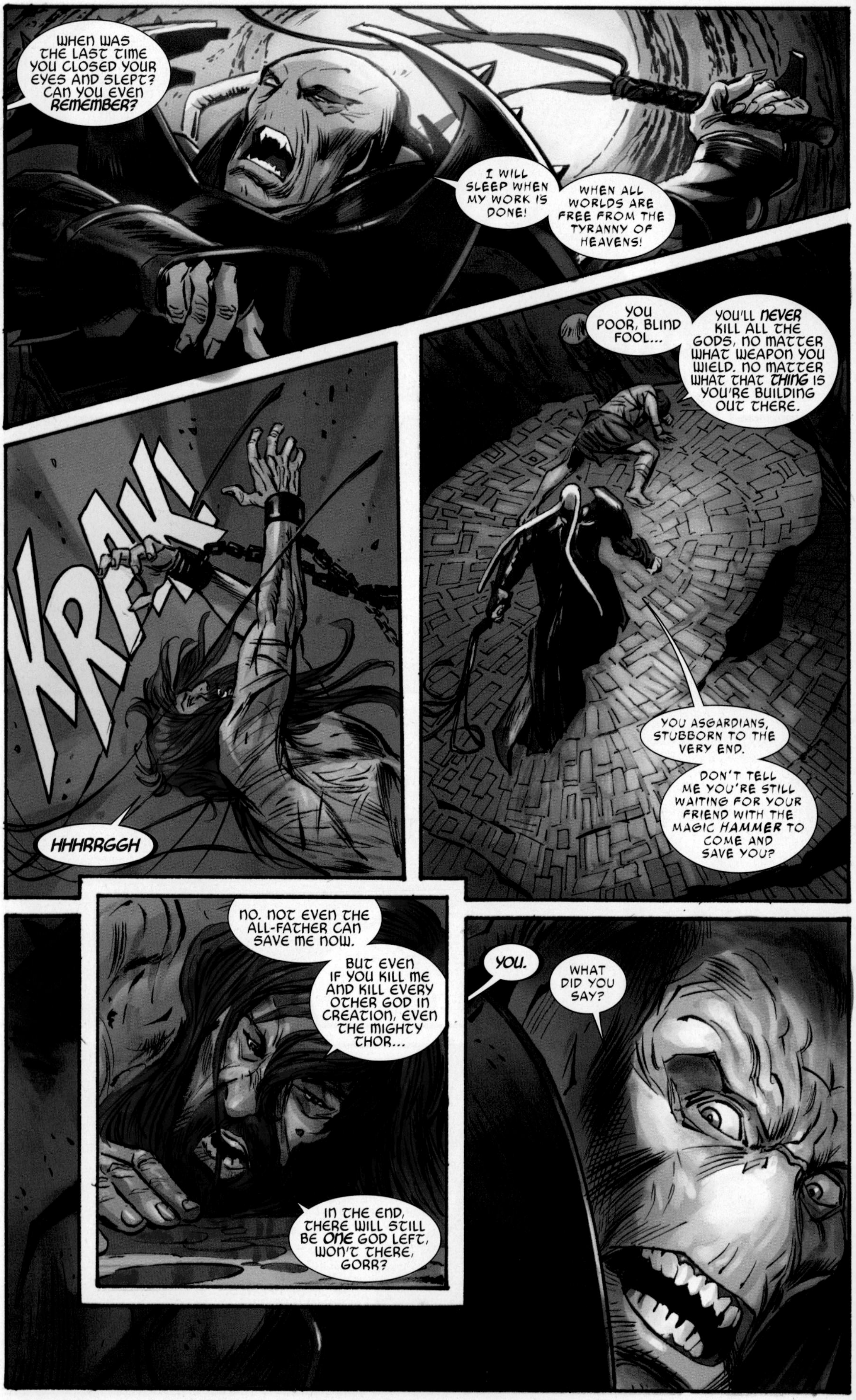
WHEN WAS THE LAST TIME YOU CLOSED YOUR EYES AND SLEPT? CAN YOU EVEN REMEMBER?
I WILL SLEEP WHEN MY WORK IS DONE!
WHEN ALL WORLDS ARE FREE FROM THE TYRANNY OF HEAVENS!
KRAK
HHHRRGGH
YOU POOR, BLIND FOOL...
YOU'LL NEVER KILL ALL THE GODS, NO MATTER WHAT WEAPON YOU WIELD. NO MATTER WHAT THAT THING IS YOU'RE BUILDING OUT THERE.
YOU ASGARDIANS, STUBBORN TO THE VERY END.
DON'T TELL ME YOU'RE STILL WAITING FOR YOUR FRIEND WITH THE MAGIC HAMMER TO COME AND SAVE YOU?
NO. NOT EVEN THE ALL-FATHER CAN SAVE ME NOW.
BUT EVEN IF YOU KILL ME AND KILL EVERY OTHER GOD IN CREATION, EVEN THE MIGHTY THOR...
IN THE END, THERE WILL STILL BE ONE GOD LEFT, WON'T THERE, GORR?
YOU.
WHAT DID YOU SAY?

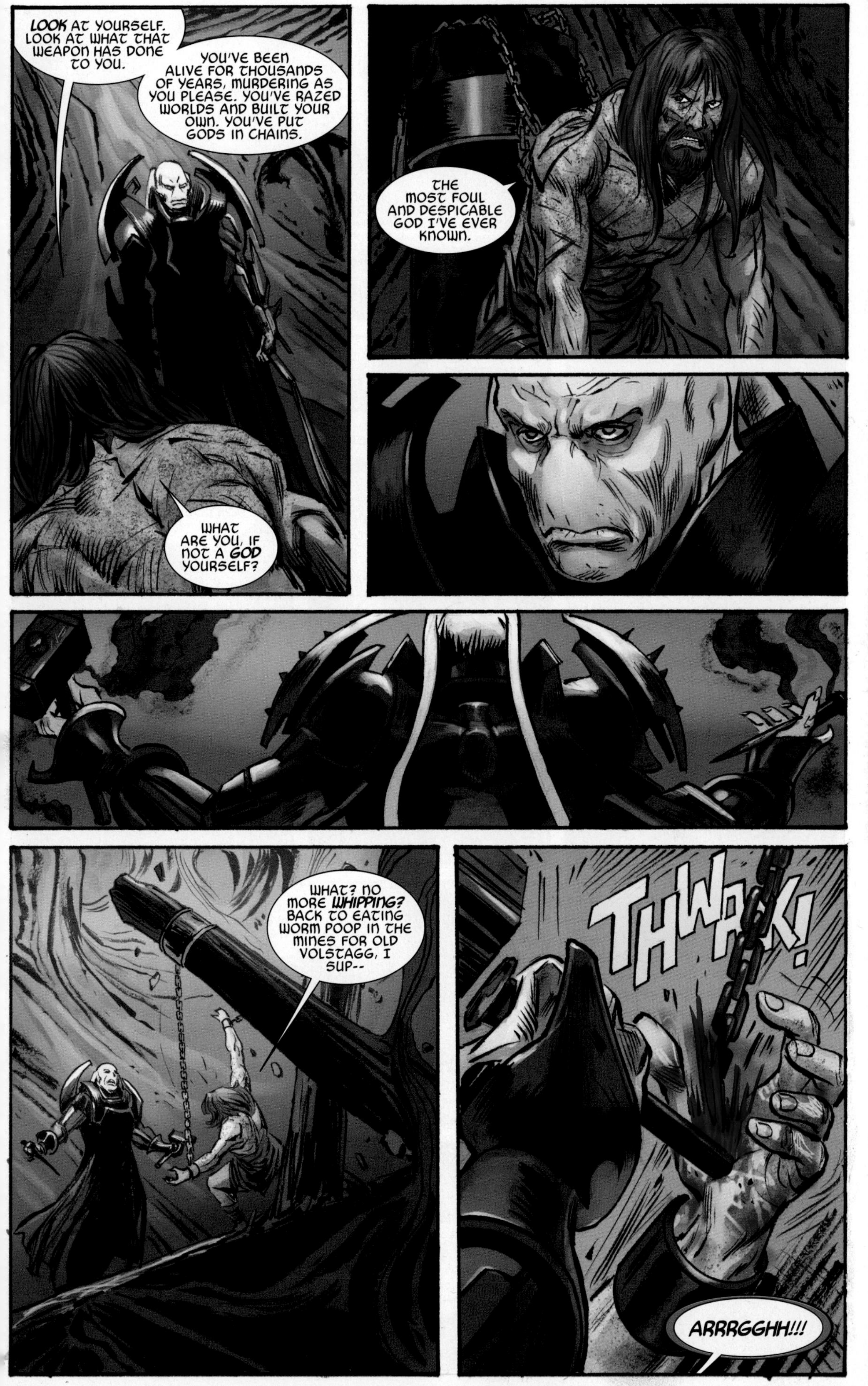

LOOK AT YOURSELF. LOOK AT WHAT THAT WEAPON HAS DONE TO YOU.
YOU'VE BEEN ALIVE FOR THOUSANDS OF YEARS, MURDERING AS YOU PLEASE. YOU'VE RAZED WORLDS AND BUILT YOUR OWN. YOU'VE PUT GODS IN CHAINS.
WHAT ARE YOU, IF NOT A GOD YOURSELF?
THE MOST FOUL AND DESPICABLE GOD I'VE EVER KNOWN.
WHAT? NO MORE WHIPPING? BACK TO EATING WORM POOP IN THE MINES FOR OLD VOLSTAGG, I SUP--
ARRRGGHH!!!

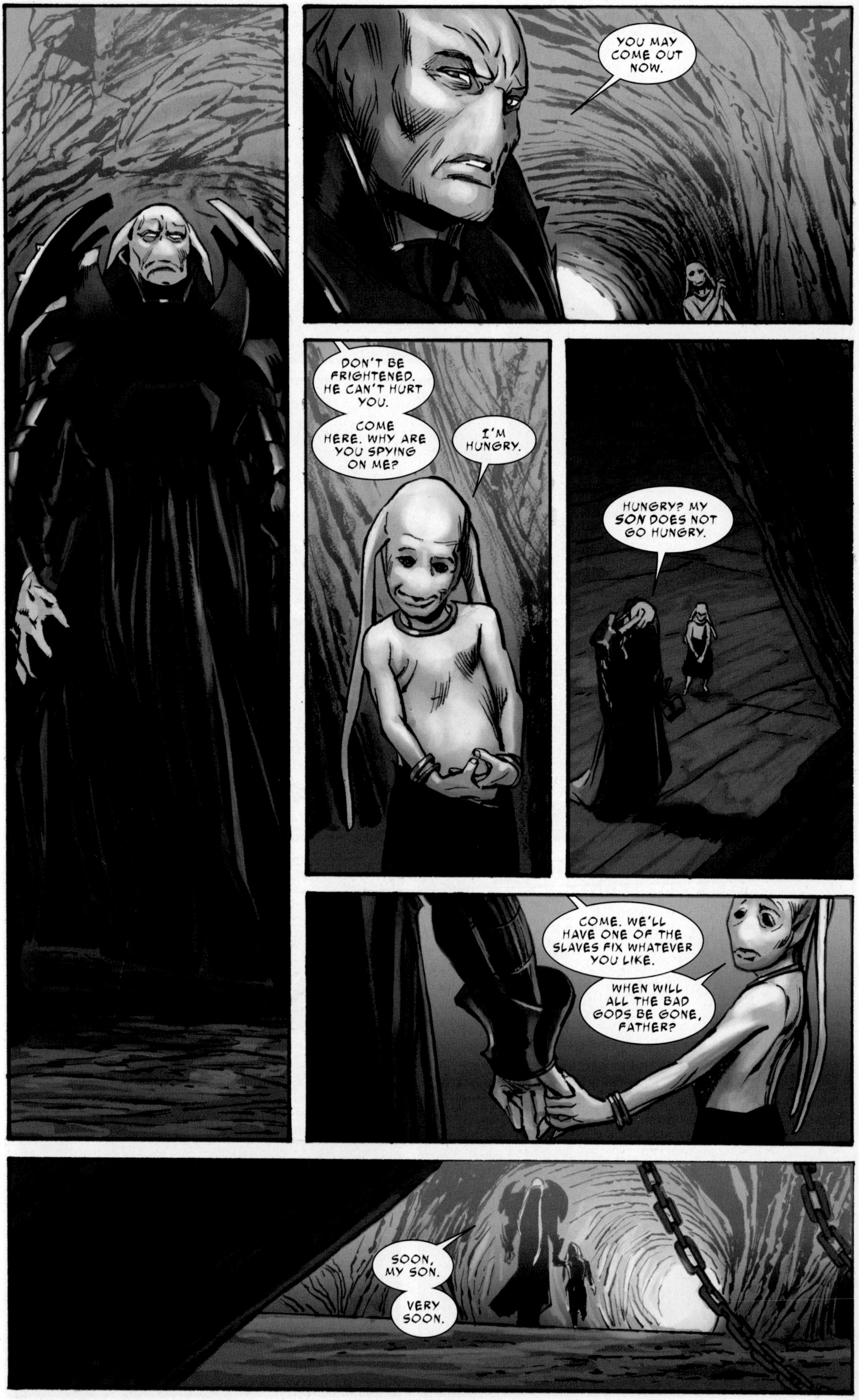
YOU MAY COME OUT NOW.
DON'T BE FRIGHTENED. HE CAN'T HURT YOU.
COME HERE. WHY ARE YOU SPYING ON ME?
I'M HUNGRY.
HUNGRY? MY SON DOES NOT GO HUNGRY.
COME. WE'LL HAVE ONE OF THE SLAVES FIX WHATEVER YOU LIKE.
WHEN WILL ALL THE BAD GODS BE GONE, FATHER?
SOON, MY SON.
VERY SOON.

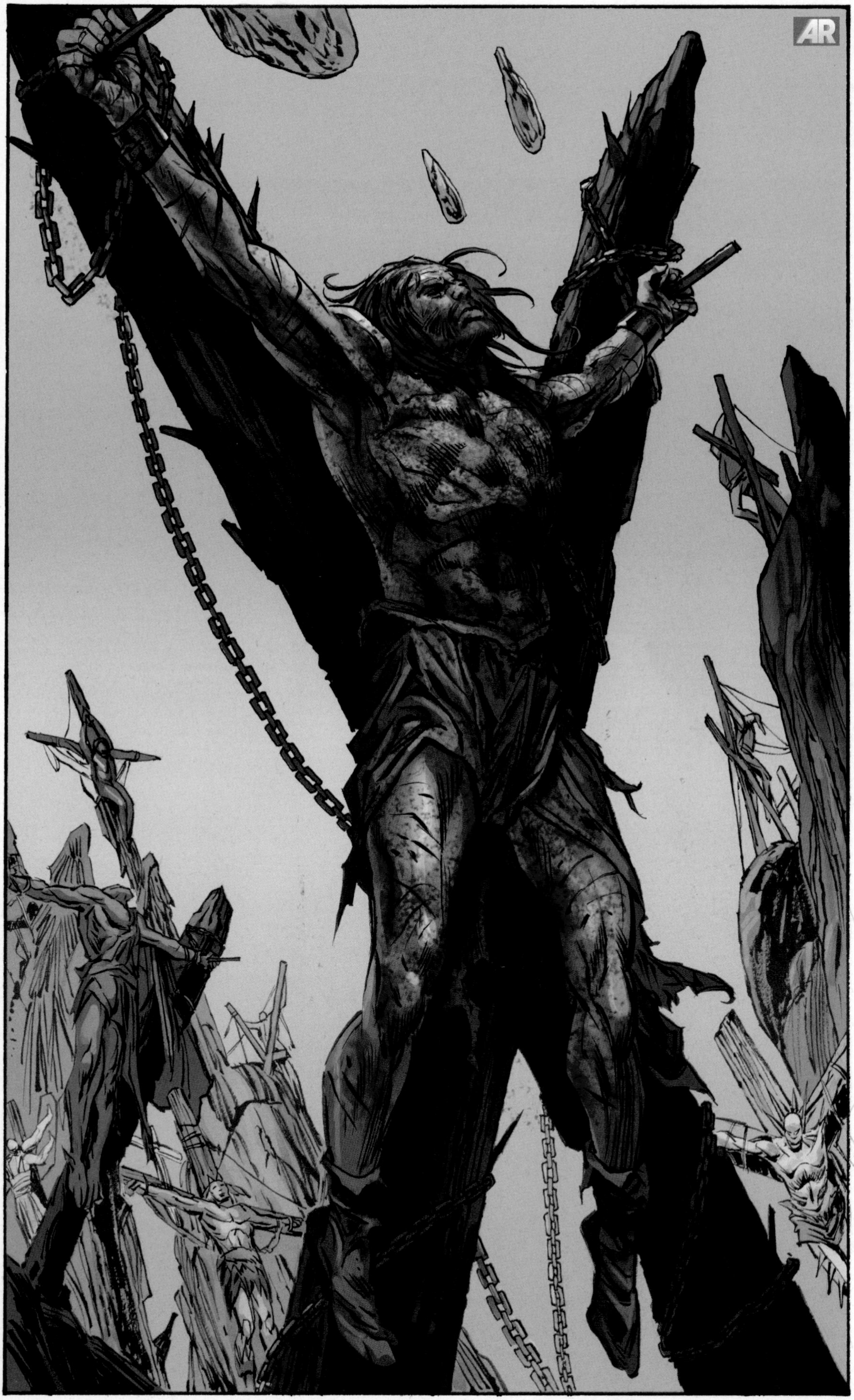

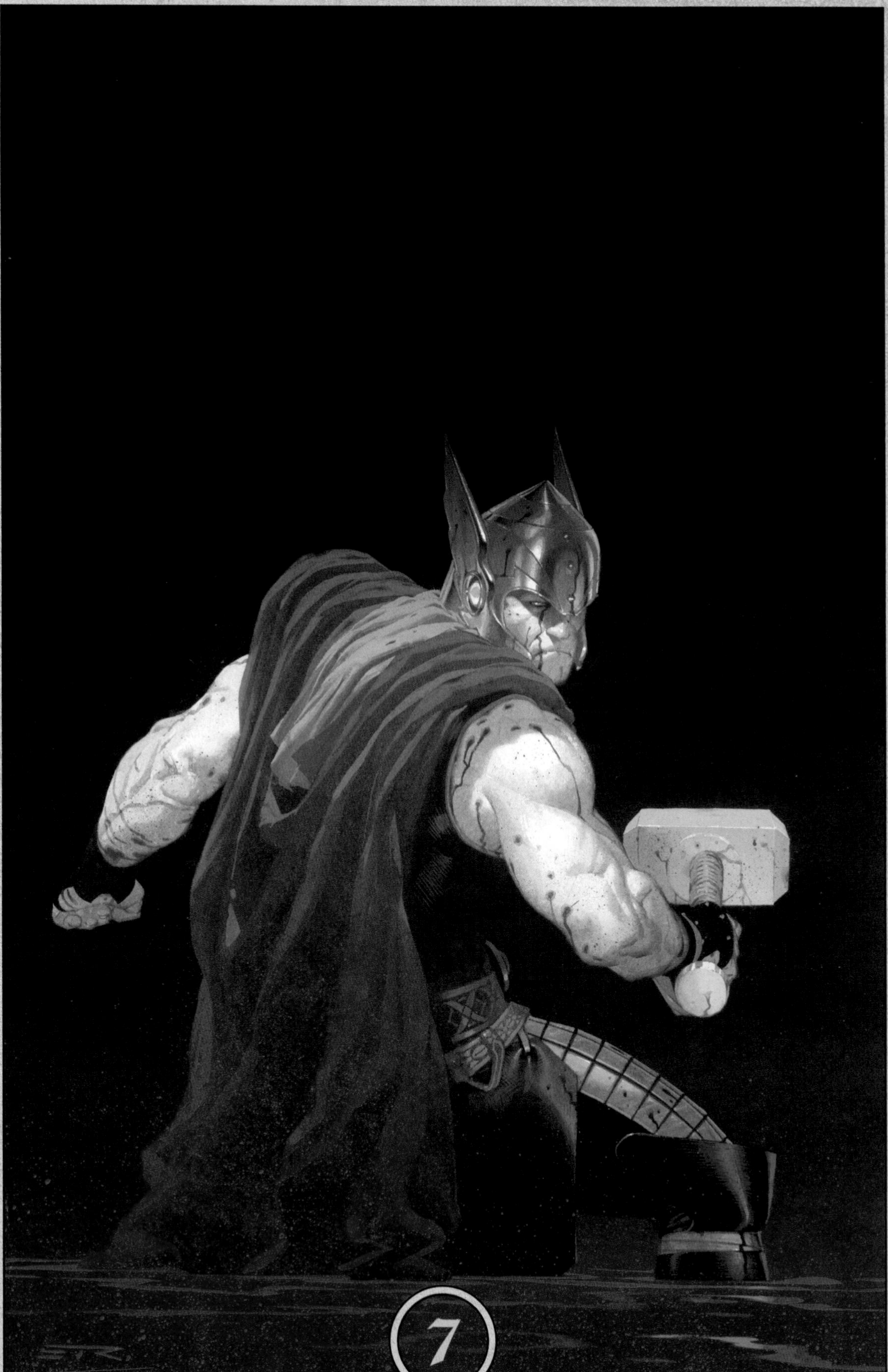
7

GODBOMB PART ONE: WHERE GODS GO TO DIE

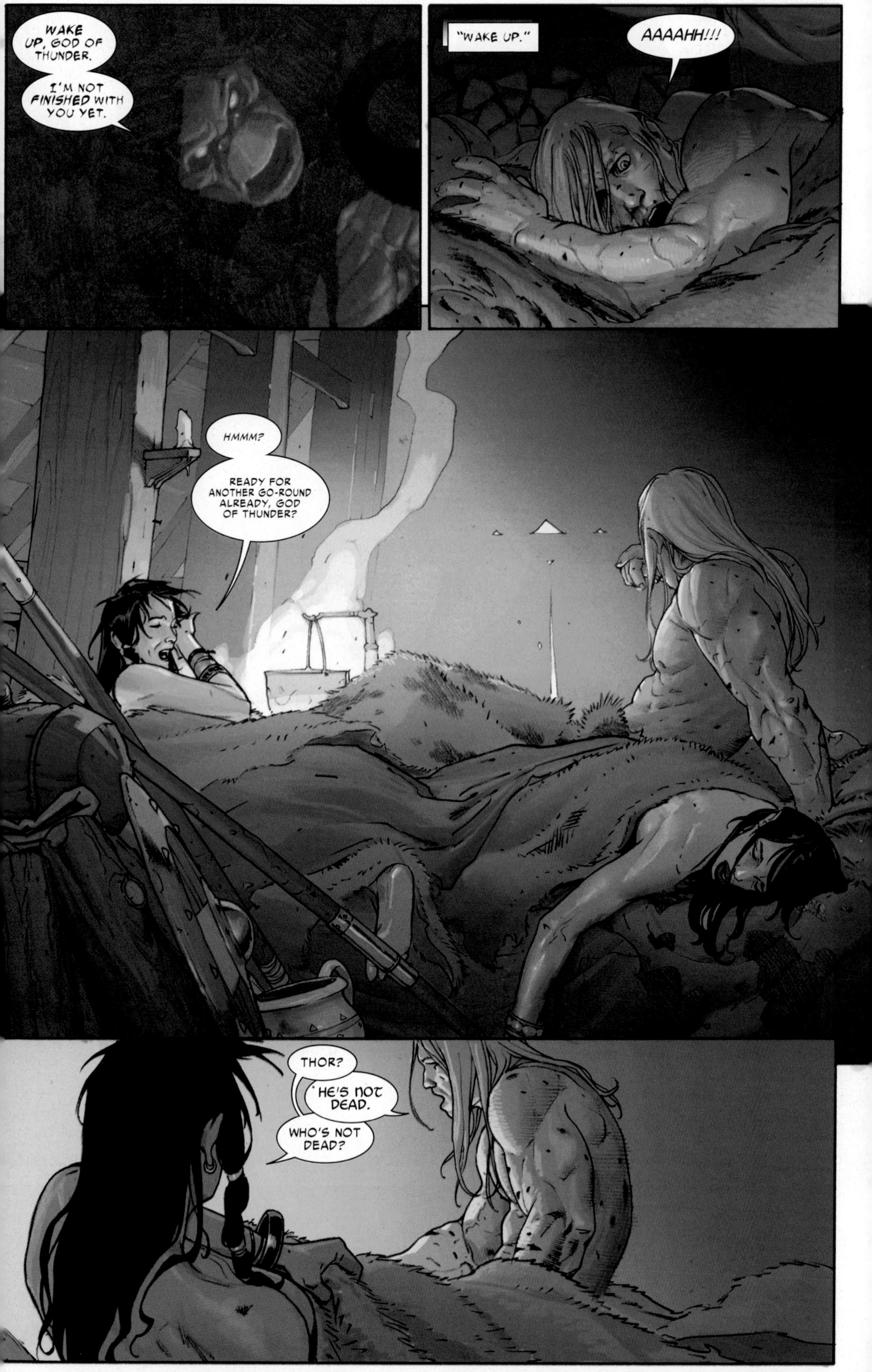
WAKE UP, GOD OF THUNDER.
I'M NOT FINISHED WITH YOU YET.
"WAKE UP."
AAAAHH!!!
HMMM?
READY FOR ANOTHER GO-ROUND ALREADY, GOD OF THUNDER?
THOR?
HE'S NOT DEAD.
WHO'S NOT DEAD?

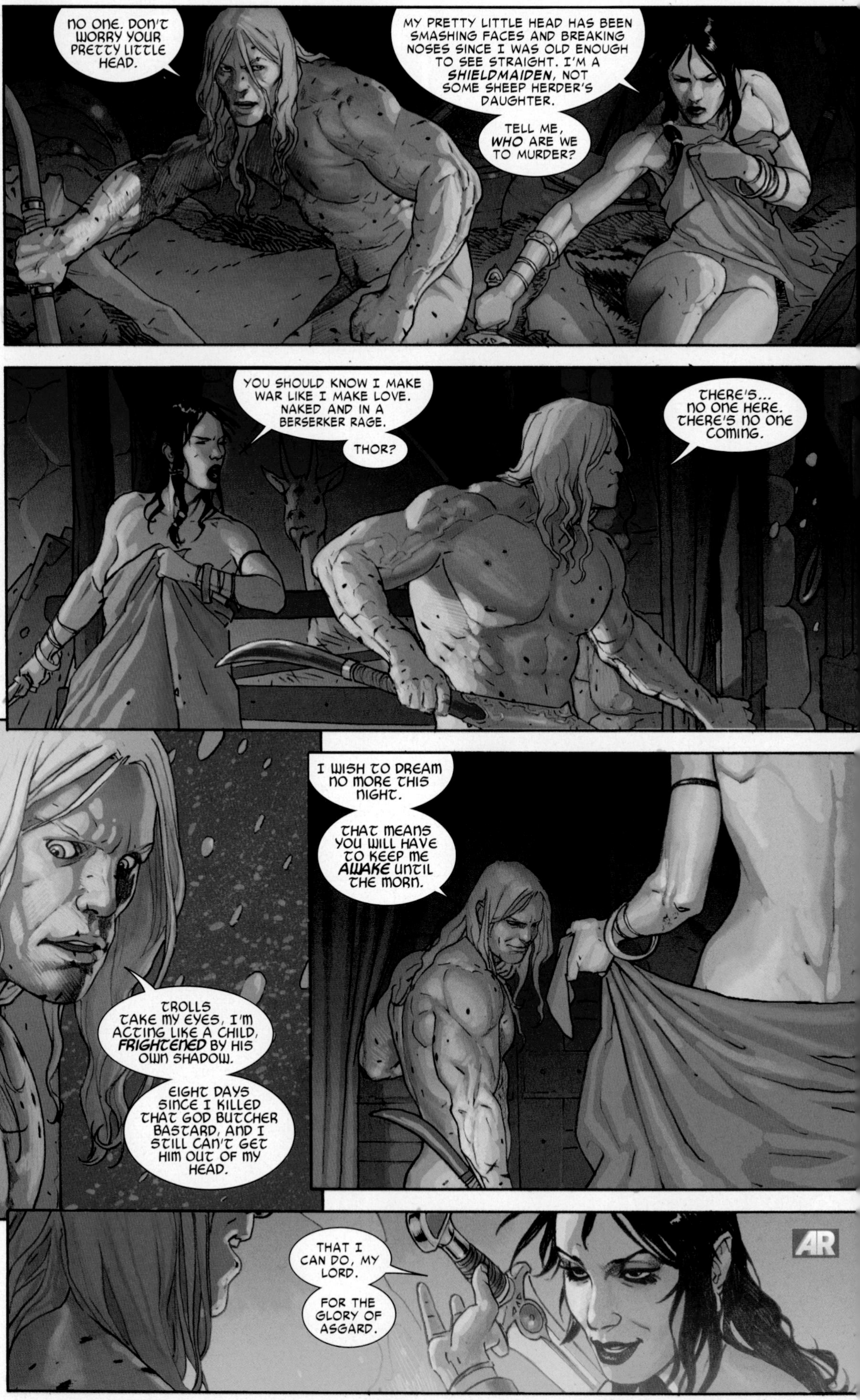
NO ONE. DON'T WORRY YOUR PRETTY LITTLE HEAD.
MY PRETTY LITTLE HEAD HAS BEEN SMASHING FACES AND BREAKING NOSES SINCE I WAS OLD ENOUGH TO SEE STRAIGHT. I'M A SHIELDMAIDEN, NOT SOME SHEEP HERDER'S DAUGHTER.
TELL ME, WHO ARE WE TO MURDER?
YOU SHOULD KNOW I MAKE WAR LIKE I MAKE LOVE. NAKED AND IN A BERSERKER RAGE.
THOR?
THERE'S... NO ONE HERE. THERE'S NO ONE COMING.
TROLLS TAKE MY EYES, I'M ACTING LIKE A CHILD, FRIGHTENED BY HIS OWN SHADOW.
EIGHT DAYS SINCE I KILLED THAT GOD BUTCHER BASTARD, AND I STILL CAN'T GET HIM OUT OF MY HEAD.
I WISH TO DREAM NO MORE THIS NIGHT.
THAT MEANS YOU WILL HAVE TO KEEP ME AWAKE UNTIL THE MORN.
THAT I CAN DO, MY LORD.
FOR THE GLORY OF ASGARD.

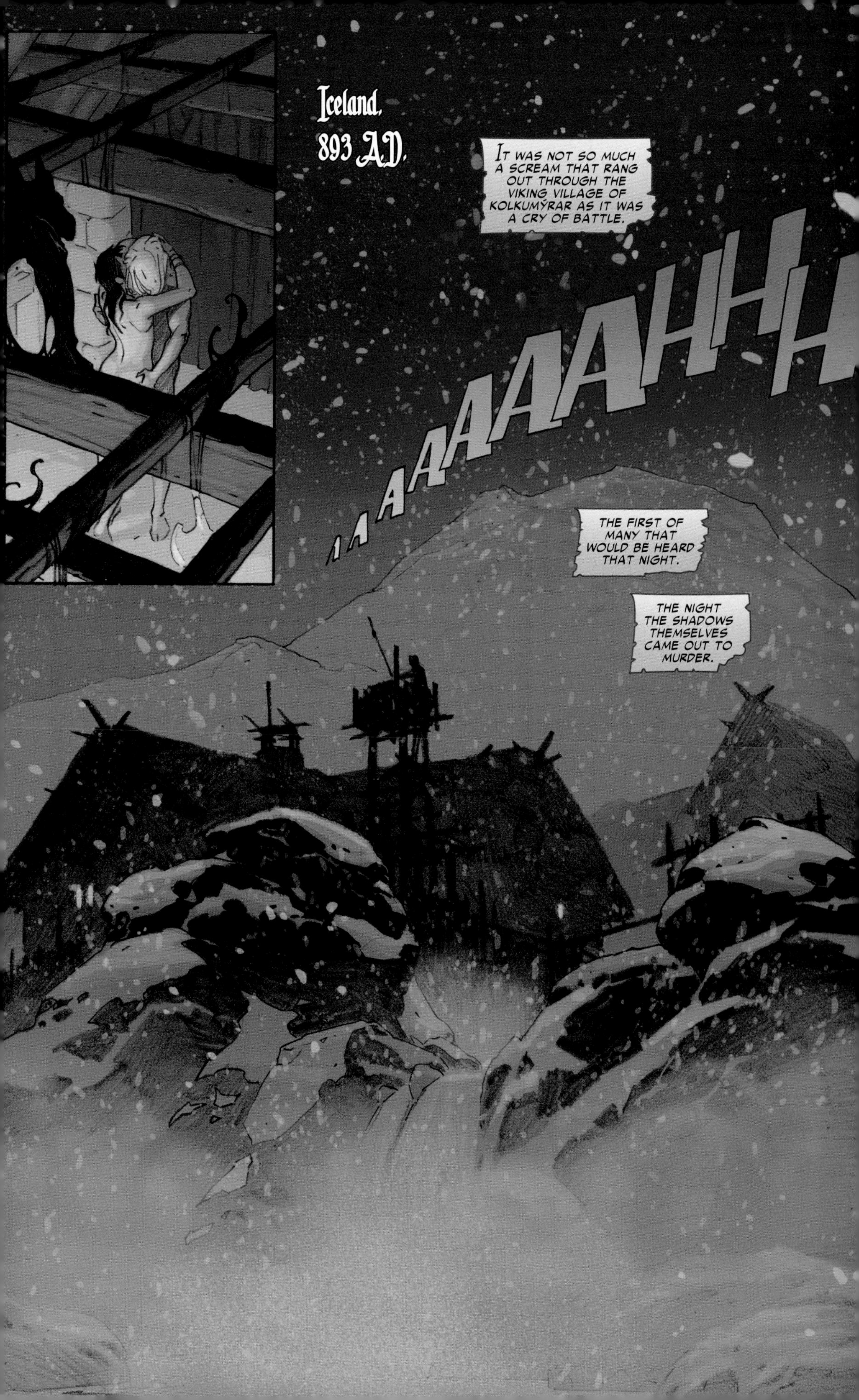
Iceland, 893 A.D.
It was not so much a scream that rang out through the Viking village of Kolkumýrar as it was a cry of battle.
AAAAAAAAHHH
The first of many that would be heard that night.
The night the shadows themselves came out to murder.

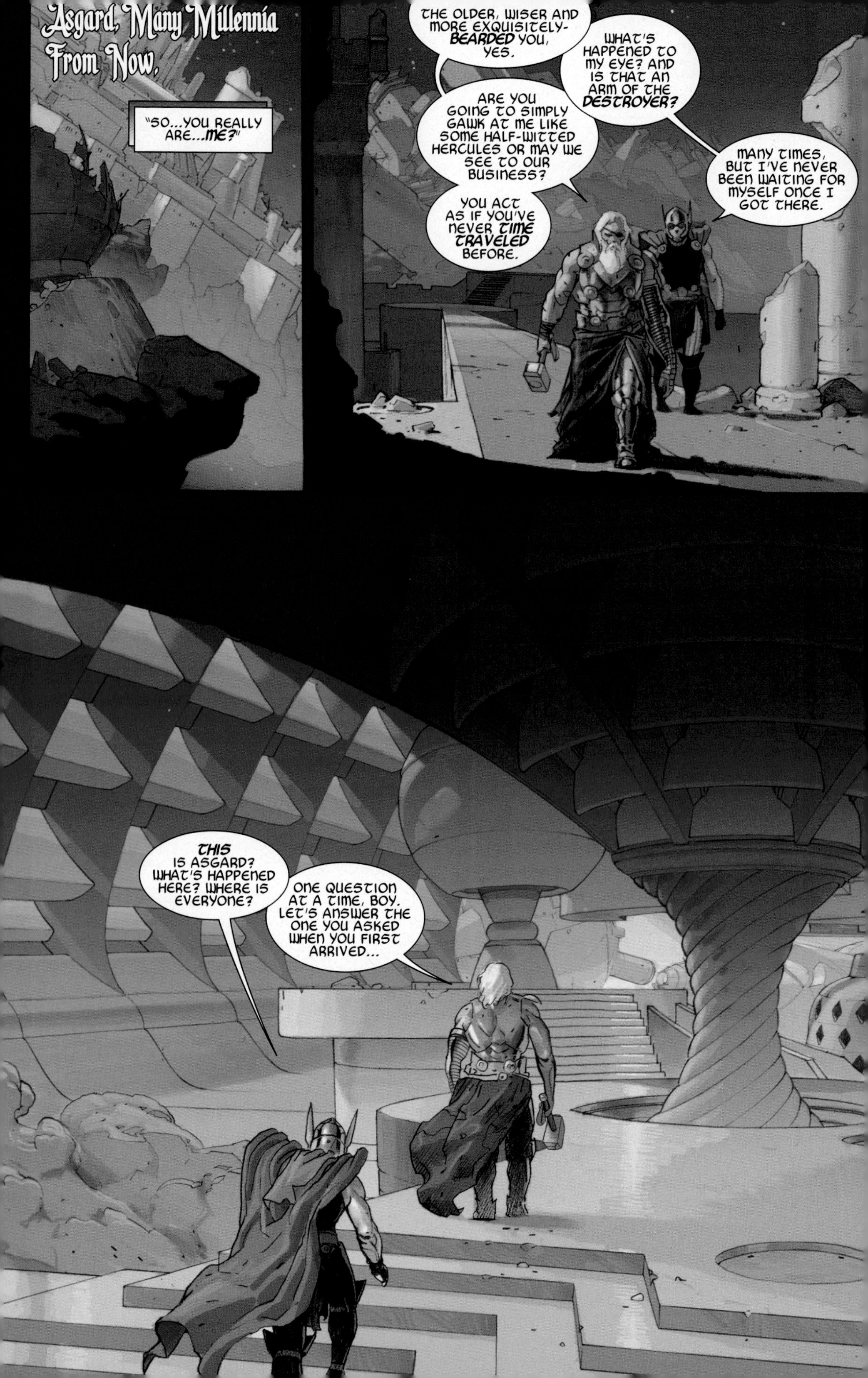
Asgard, Many Millennia From Now,
"SO...YOU REALLY ARE...ME?"
THE OLDER, WISER AND MORE EXQUISITELY-BEARDED YOU, YES.
ARE YOU GOING TO SIMPLY GAWK AT ME LIKE SOME HALF-WITTED HERCULES OR MAY WE SEE TO OUR BUSINESS?
WHAT'S HAPPENED TO MY EYE? AND IS THAT AN ARM OF THE DESTROYER?
YOU ACT AS IF YOU'VE NEVER TIME TRAVELED BEFORE.
MANY TIMES, BUT I'VE NEVER BEEN WAITING FOR MYSELF ONCE I GOT THERE.
THIS IS ASGARD? WHAT'S HAPPENED HERE? WHERE IS EVERYONE?
ONE QUESTION AT A TIME, BOY. LET'S ANSWER THE ONE YOU ASKED WHEN YOU FIRST ARRIVED...

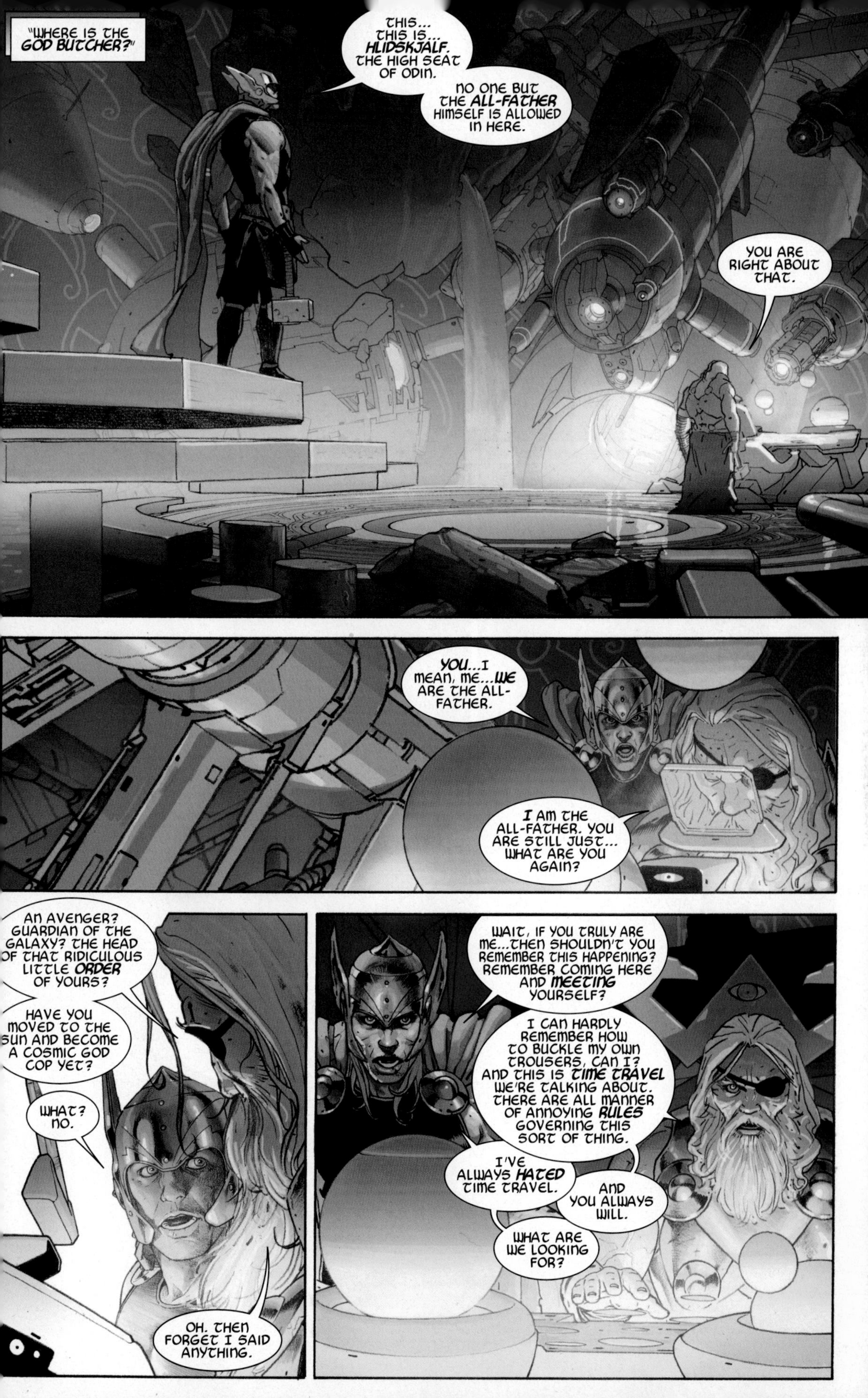
"WHERE IS THE GOD BUTCHER?"
THIS... THIS IS... HLIDSKJALF. THE HIGH SEAT OF ODIN.
NO ONE BUT THE ALL-FATHER HIMSELF IS ALLOWED IN HERE.
YOU ARE RIGHT ABOUT THAT.
YOU...I MEAN, ME...WE ARE THE ALL-FATHER.
I AM THE ALL-FATHER. YOU ARE STILL JUST... WHAT ARE YOU AGAIN?
AN AVENGER? GUARDIAN OF THE GALAXY? THE HEAD OF THAT RIDICULOUS LITTLE ORDER OF YOURS?
HAVE YOU MOVED TO THE SUN AND BECOME A COSMIC GOD COP YET?
WHAT? NO.
OH. THEN FORGET I SAID ANYTHING.
WAIT, IF YOU TRULY ARE ME...THEN SHOULDN'T YOU REMEMBER THIS HAPPENING? REMEMBER COMING HERE AND MEETING YOURSELF?
I CAN HARDLY REMEMBER HOW TO BUCKLE MY OWN TROUSERS, CAN I? AND THIS IS TIME TRAVEL WE'RE TALKING ABOUT. THERE ARE ALL MANNER OF ANNOYING RULES GOVERNING THIS SORT OF THING.
I'VE ALWAYS HATED TIME TRAVEL.
AND YOU ALWAYS WILL.
WHAT ARE WE LOOKING FOR?

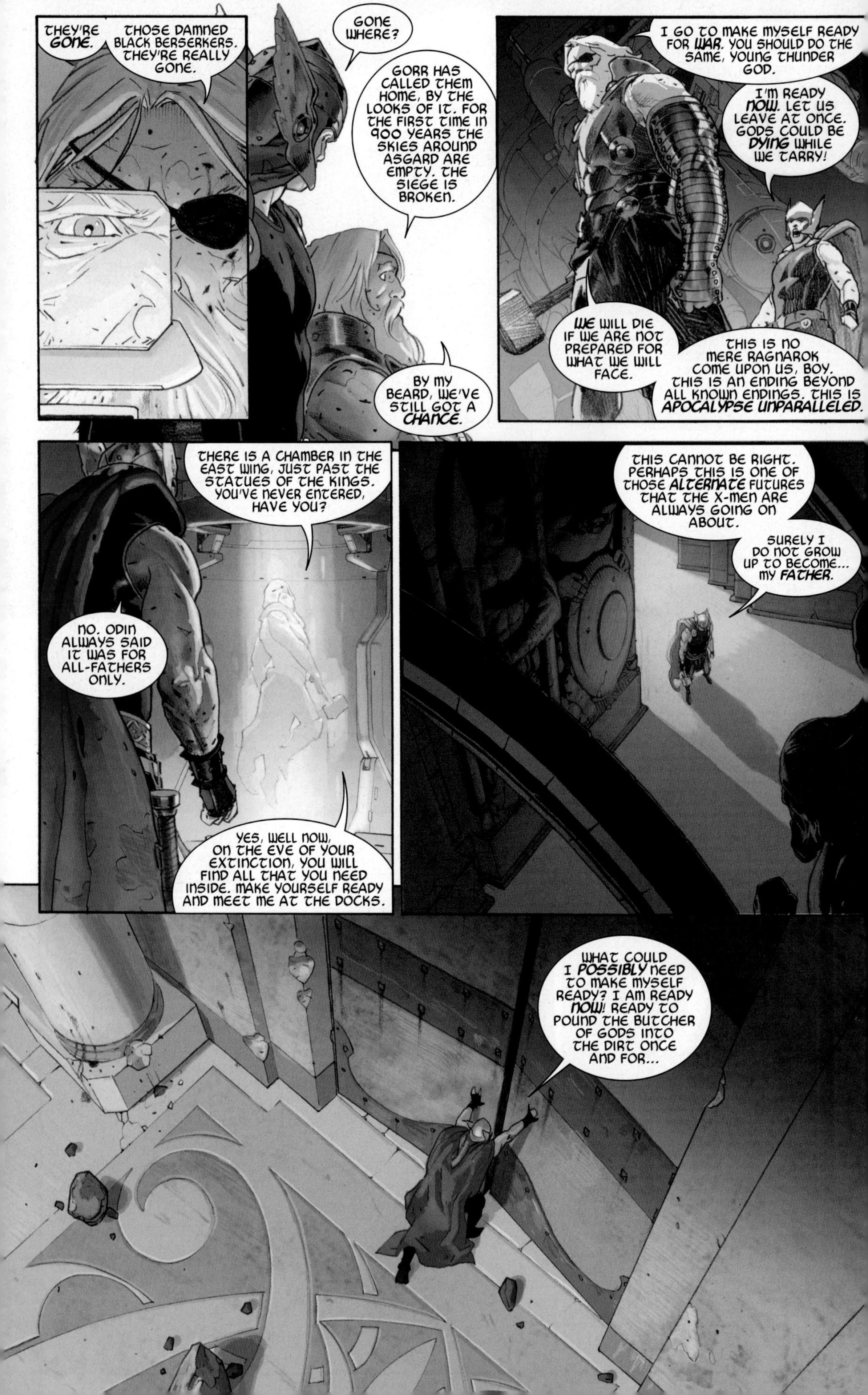
THEY'RE GONE.
THOSE DAMNED BLACK BERSERKERS. THEY'RE REALLY GONE.
GONE WHERE?
GORR HAS CALLED THEM HOME, BY THE LOOKS OF IT. FOR THE FIRST TIME IN 900 YEARS THE SKIES AROUND ASGARD ARE EMPTY. THE SIEGE IS BROKEN.
BY MY BEARD, WE'VE STILL GOT A CHANCE.
I GO TO MAKE MYSELF READY FOR WAR. YOU SHOULD DO THE SAME, YOUNG THUNDER GOD.
I'M READY NOW. LET US LEAVE AT ONCE. GODS COULD BE DYING WHILE WE TARRY!
WE WILL DIE IF WE ARE NOT PREPARED FOR WHAT WE WILL FACE.
THIS IS NO MERE RAGNAROK COME UPON US, BOY. THIS IS AN ENDING BEYOND ALL KNOWN ENDINGS. THIS IS APOCALYPSE UNPARALLELED.
THERE IS A CHAMBER IN THE EAST WING, JUST PAST THE STATUES OF THE KINGS. YOU'VE NEVER ENTERED, HAVE YOU?
NO. ODIN ALWAYS SAID IT WAS FOR ALL-FATHERS ONLY.
YES, WELL NOW, ON THE EVE OF YOUR EXTINCTION, YOU WILL FIND ALL THAT YOU NEED INSIDE. MAKE YOURSELF READY AND MEET ME AT THE DOCKS.
THIS CANNOT BE RIGHT. PERHAPS THIS IS ONE OF THOSE ALTERNATE FUTURES THAT THE X-MEN ARE ALWAYS GOING ON ABOUT.
SURELY I DO NOT GROW UP TO BECOME... MY FATHER.
WHAT COULD I POSSIBLY NEED TO MAKE MYSELF READY? I AM READY NOW! READY TO POUND THE BUTCHER OF GODS INTO THE DIRT ONCE AND FOR...

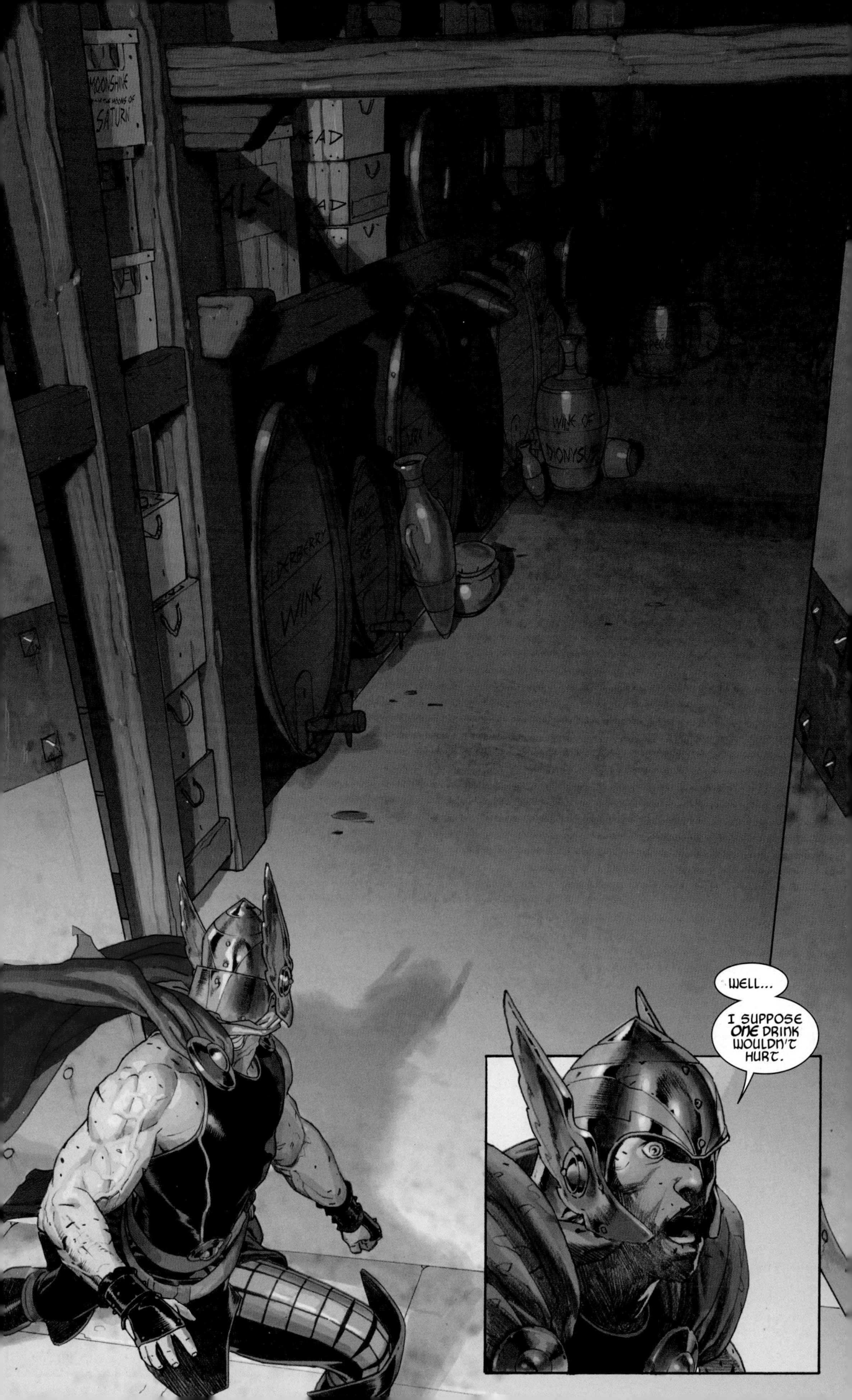
MOONSHINE
SATURN
ELDERBERRY WINE
WINE OF DIONYSUS
WELL...
I SUPPOSE ONE DRINK WOULDN'T HURT.

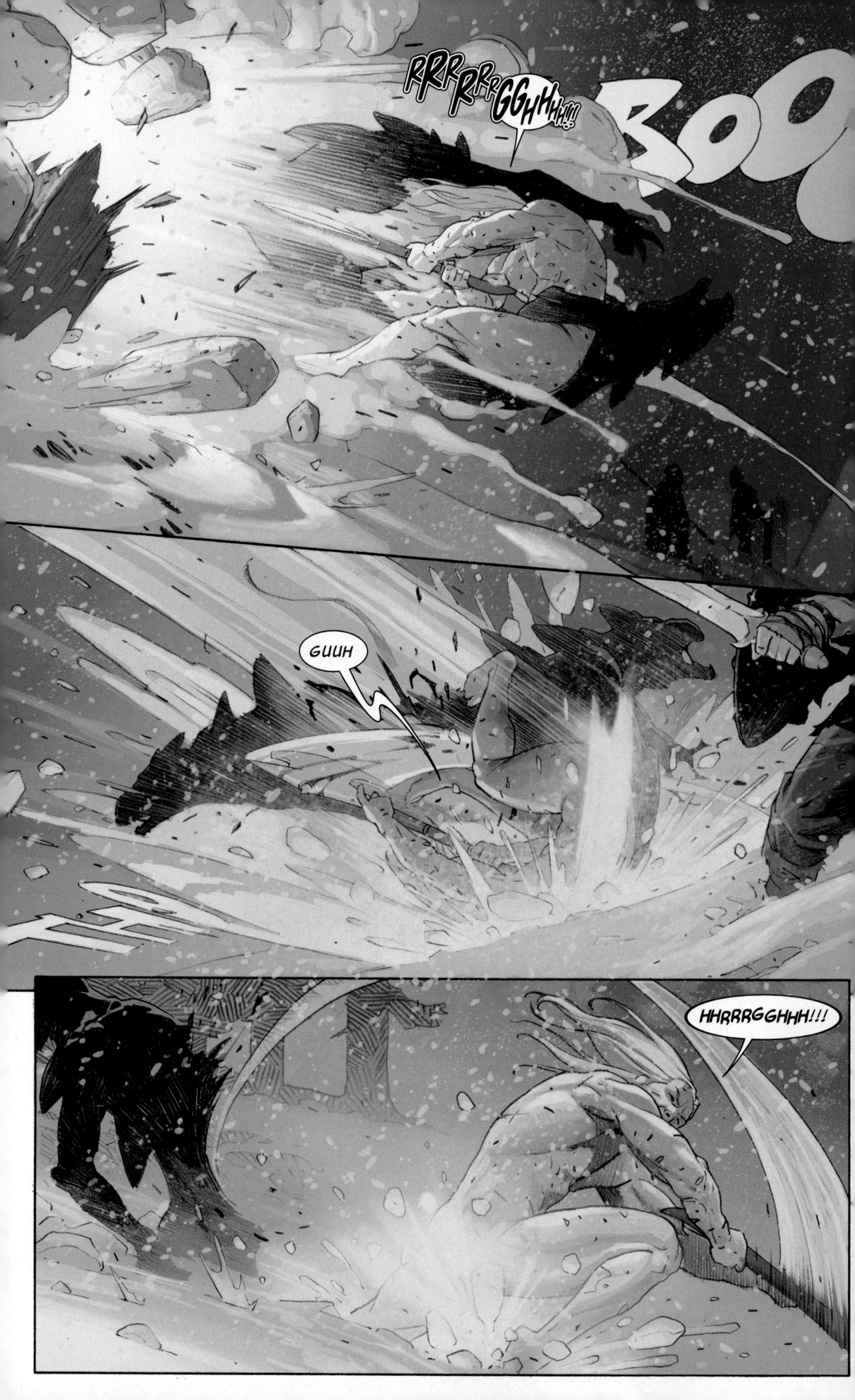
RRRRRRGGHHHH!!!
BOO
GUUH
HHRRRGGHHH!!!

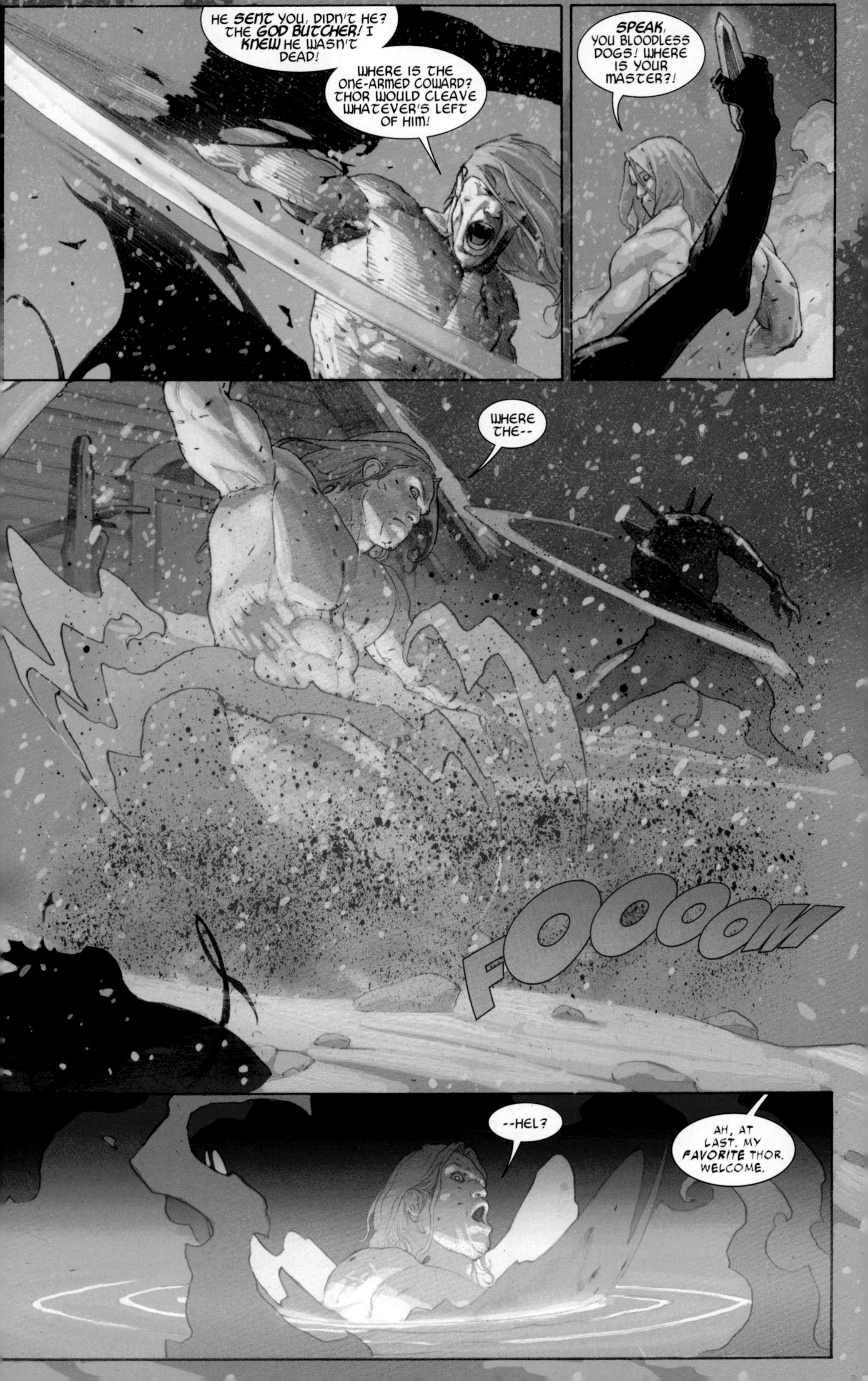
HE SENT YOU, DIDN'T HE? THE GOD BUTCHER! I KNEW HE WASN'T DEAD!
WHERE IS THE ONE-ARMED COWARD? THOR WOULD CLEAVE WHATEVER'S LEFT OF HIM!
SPEAK, YOU BLOODLESS DOGS! WHERE IS YOUR MASTER?!
WHERE THE--
FOOOOM
--HEL?
AH, AT LAST. MY FAVORITE THOR. WELCOME.

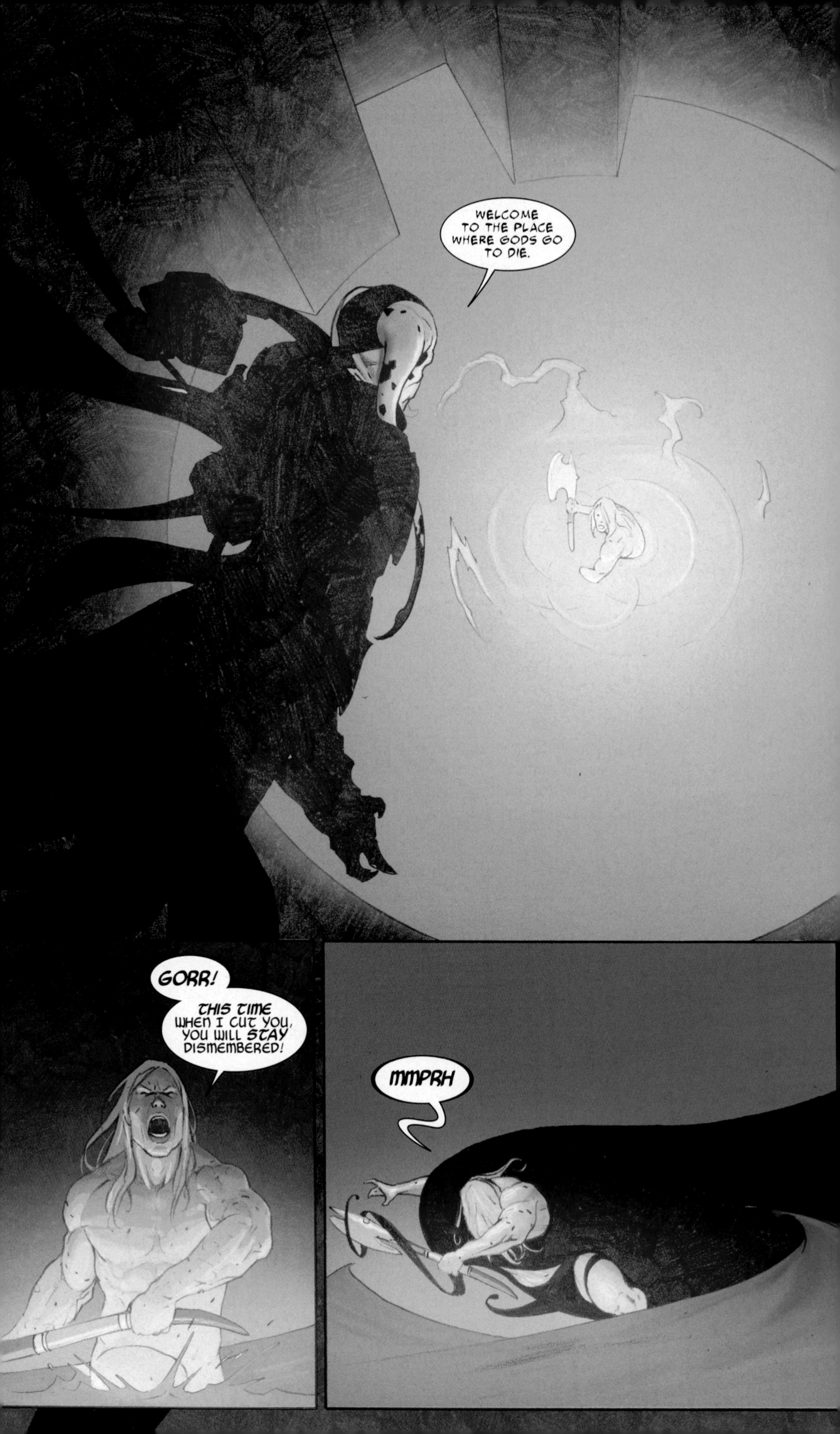
WELCOME TO THE PLACE WHERE GODS GO TO DIE.
GORR!
THIS TIME WHEN I CUT YOU, YOU WILL STAY DISMEMBERED!
MMPRH

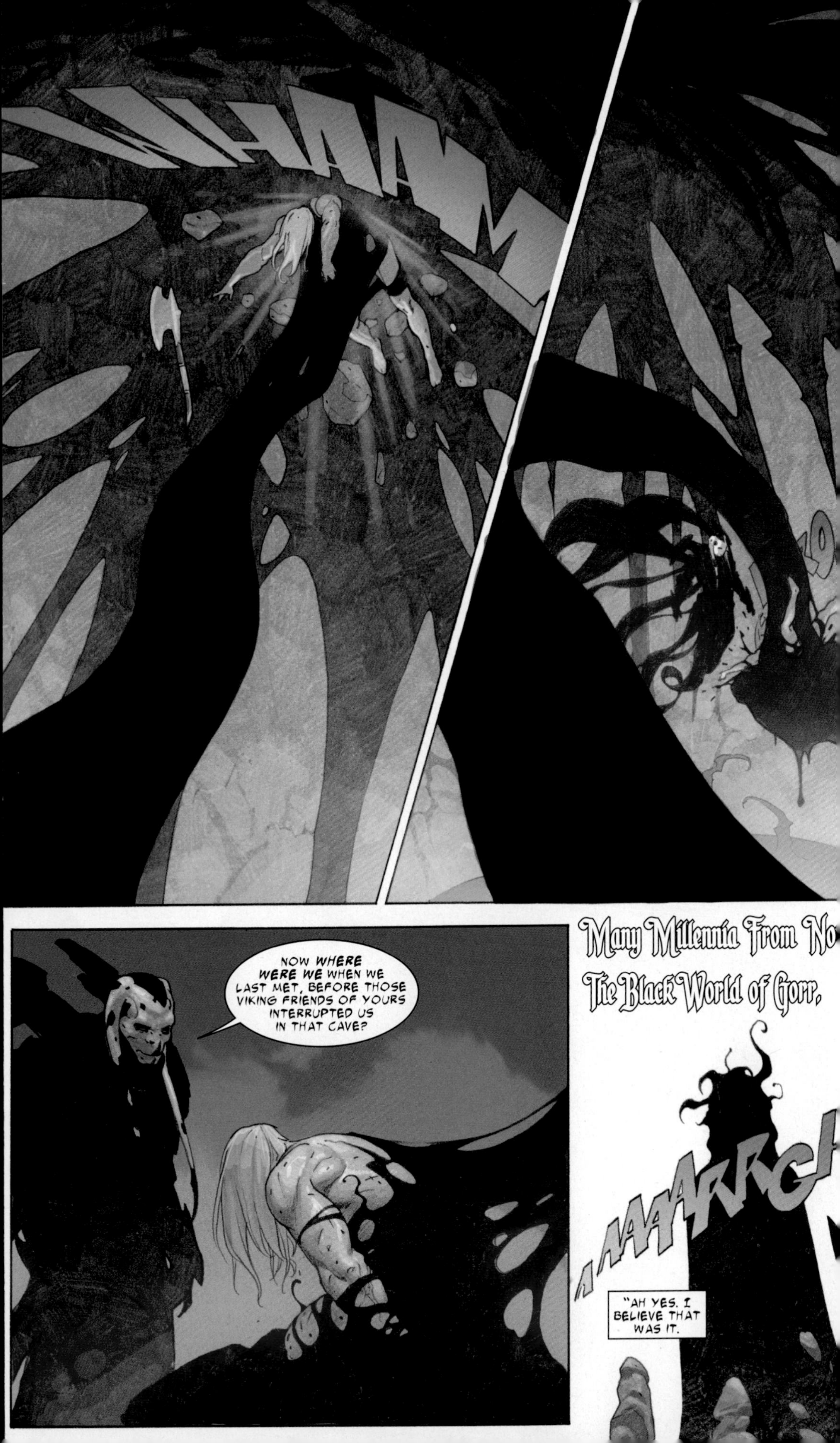
NOW WHERE WERE WE WHEN WE LAST MET, BEFORE THOSE VIKING FRIENDS OF YOURS INTERRUPTED US IN THAT CAVE?
Many Millennia From No
The Black World of Gorr,
AAAARRGH
"AH YES. I BELIEVE THAT WAS IT.

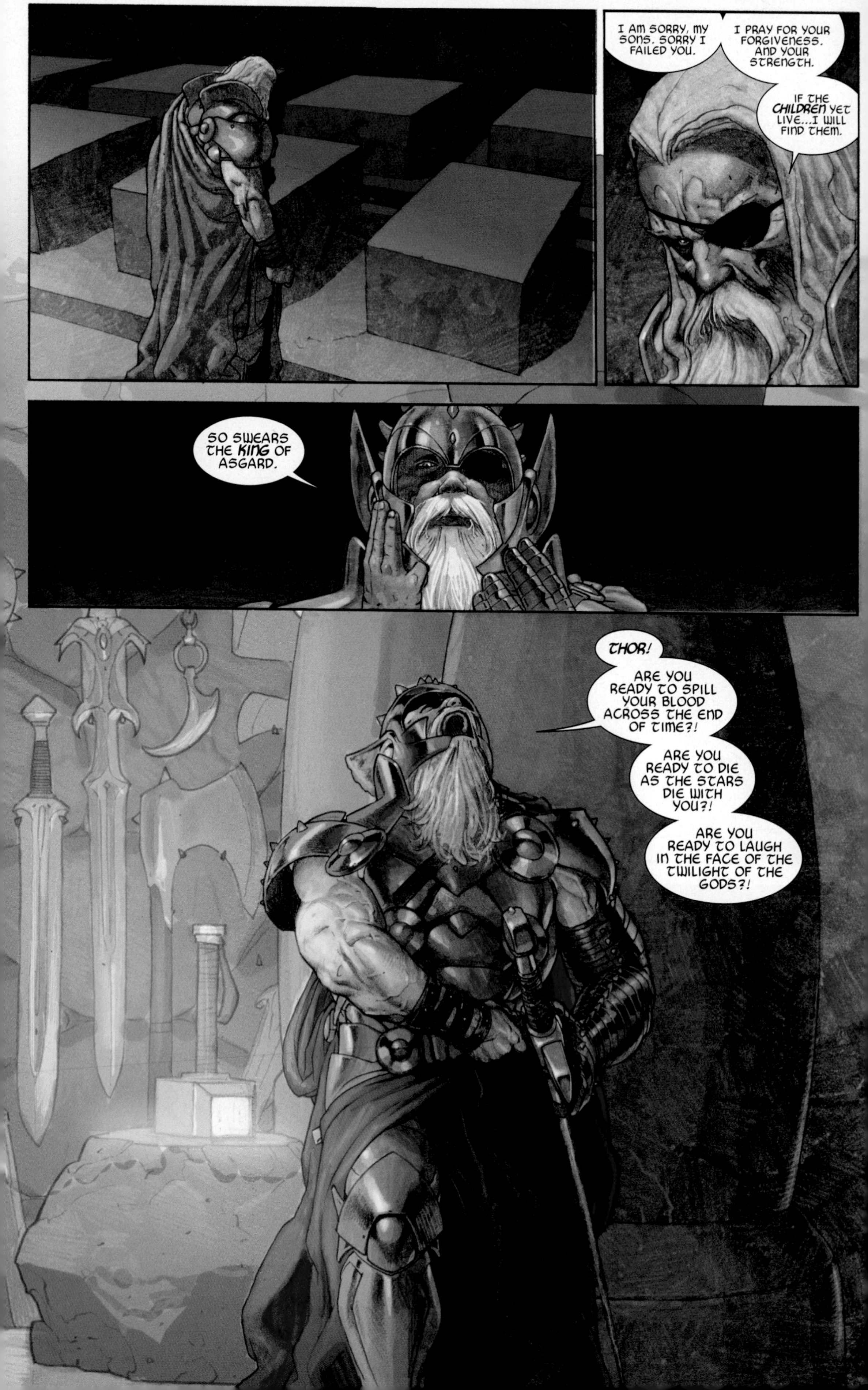
I AM SORRY, MY SONS. SORRY I FAILED YOU.
I PRAY FOR YOUR FORGIVENESS. AND YOUR STRENGTH.
IF THE CHILDREN YET LIVE...I WILL FIND THEM.
SO SWEARS THE KING OF ASGARD.
THOR!
ARE YOU READY TO SPILL YOUR BLOOD ACROSS THE END OF TIME?!
ARE YOU READY TO DIE AS THE STARS DIE WITH YOU?!
ARE YOU READY TO LAUGH IN THE FACE OF THE TWILIGHT OF THE GODS?!

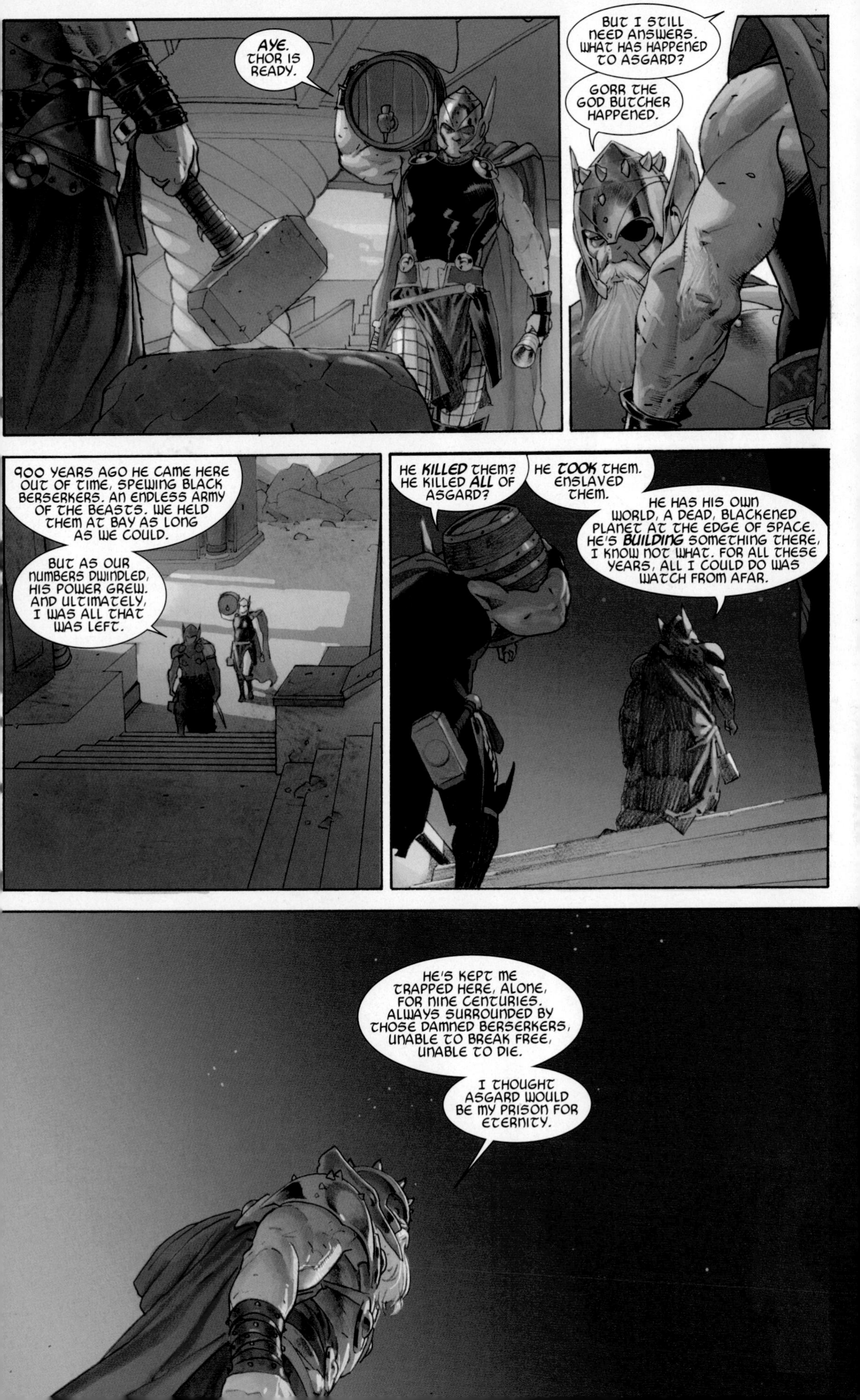
AYE. THOR IS READY.
BUT I STILL NEED ANSWERS. WHAT HAS HAPPENED TO ASGARD?
GORR THE GOD BUTCHER HAPPENED.
900 YEARS AGO HE CAME HERE OUT OF TIME, SPEWING BLACK BERSERKERS. AN ENDLESS ARMY OF THE BEASTS. WE HELD THEM AT BAY AS LONG AS WE COULD.
BUT AS OUR NUMBERS DWINDLED, HIS POWER GREW. AND ULTIMATELY, I WAS ALL THAT WAS LEFT.
HE KILLED THEM? HE KILLED ALL OF ASGARD?
HE TOOK THEM. ENSLAVED THEM.
HE HAS HIS OWN WORLD, A DEAD, BLACKENED PLANET AT THE EDGE OF SPACE. HE'S BUILDING SOMETHING THERE, I KNOW NOT WHAT. FOR ALL THESE YEARS, ALL I COULD DO WAS WATCH FROM AFAR.
HE'S KEPT ME TRAPPED HERE, ALONE, FOR NINE CENTURIES. ALWAYS SURROUNDED BY THOSE DAMNED BERSERKERS, UNABLE TO BREAK FREE, UNABLE TO DIE.
I THOUGHT ASGARD WOULD BE MY PRISON FOR ETERNITY.

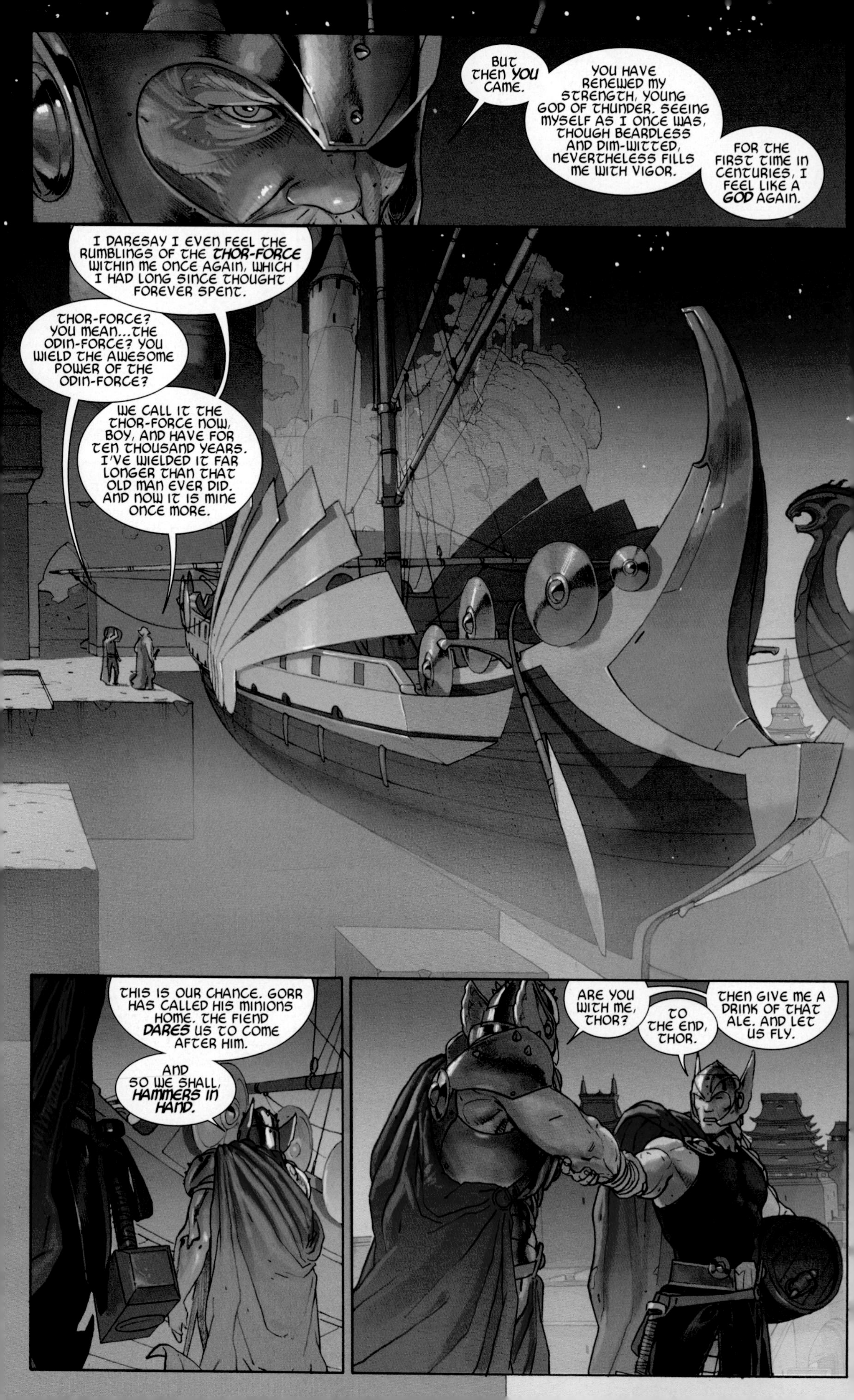
BUT THEN *YOU* CAME.
YOU HAVE RENEWED MY STRENGTH, YOUNG GOD OF THUNDER. SEEING MYSELF AS I ONCE WAS, THOUGH BEARDLESS AND DIM-WITTED, NEVERTHELESS FILLS ME WITH VIGOR.
FOR THE FIRST TIME IN CENTURIES, I FEEL LIKE A *GOD* AGAIN.
I DARESAY I EVEN FEEL THE RUMBLINGS OF THE *THOR-FORCE* WITHIN ME ONCE AGAIN, WHICH I HAD LONG SINCE THOUGHT FOREVER SPENT.
THOR-FORCE? YOU MEAN...THE ODIN-FORCE? YOU WIELD THE AWESOME POWER OF THE ODIN-FORCE?
WE CALL IT THE THOR-FORCE NOW, BOY, AND HAVE FOR TEN THOUSAND YEARS. I'VE WIELDED IT FAR LONGER THAN THAT OLD MAN EVER DID. AND NOW IT IS MINE ONCE MORE.
THIS IS OUR CHANCE. GORR HAS CALLED HIS MINIONS HOME. THE FIEND *DARES* US TO COME AFTER HIM.
AND SO WE SHALL, *HAMMERS IN HAND.*
ARE YOU WITH ME, THOR?
TO THE END, THOR.
THEN GIVE ME A DRINK OF THAT ALE. AND LET US FLY.

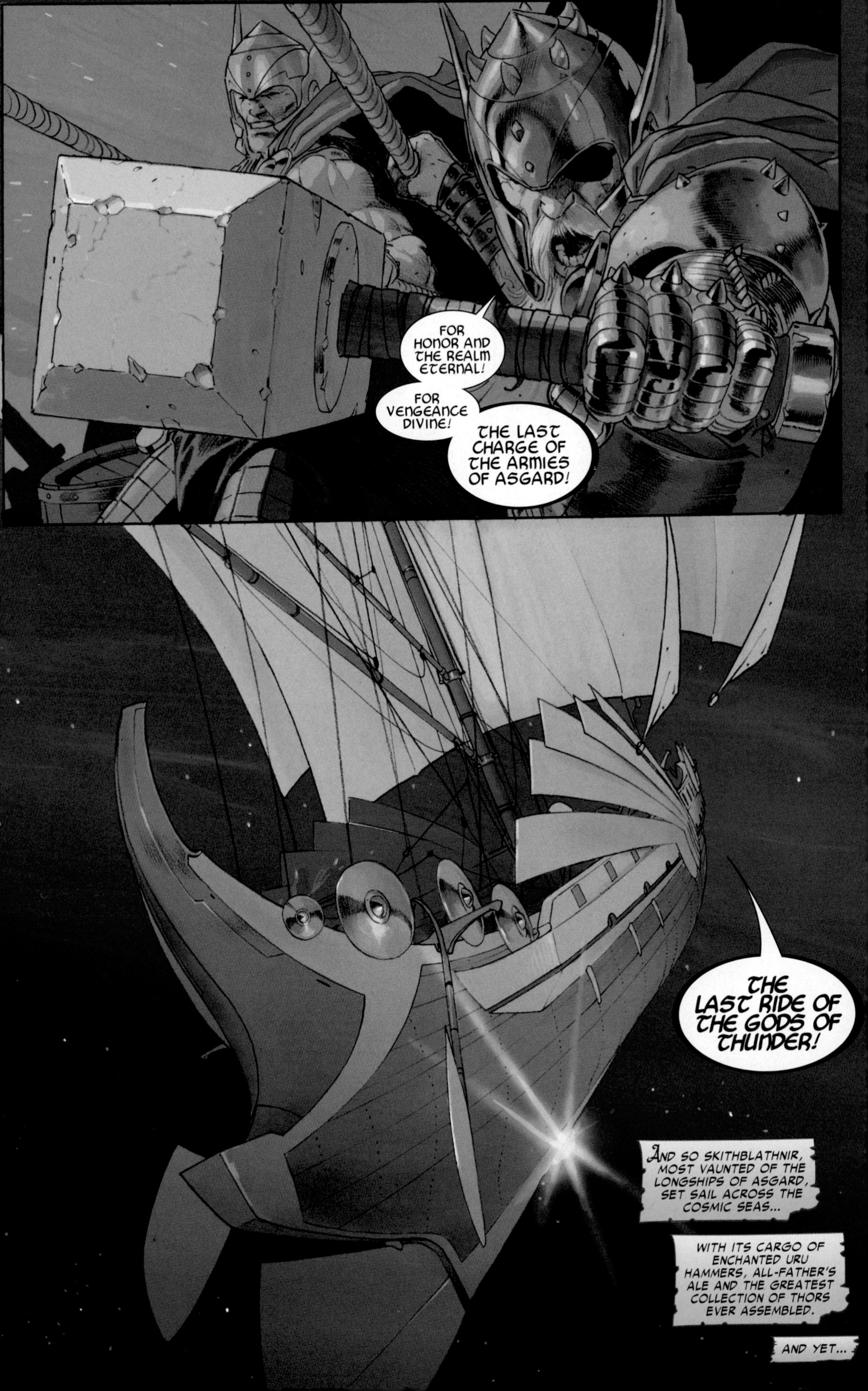
FOR HONOR AND THE REALM ETERNAL!
FOR VENGEANCE DIVINE!
THE LAST CHARGE OF THE ARMIES OF ASGARD!
THE LAST RIDE OF THE GODS OF THUNDER!
AND SO SKITHBLATHNIR, MOST VAUNTED OF THE LONGSHIPS OF ASGARD, SET SAIL ACROSS THE COSMIC SEAS...
WITH ITS CARGO OF ENCHANTED URU HAMMERS, ALL-FATHER'S ALE AND THE GREATEST COLLECTION OF THORS EVER ASSEMBLED.
AND YET...

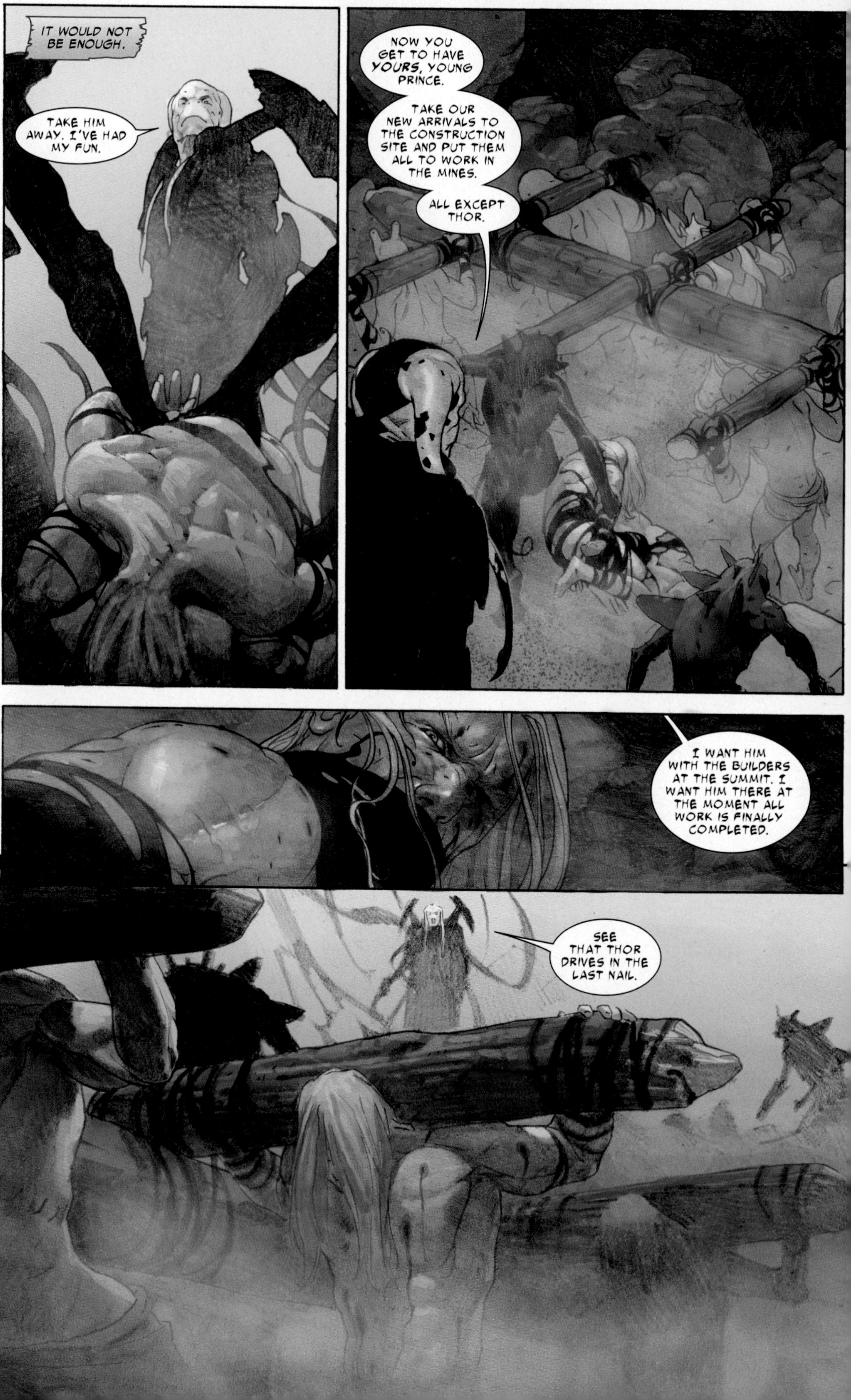
IT WOULD NOT BE ENOUGH.
TAKE HIM AWAY. I'VE HAD MY FUN.
NOW YOU GET TO HAVE YOURS, YOUNG PRINCE.
TAKE OUR NEW ARRIVALS TO THE CONSTRUCTION SITE AND PUT THEM ALL TO WORK IN THE MINES.
ALL EXCEPT THOR.
I WANT HIM WITH THE BUILDERS AT THE SUMMIT. I WANT HIM THERE AT THE MOMENT ALL WORK IS FINALLY COMPLETED.
SEE THAT THOR DRIVES IN THE LAST NAIL.

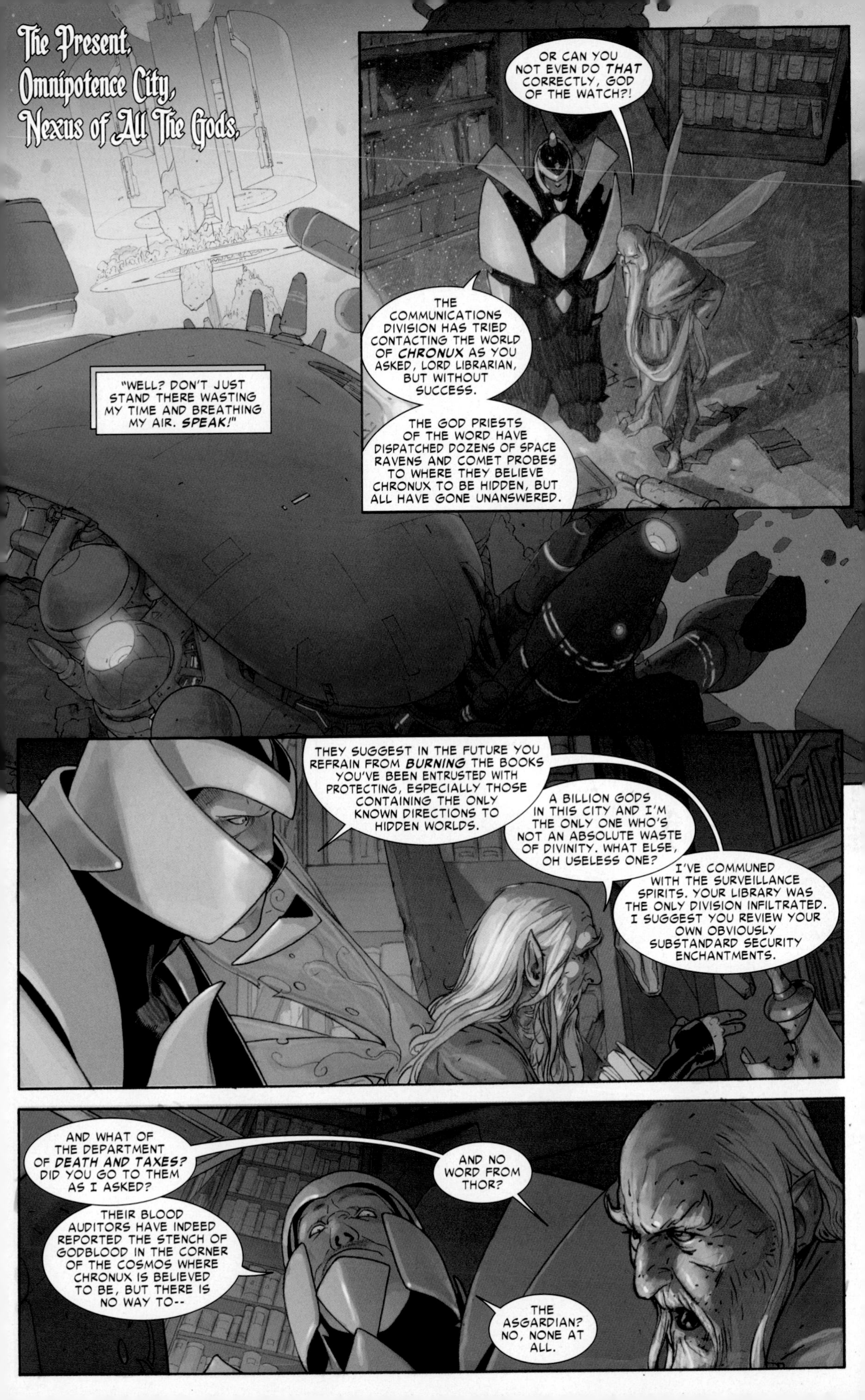
The Present, Omnipotence City, Nexus of All The Gods,
"WELL? DON'T JUST STAND THERE WASTING MY TIME AND BREATHING MY AIR. SPEAK!"
OR CAN YOU NOT EVEN DO THAT CORRECTLY, GOD OF THE WATCH?!
THE COMMUNICATIONS DIVISION HAS TRIED CONTACTING THE WORLD OF CHRONUX AS YOU ASKED, LORD LIBRARIAN, BUT WITHOUT SUCCESS.
THE GOD PRIESTS OF THE WORD HAVE DISPATCHED DOZENS OF SPACE RAVENS AND COMET PROBES TO WHERE THEY BELIEVE CHRONUX TO BE HIDDEN, BUT ALL HAVE GONE UNANSWERED.
THEY SUGGEST IN THE FUTURE YOU REFRAIN FROM BURNING THE BOOKS YOU'VE BEEN ENTRUSTED WITH PROTECTING, ESPECIALLY THOSE CONTAINING THE ONLY KNOWN DIRECTIONS TO HIDDEN WORLDS.
A BILLION GODS IN THIS CITY AND I'M THE ONLY ONE WHO'S NOT AN ABSOLUTE WASTE OF DIVINITY. WHAT ELSE, OH USELESS ONE?
I'VE COMMUNED WITH THE SURVEILLANCE SPIRITS. YOUR LIBRARY WAS THE ONLY DIVISION INFILTRATED. I SUGGEST YOU REVIEW YOUR OWN OBVIOUSLY SUBSTANDARD SECURITY ENCHANTMENTS.
AND WHAT OF THE DEPARTMENT OF DEATH AND TAXES? DID YOU GO TO THEM AS I ASKED?
THEIR BLOOD AUDITORS HAVE INDEED REPORTED THE STENCH OF GODBLOOD IN THE CORNER OF THE COSMOS WHERE CHRONUX IS BELIEVED TO BE, BUT THERE IS NO WAY TO--
AND NO WORD FROM THOR?
THE ASGARDIAN? NO, NONE AT ALL.

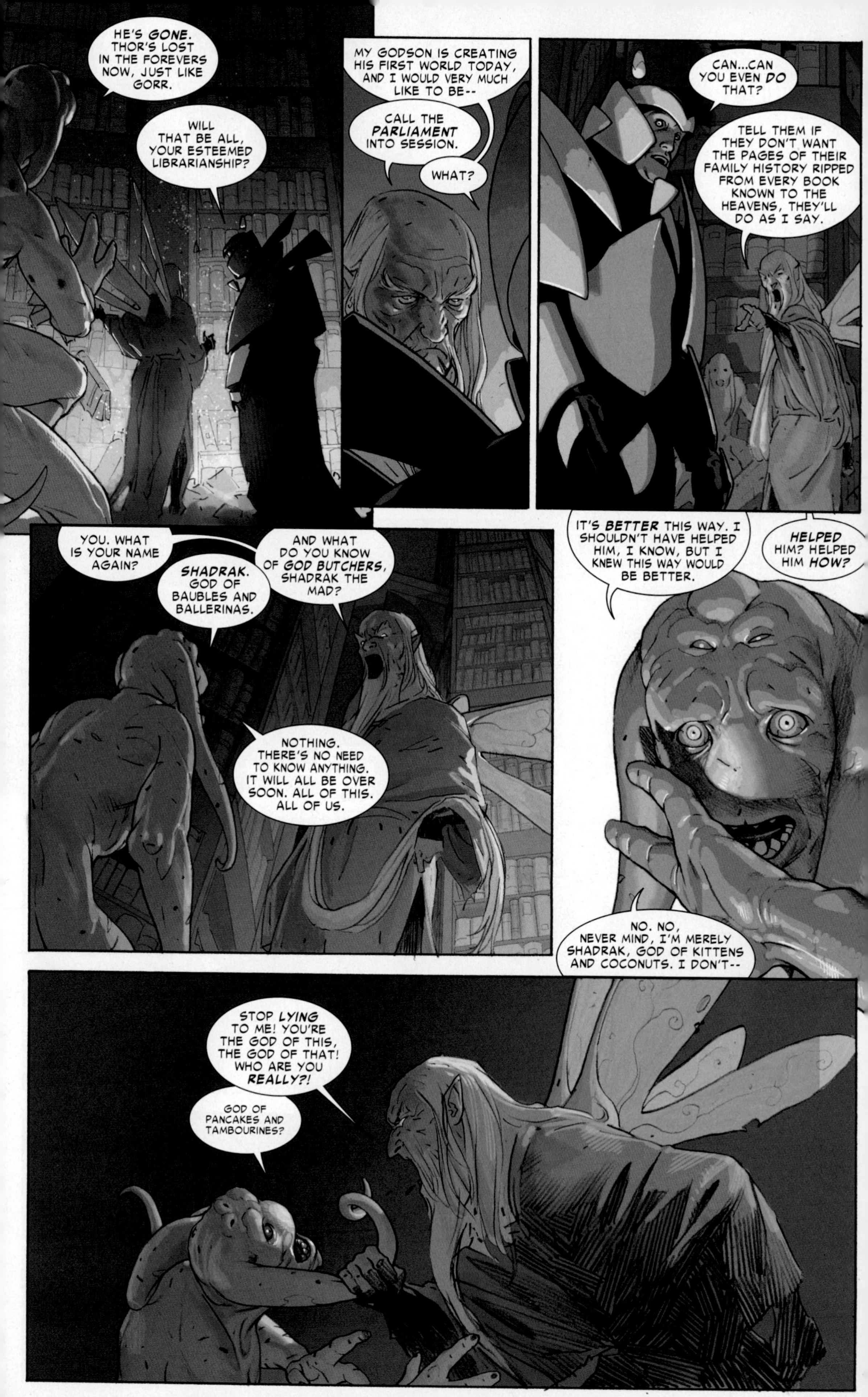
HE'S GONE. THOR'S LOST IN THE FOREVERS NOW, JUST LIKE GORR.
WILL THAT BE ALL, YOUR ESTEEMED LIBRARIANSHIP?
MY GODSON IS CREATING HIS FIRST WORLD TODAY, AND I WOULD VERY MUCH LIKE TO BE--
CALL THE PARLIAMENT INTO SESSION.
WHAT?
CAN...CAN YOU EVEN DO THAT?
TELL THEM IF THEY DON'T WANT THE PAGES OF THEIR FAMILY HISTORY RIPPED FROM EVERY BOOK KNOWN TO THE HEAVENS, THEY'LL DO AS I SAY.
YOU. WHAT IS YOUR NAME AGAIN?
SHADRAK. GOD OF BAUBLES AND BALLERINAS.
AND WHAT DO YOU KNOW OF GOD BUTCHERS, SHADRAK THE MAD?
NOTHING. THERE'S NO NEED TO KNOW ANYTHING. IT WILL ALL BE OVER SOON. ALL OF THIS. ALL OF US.
IT'S BETTER THIS WAY. I SHOULDN'T HAVE HELPED HIM, I KNOW, BUT I KNEW THIS WAY WOULD BE BETTER.
HELPED HIM? HELPED HIM HOW?
NO. NO, NEVER MIND, I'M MERELY SHADRAK, GOD OF KITTENS AND COCONUTS. I DON'T--
STOP LYING TO ME! YOU'RE THE GOD OF THIS, THE GOD OF THAT! WHO ARE YOU REALLY?!
GOD OF PANCAKES AND TAMBOURINES?

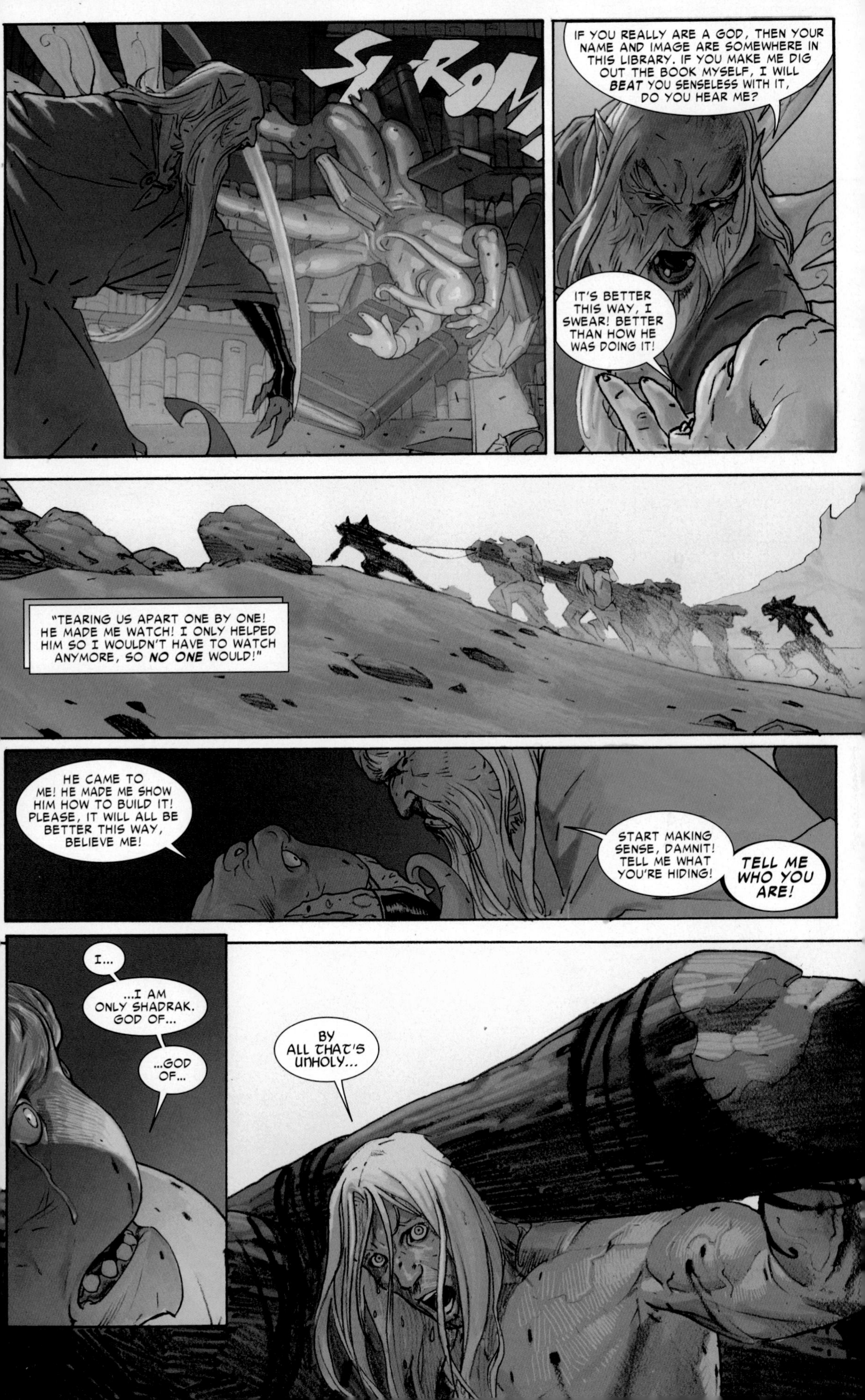
SKROM
IF YOU REALLY ARE A GOD, THEN YOUR NAME AND IMAGE ARE SOMEWHERE IN THIS LIBRARY. IF YOU MAKE ME DIG OUT THE BOOK MYSELF, I WILL BEAT YOU SENSELESS WITH IT, DO YOU HEAR ME?
IT'S BETTER THIS WAY, I SWEAR! BETTER THAN HOW HE WAS DOING IT!
"TEARING US APART ONE BY ONE! HE MADE ME WATCH! I ONLY HELPED HIM SO I WOULDN'T HAVE TO WATCH ANYMORE, SO NO ONE WOULD!"
HE CAME TO ME! HE MADE ME SHOW HIM HOW TO BUILD IT! PLEASE, IT WILL ALL BE BETTER THIS WAY, BELIEVE ME!
START MAKING SENSE, DAMNIT! TELL ME WHAT YOU'RE HIDING!
TELL ME WHO YOU ARE!
I...
...I AM ONLY SHADRAK. GOD OF...
...GOD OF...
BY ALL THAT'S UNHOLY...

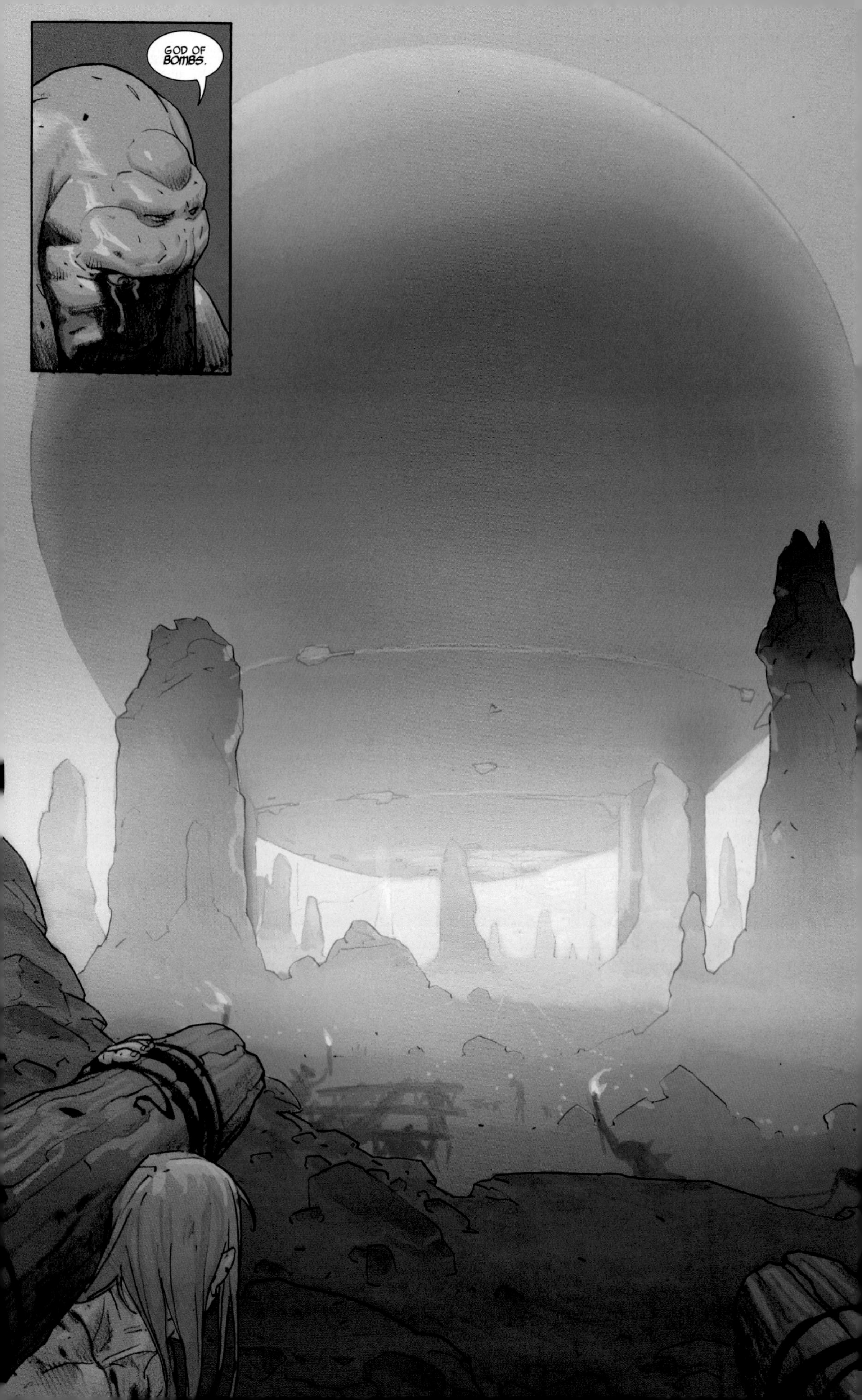
GOD OF BOMBS.

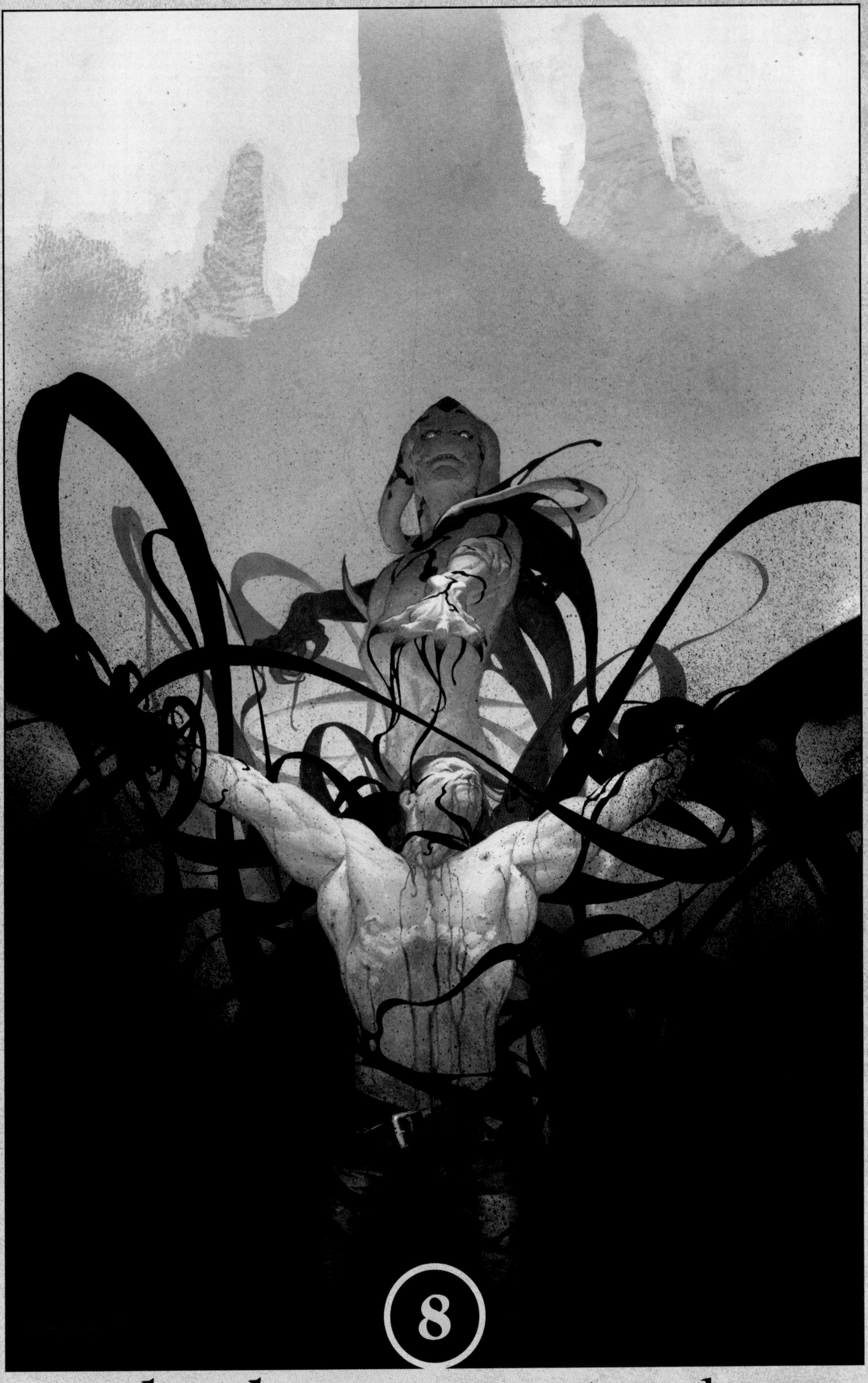
8

GODBOMB PART TWO: GOD IN CHAINS

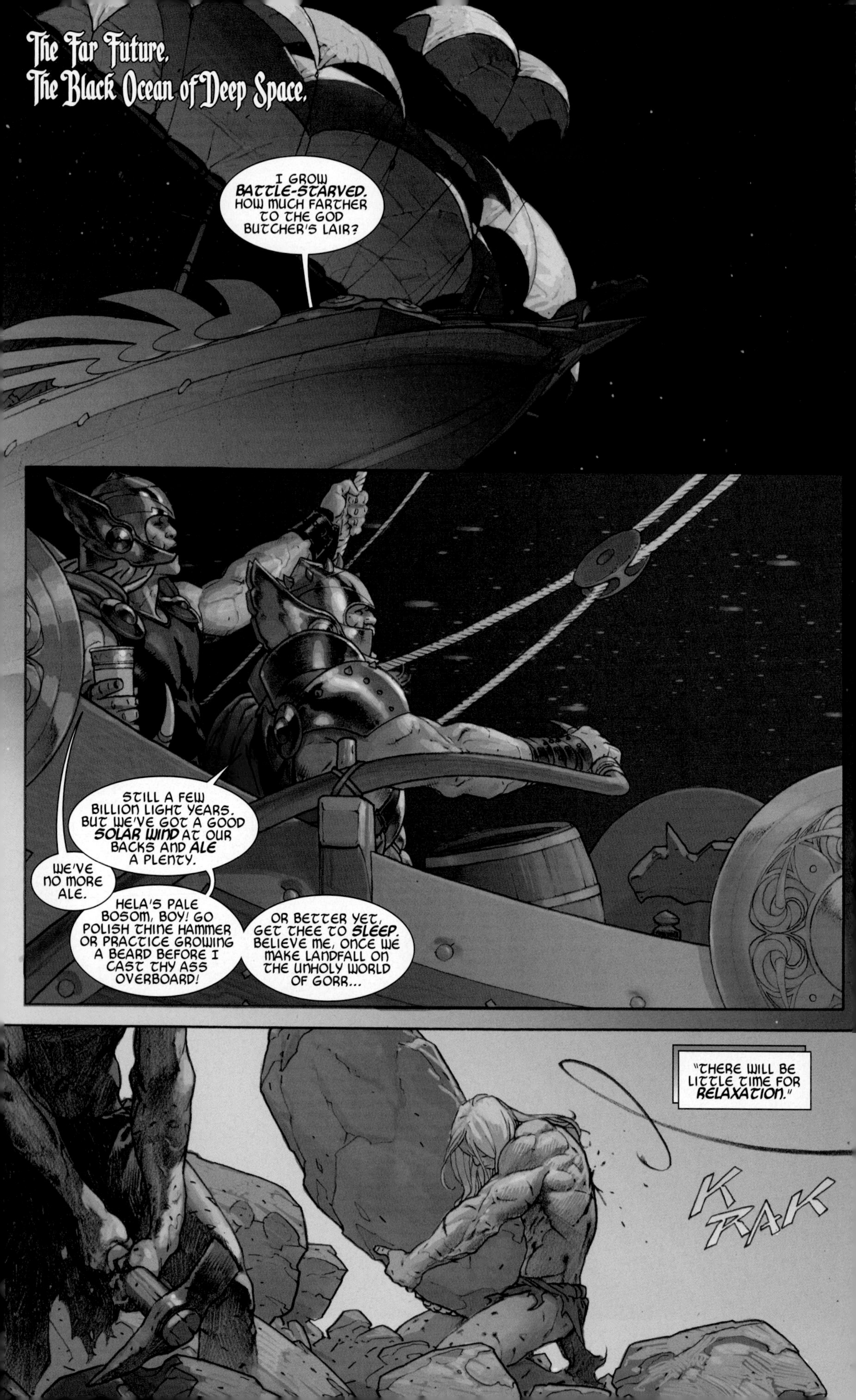
The Far Future.
The Black Ocean of Deep Space.
I GROW BATTLE-STARVED. HOW MUCH FARTHER TO THE GOD BUTCHER'S LAIR?
STILL A FEW BILLION LIGHT YEARS. BUT WE'VE GOT A GOOD SOLAR WIND AT OUR BACKS AND ALE A PLENTY.
WE'VE NO MORE ALE.
HELA'S PALE BOSOM, BOY! GO POLISH THINE HAMMER OR PRACTICE GROWING A BEARD BEFORE I CAST THY ASS OVERBOARD!
OR BETTER YET, GET THEE TO SLEEP. BELIEVE ME, ONCE WE MAKE LANDFALL ON THE UNHOLY WORLD OF GORR...
"THERE WILL BE LITTLE TIME FOR RELAXATION."
KRAK

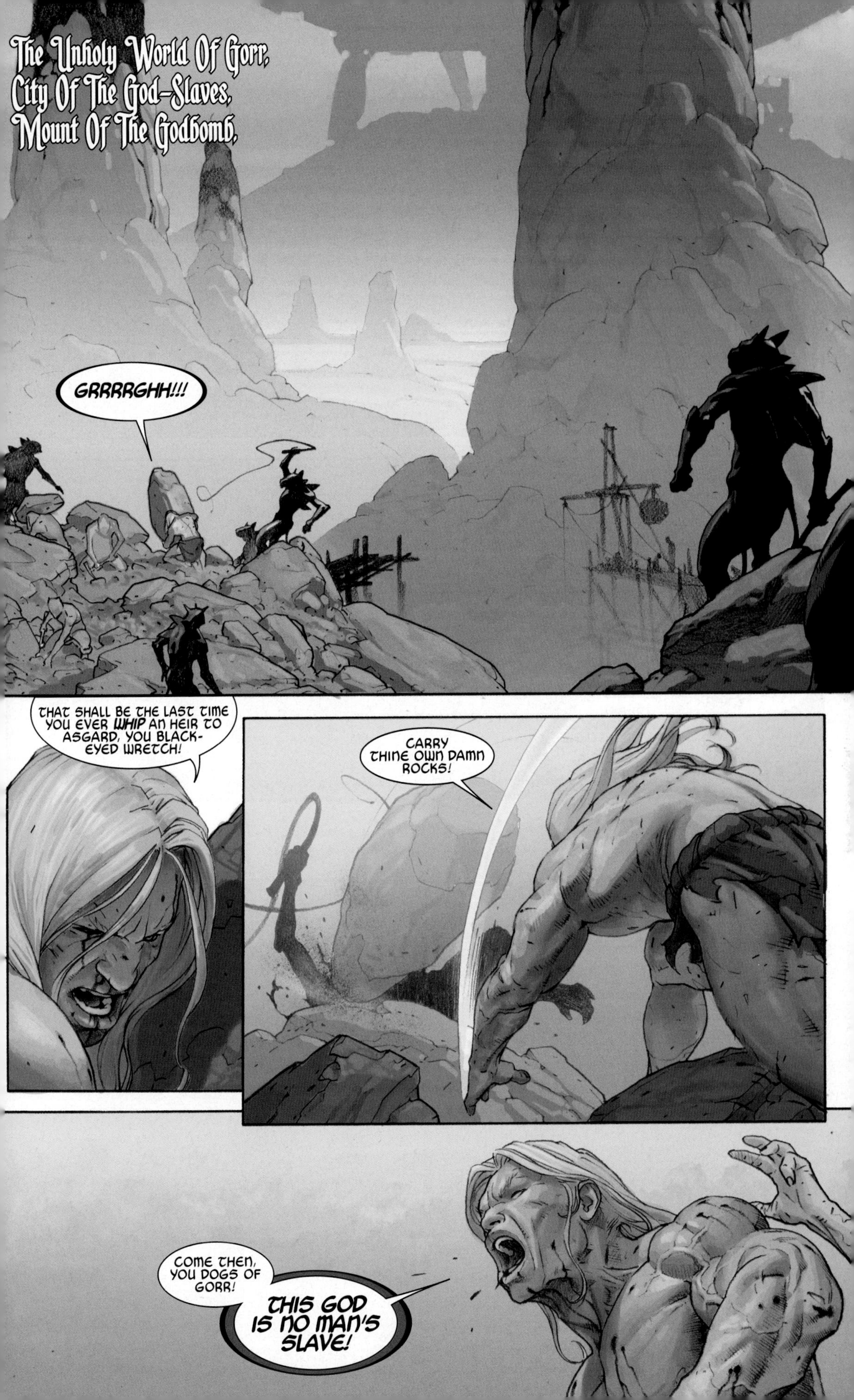
The Unholy World Of Gorr,
City Of The God-Slaves,
Mount Of The Godbomb.
GRRRRGHH!!!
THAT SHALL BE THE LAST TIME YOU EVER WHIP AN HEIR TO ASGARD, YOU BLACK-EYED WRETCH!
CARRY THINE OWN DAMN ROCKS!
COME THEN, YOU DOGS OF GORR!
THIS GOD IS NO MAN'S SLAVE!

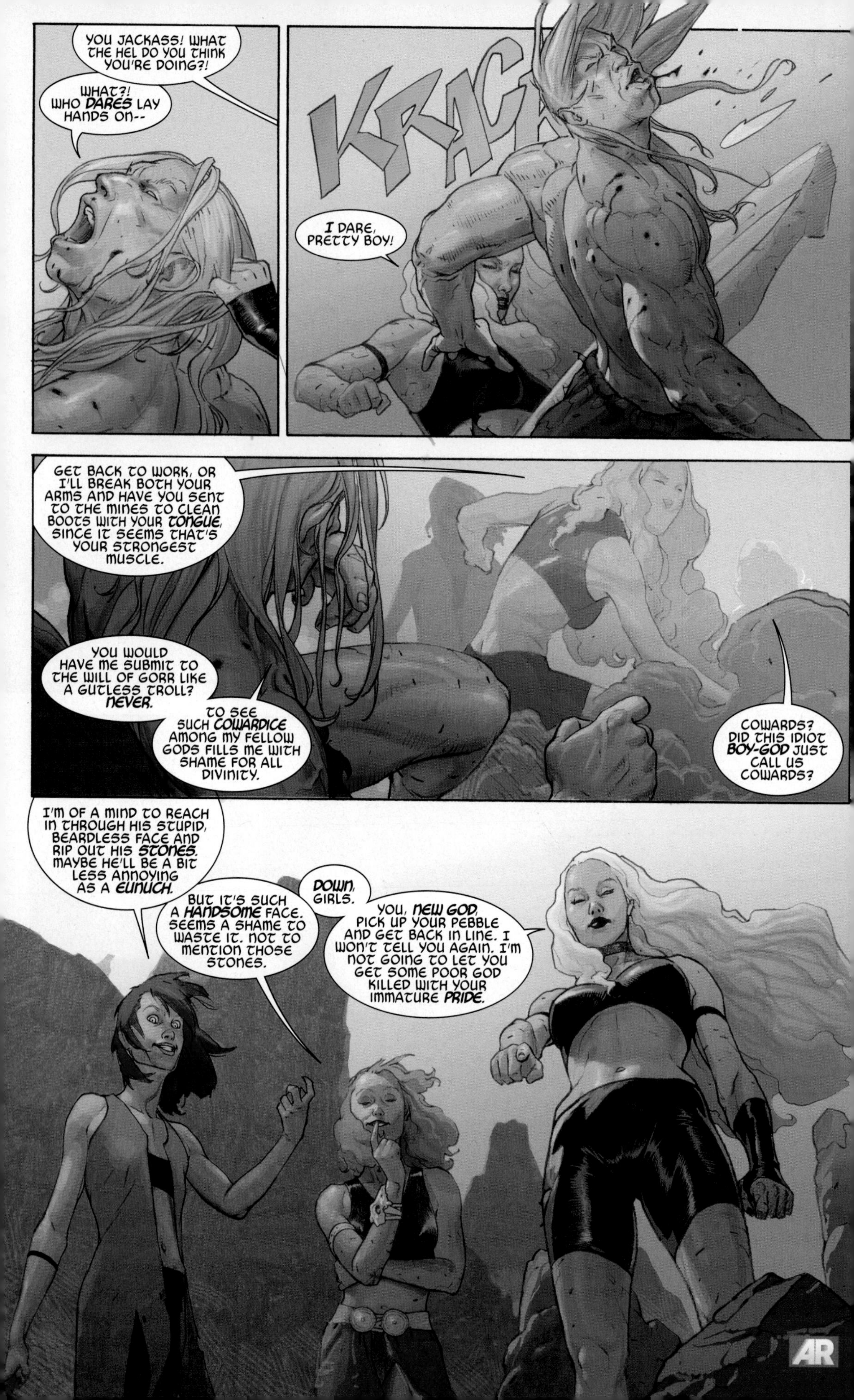

YOU JACKASS! WHAT THE HEL DO YOU THINK YOU'RE DOING?!
WHAT?! WHO DARES LAY HANDS ON--
KRACK
I DARE, PRETTY BOY!
GET BACK TO WORK, OR I'LL BREAK BOTH YOUR ARMS AND HAVE YOU SENT TO THE MINES TO CLEAN BOOTS WITH YOUR TONGUE, SINCE IT SEEMS THAT'S YOUR STRONGEST MUSCLE.
YOU WOULD HAVE ME SUBMIT TO THE WILL OF GORR LIKE A GUTLESS TROLL? NEVER.
TO SEE SUCH COWARDICE AMONG MY FELLOW GODS FILLS ME WITH SHAME FOR ALL DIVINITY.
COWARDS? DID THIS IDIOT BOY-GOD JUST CALL US COWARDS?
I'M OF A MIND TO REACH IN THROUGH HIS STUPID, BEARDLESS FACE AND RIP OUT HIS STONES. MAYBE HE'LL BE A BIT LESS ANNOYING AS A EUNUCH.
BUT IT'S SUCH A HANDSOME FACE. SEEMS A SHAME TO WASTE IT. NOT TO MENTION THOSE STONES.
DOWN, GIRLS.
YOU, NEW GOD, PICK UP YOUR PEBBLE AND GET BACK IN LINE. I WON'T TELL YOU AGAIN. I'M NOT GOING TO LET YOU GET SOME POOR GOD KILLED WITH YOUR IMMATURE PRIDE.

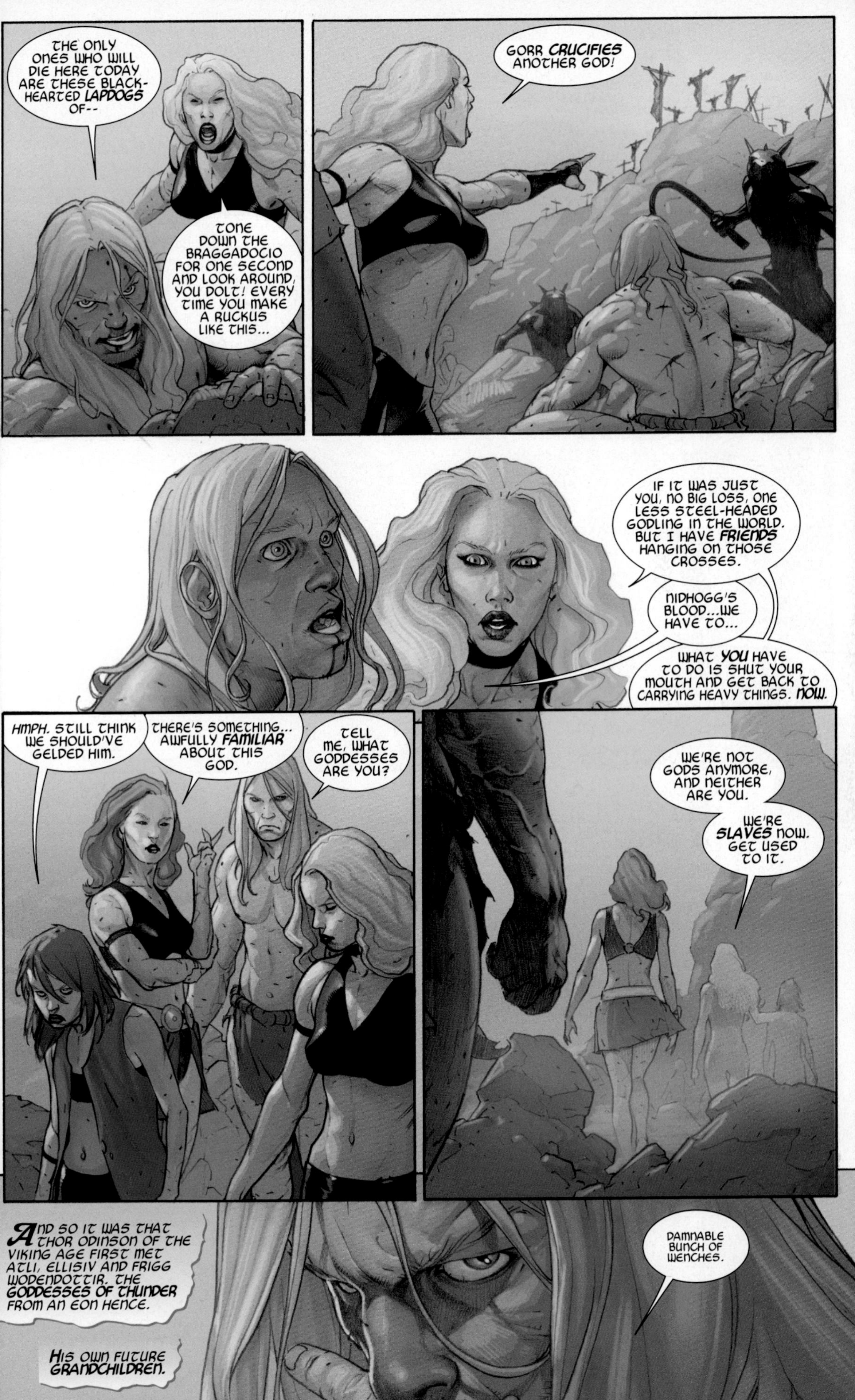
THE ONLY ONES WHO WILL DIE HERE TODAY ARE THESE BLACK-HEARTED LAPDOGS OF--
TONE DOWN THE BRAGGADOCIO FOR ONE SECOND AND LOOK AROUND, YOU DOLT! EVERY TIME YOU MAKE A RUCKUS LIKE THIS...
GORR CRUCIFIES ANOTHER GOD!
IF IT WAS JUST YOU, NO BIG LOSS. ONE LESS STEEL-HEADED GODLING IN THE WORLD. BUT I HAVE FRIENDS HANGING ON THOSE CROSSES.
NIDHOGG'S BLOOD...WE HAVE TO...
WHAT YOU HAVE TO DO IS SHUT YOUR MOUTH AND GET BACK TO CARRYING HEAVY THINGS. NOW.
HMPH. STILL THINK WE SHOULD'VE GELDED HIM.
THERE'S SOMETHING... AWFULLY FAMILIAR ABOUT THIS GOD.
TELL ME, WHAT GODDESSES ARE YOU?
WE'RE NOT GODS ANYMORE, AND NEITHER ARE YOU.
WE'RE SLAVES NOW. GET USED TO IT.
AND SO IT WAS THAT THOR ODINSON OF THE VIKING AGE FIRST MET ATLI, ELLISIV AND FRIGG WODENDOTTIR. THE GODDESSES OF THUNDER FROM AN EON HENCE.
DAMNABLE BUNCH OF WENCHES.
HIS OWN FUTURE GRANDCHILDREN.

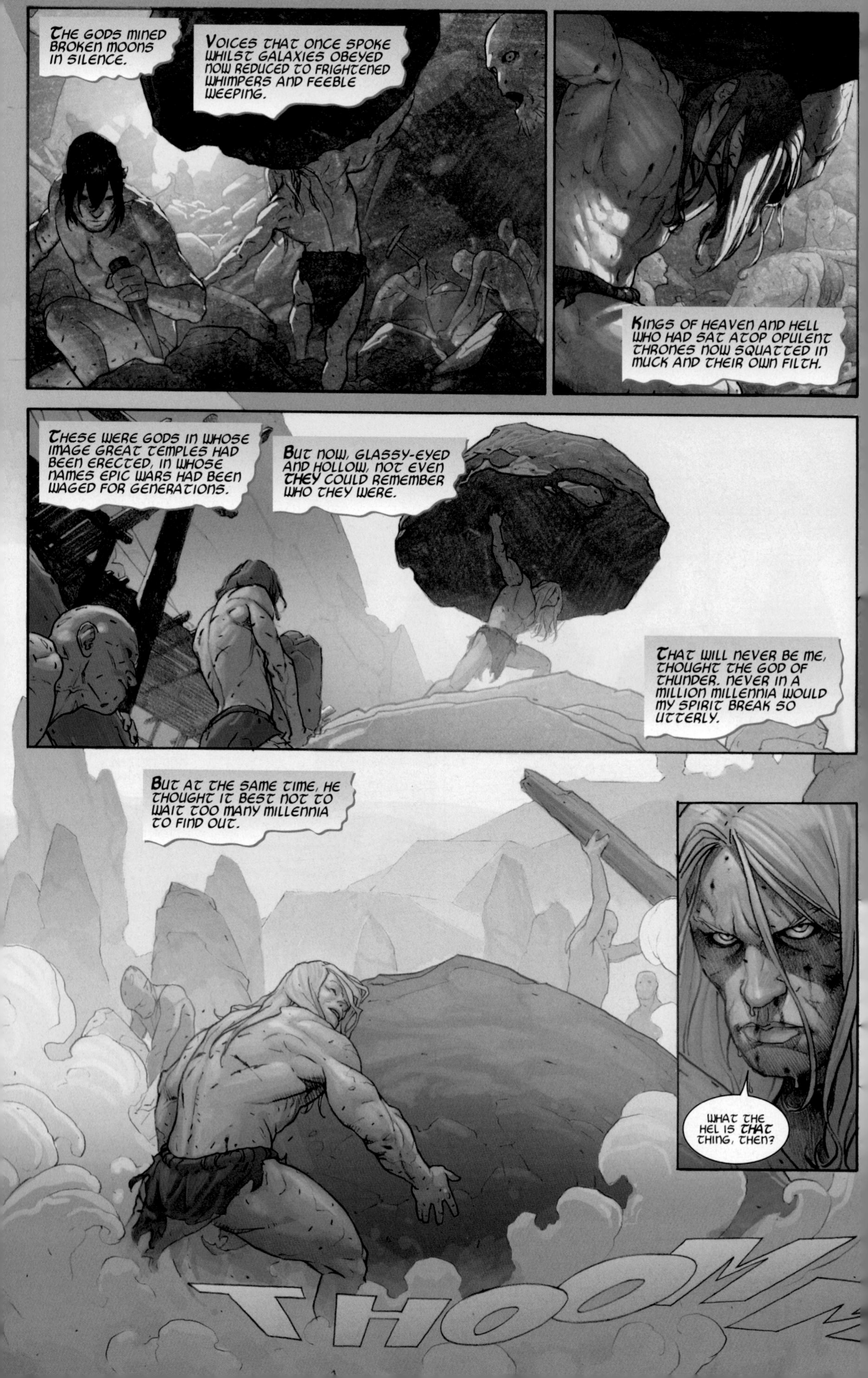
THE GODS MINED BROKEN MOONS IN SILENCE.
VOICES THAT ONCE SPOKE WHILST GALAXIES OBEYED NOW REDUCED TO FRIGHTENED WHIMPERS AND FEEBLE WEEPING.
KINGS OF HEAVEN AND HELL WHO HAD SAT ATOP OPULENT THRONES NOW SQUATTED IN MUCK AND THEIR OWN FILTH.
THESE WERE GODS IN WHOSE IMAGE GREAT TEMPLES HAD BEEN ERECTED, IN WHOSE NAMES EPIC WARS HAD BEEN WAGED FOR GENERATIONS.
BUT NOW, GLASSY-EYED AND HOLLOW, NOT EVEN THEY COULD REMEMBER WHO THEY WERE.
THAT WILL NEVER BE ME, THOUGHT THE GOD OF THUNDER. NEVER IN A MILLION MILLENNIA WOULD MY SPIRIT BREAK SO UTTERLY.
BUT AT THE SAME TIME, HE THOUGHT IT BEST NOT TO WAIT TOO MANY MILLENNIA TO FIND OUT.
WHAT THE HEL IS THAT THING, THEN?
THOOM

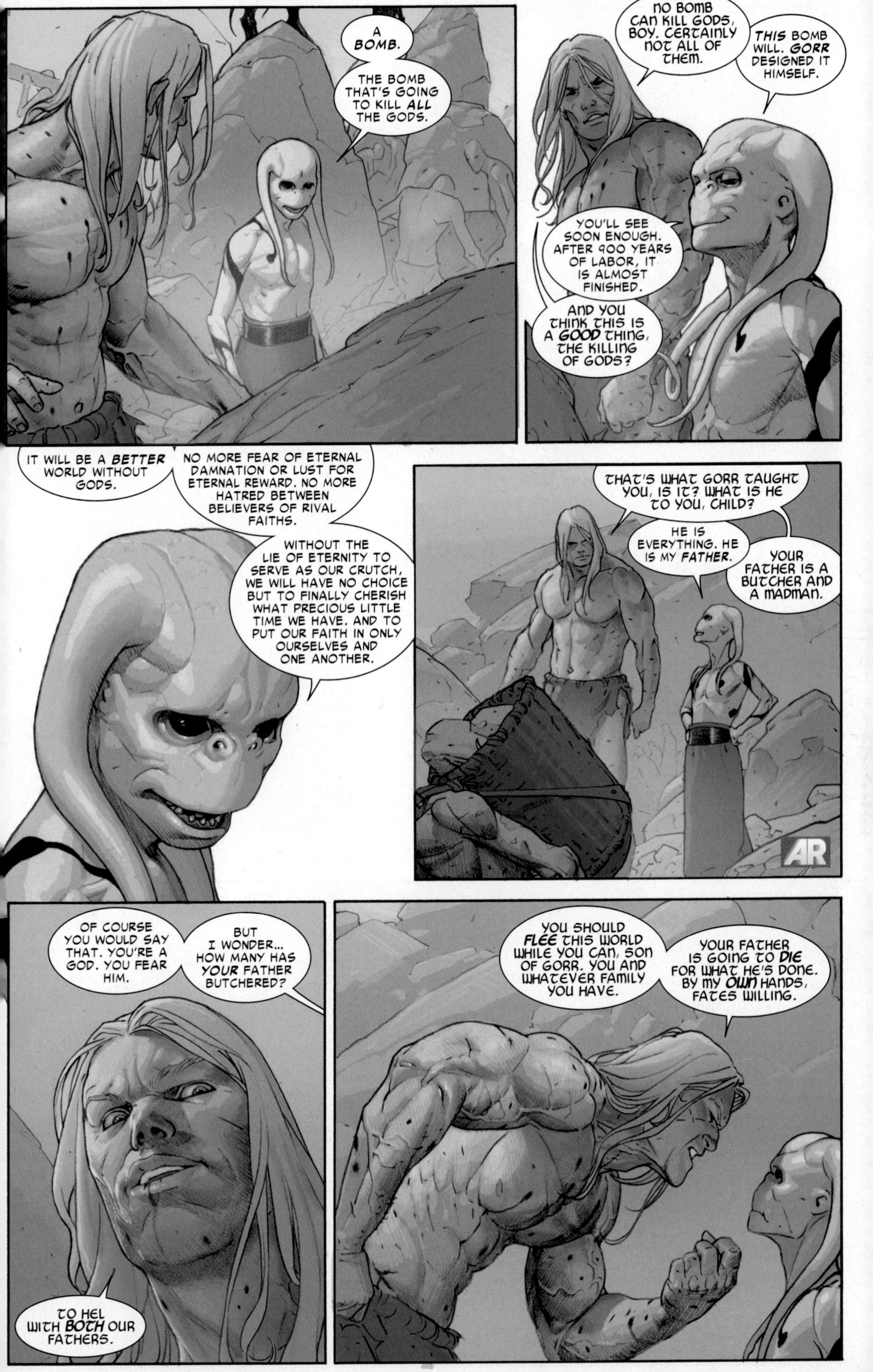
A BOMB.
THE BOMB THAT'S GOING TO KILL ALL THE GODS.
NO BOMB CAN KILL GODS, BOY. CERTAINLY NOT ALL OF THEM.
THIS BOMB WILL. GORR DESIGNED IT HIMSELF.
YOU'LL SEE SOON ENOUGH. AFTER 900 YEARS OF LABOR, IT IS ALMOST FINISHED.
AND YOU THINK THIS IS A GOOD THING, THE KILLING OF GODS?
IT WILL BE A BETTER WORLD WITHOUT GODS.
NO MORE FEAR OF ETERNAL DAMNATION OR LUST FOR ETERNAL REWARD. NO MORE HATRED BETWEEN BELIEVERS OF RIVAL FAITHS.
WITHOUT THE LIE OF ETERNITY TO SERVE AS OUR CRUTCH, WE WILL HAVE NO CHOICE BUT TO FINALLY CHERISH WHAT PRECIOUS LITTLE TIME WE HAVE. AND TO PUT OUR FAITH IN ONLY OURSELVES AND ONE ANOTHER.
THAT'S WHAT GORR TAUGHT YOU, IS IT? WHAT IS HE TO YOU, CHILD?
HE IS EVERYTHING. HE IS MY FATHER.
YOUR FATHER IS A BUTCHER AND A MADMAN.
OF COURSE YOU WOULD SAY THAT. YOU'RE A GOD. YOU FEAR HIM.
BUT I WONDER... HOW MANY HAS YOUR FATHER BUTCHERED?
TO HEL WITH BOTH OUR FATHERS.
YOU SHOULD FLEE THIS WORLD WHILE YOU CAN, SON OF GORR. YOU AND WHATEVER FAMILY YOU HAVE.
YOUR FATHER IS GOING TO DIE FOR WHAT HE'S DONE. BY MY OWN HANDS, FATES WILLING.

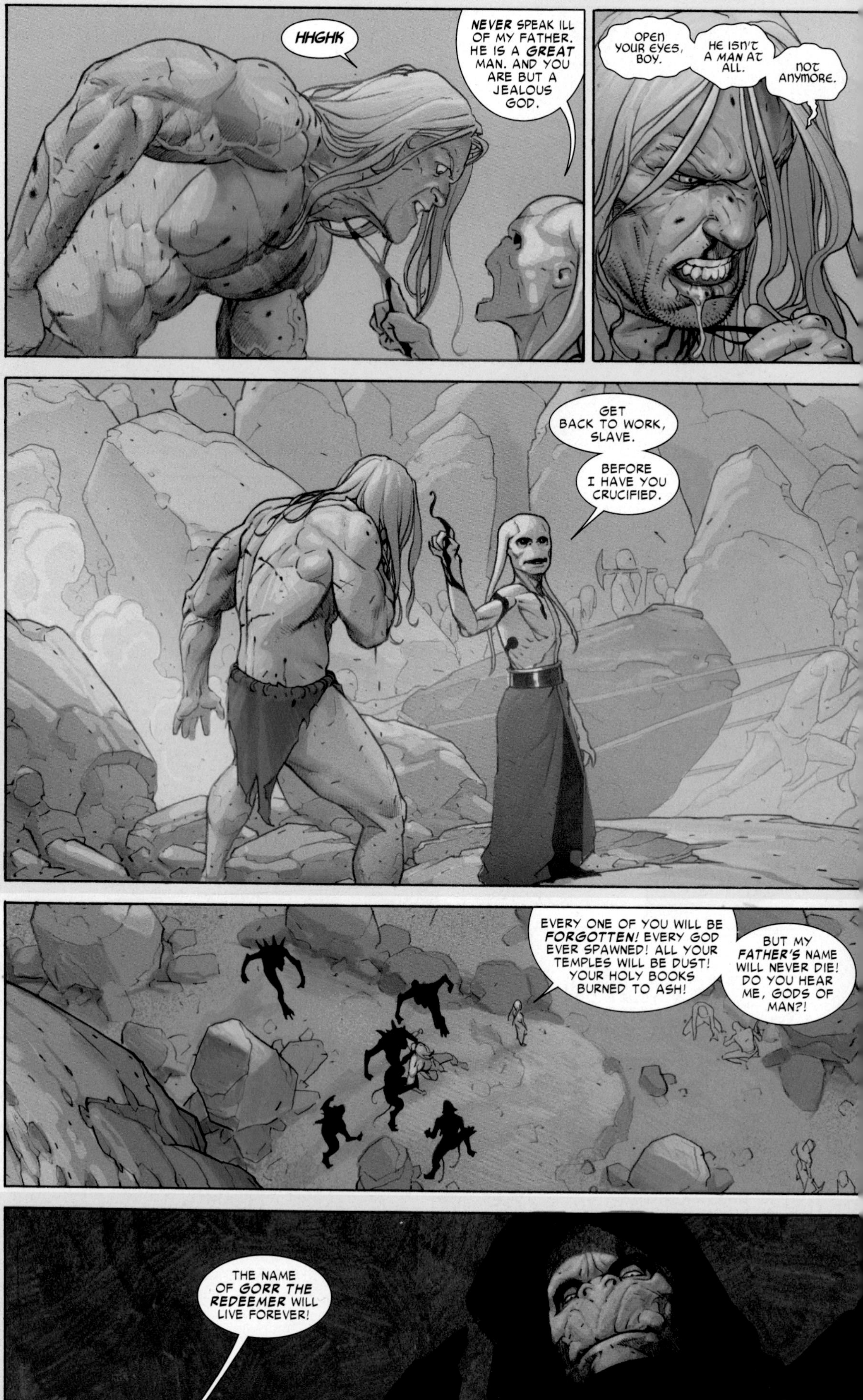
HHGHK
NEVER SPEAK ILL OF MY FATHER. HE IS A GREAT MAN. AND YOU ARE BUT A JEALOUS GOD.
OPEN YOUR EYES, BOY.
HE ISN'T A MAN AT ALL.
NOT ANYMORE.
GET BACK TO WORK, SLAVE.
BEFORE I HAVE YOU CRUCIFIED.
EVERY ONE OF YOU WILL BE FORGOTTEN! EVERY GOD EVER SPAWNED! ALL YOUR TEMPLES WILL BE DUST! YOUR HOLY BOOKS BURNED TO ASH!
BUT MY FATHER'S NAME WILL NEVER DIE! DO YOU HEAR ME, GODS OF MAN?!
THE NAME OF GORR THE REDEEMER WILL LIVE FOREVER!

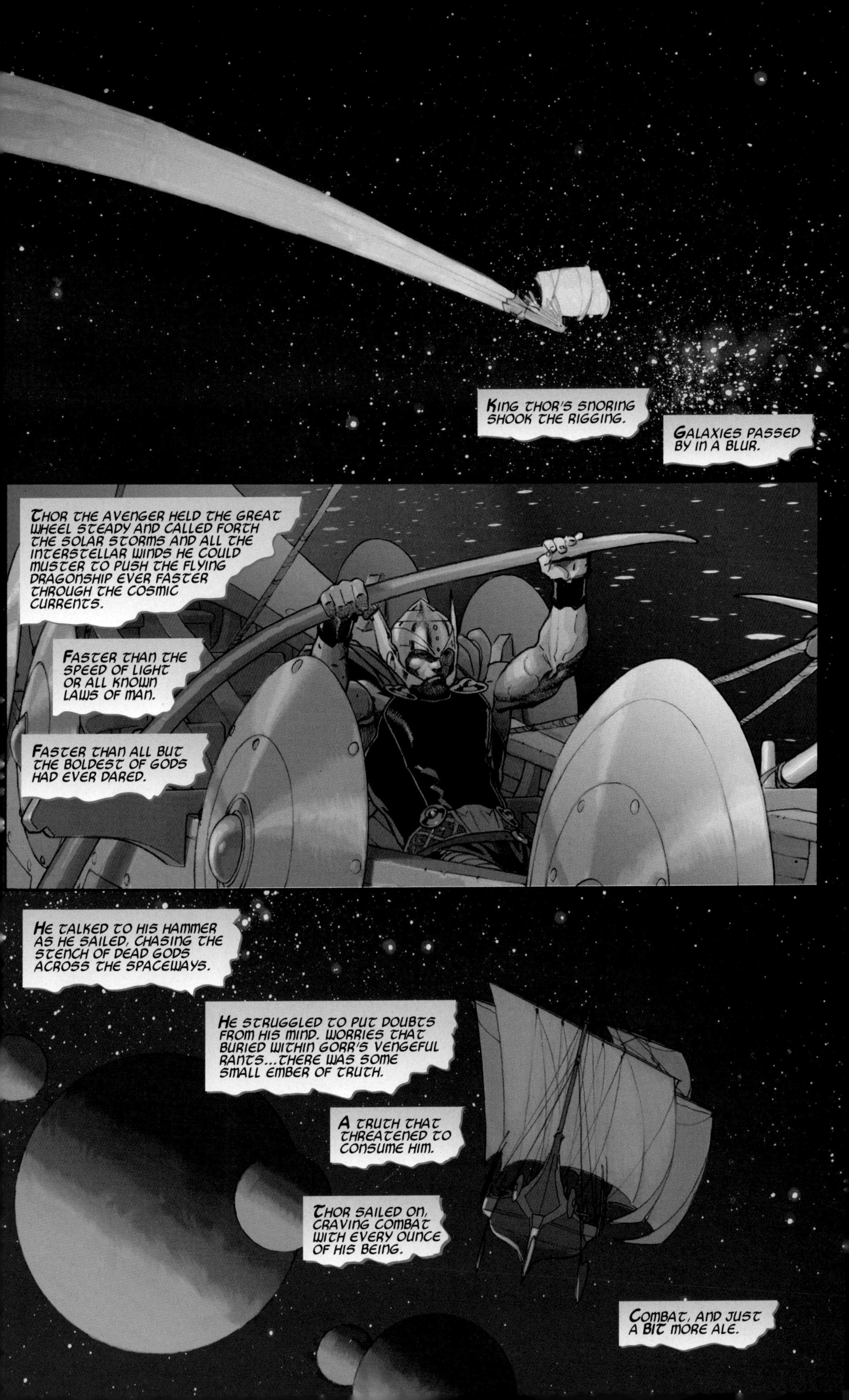

KING THOR'S SNORING SHOOK THE RIGGING.
GALAXIES PASSED BY IN A BLUR.
THOR THE AVENGER HELD THE GREAT WHEEL STEADY AND CALLED FORTH THE SOLAR STORMS AND ALL THE INTERSTELLAR WINDS HE COULD MUSTER TO PUSH THE FLYING DRAGONSHIP EVER FASTER THROUGH THE COSMIC CURRENTS.
FASTER THAN THE SPEED OF LIGHT OR ALL KNOWN LAWS OF MAN.
FASTER THAN ALL BUT THE BOLDEST OF GODS HAD EVER DARED.
HE TALKED TO HIS HAMMER AS HE SAILED, CHASING THE STENCH OF DEAD GODS ACROSS THE SPACEWAYS.
HE STRUGGLED TO PUT DOUBTS FROM HIS MIND. WORRIES THAT BURIED WITHIN GORR'S VENGEFUL RANTS...THERE WAS SOME SMALL EMBER OF TRUTH.
A TRUTH THAT THREATENED TO CONSUME HIM.
THOR SAILED ON, CRAVING COMBAT WITH EVERY OUNCE OF HIS BEING.
COMBAT, AND JUST A BIT MORE ALE.

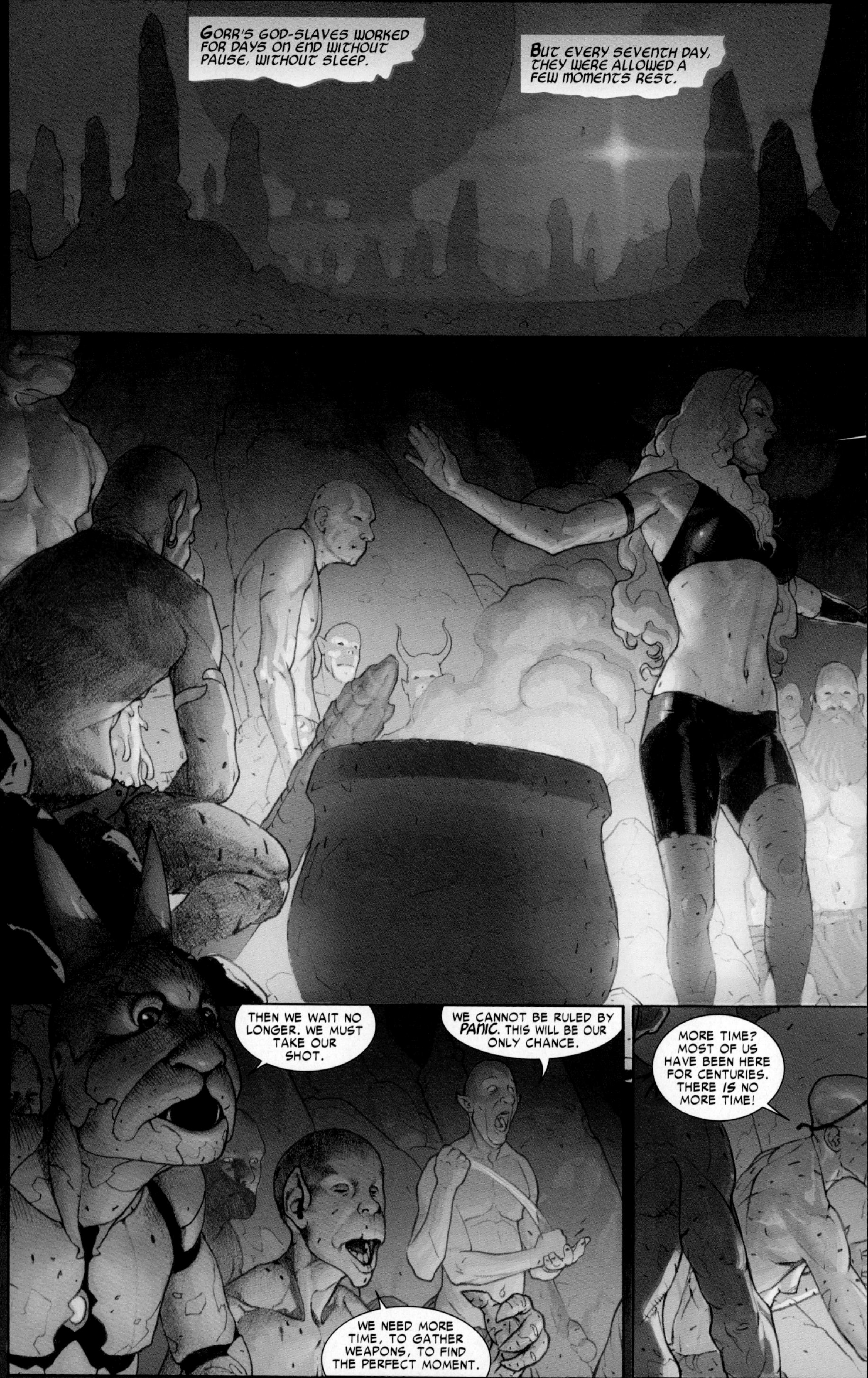
GORR'S GOD-SLAVES WORKED FOR DAYS ON END WITHOUT PAUSE, WITHOUT SLEEP.
BUT EVERY SEVENTH DAY, THEY WERE ALLOWED A FEW MOMENTS REST.
THEN WE WAIT NO LONGER. WE MUST TAKE OUR SHOT.
WE NEED MORE TIME, TO GATHER WEAPONS, TO FIND THE PERFECT MOMENT.
WE CANNOT BE RULED BY PANIC. THIS WILL BE OUR ONLY CHANCE.
MORE TIME? MOST OF US HAVE BEEN HERE FOR CENTURIES. THERE IS NO MORE TIME!

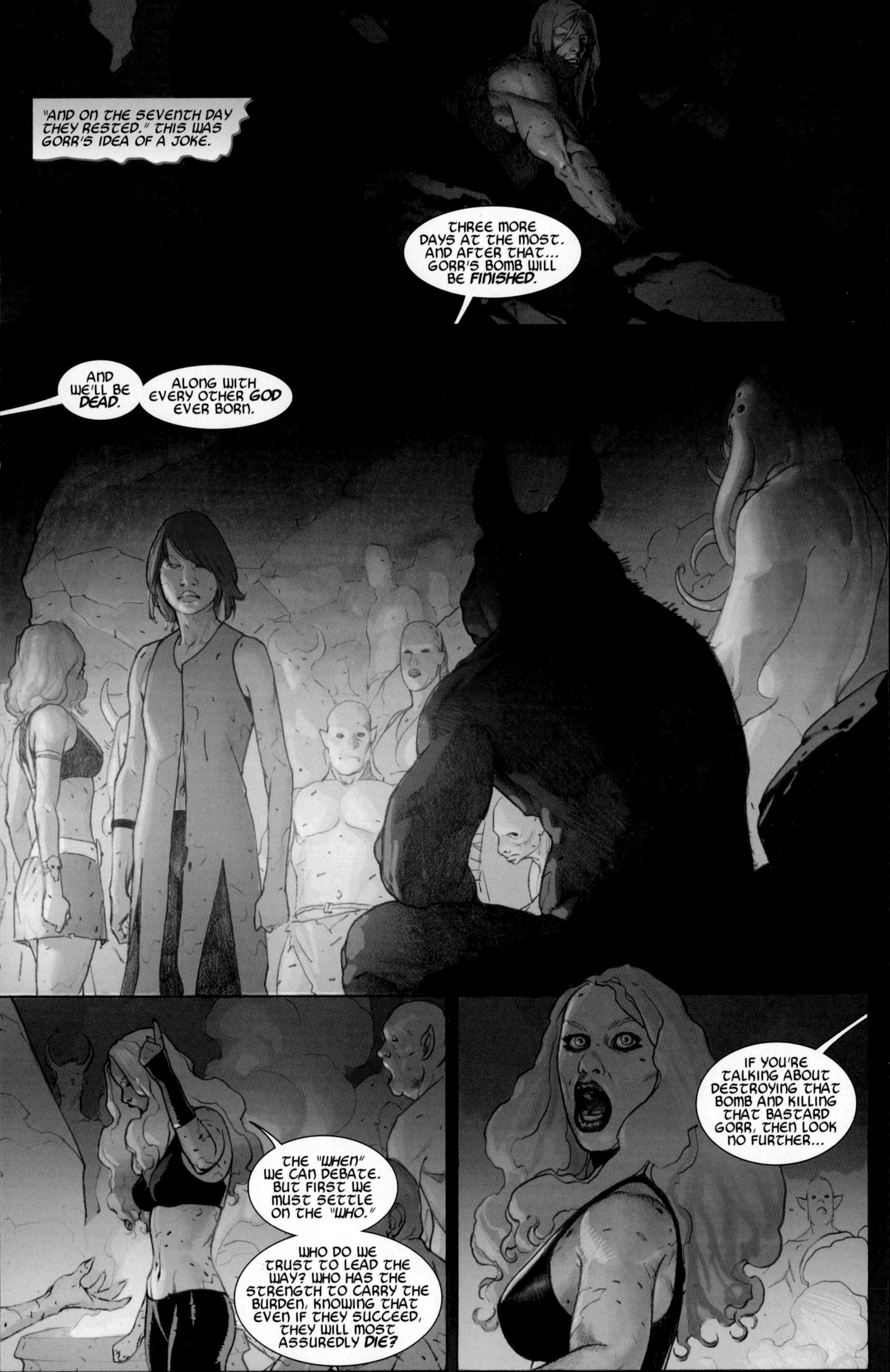
"AND ON THE SEVENTH DAY THEY RESTED." THIS WAS GORR'S IDEA OF A JOKE.
THREE MORE DAYS AT THE MOST. AND AFTER THAT... GORR'S BOMB WILL BE FINISHED.
AND WE'LL BE DEAD.
ALONG WITH EVERY OTHER GOD EVER BORN.
THE "WHEN" WE CAN DEBATE. BUT FIRST WE MUST SETTLE ON THE "WHO."
WHO DO WE TRUST TO LEAD THE WAY? WHO HAS THE STRENGTH TO CARRY THE BURDEN, KNOWING THAT EVEN IF THEY SUCCEED, THEY WILL MOST ASSUREDLY DIE?
IF YOU'RE TALKING ABOUT DESTROYING THAT BOMB AND KILLING THAT BASTARD GORR, THEN LOOK NO FURTHER...

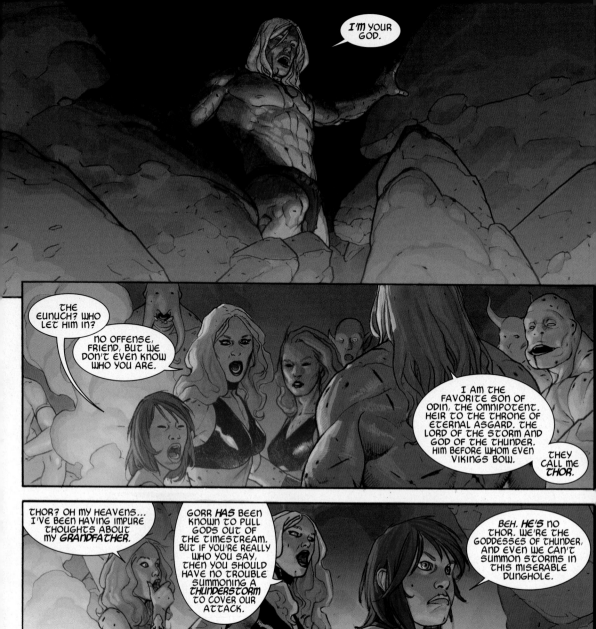

I'M YOUR GOD.

THE EUNUCH? WHO LET HIM IN?

NO OFFENSE, FRIEND, BUT WE DON'T EVEN KNOW WHO YOU ARE.

I AM THE FAVORITE SON OF ODIN, THE OMNIPOTENT. HEIR TO THE THRONE OF ETERNAL ASGARD. THE LORD OF THE STORM AND GOD OF THE THUNDER. HIM BEFORE WHOM EVEN VIKINGS BOW.

THEY CALL ME THOR.

THOR? OH MY HEAVENS... I'VE BEEN HAVING IMPURE THOUGHTS ABOUT MY GRANDFATHER.

GORR HAS BEEN KNOWN TO PULL GODS OUT OF THE TIMESTREAM. BUT IF YOU'RE REALLY WHO YOU SAY, THEN YOU SHOULD HAVE NO TROUBLE SUMMONING A THUNDERSTORM TO COVER OUR ATTACK.

BEH. HE'S NO THOR. WE'RE THE GODDESSES OF THUNDER, AND EVEN WE CAN'T SUMMON STORMS IN THIS MISERABLE DUNGHOLE.

I'VE TRIED, BUT...THIS WORLD IS TOO BARREN.

THERE ARE NO STORMS HERE THAT ANSWER THOR'S CALL.

DON'T FEEL TOO BAD. HAINT, THE RAIN GOD, CAN'T EVEN MAKE IT DEW ANYMORE. AND GORD, THE WINE LORD, CAN ONLY TURN WATER INTO VINEGAR.

WE NEED MORE WEAPONS IF WE'RE GOING TO CROSS THE BLACK PLAIN AND REACH THAT BOMB. CLUBS, SHARP STONES, WHATEVER WE CAN FIND.

THIS BOMB... CAN IT REALLY KILL ALL THE GODS?

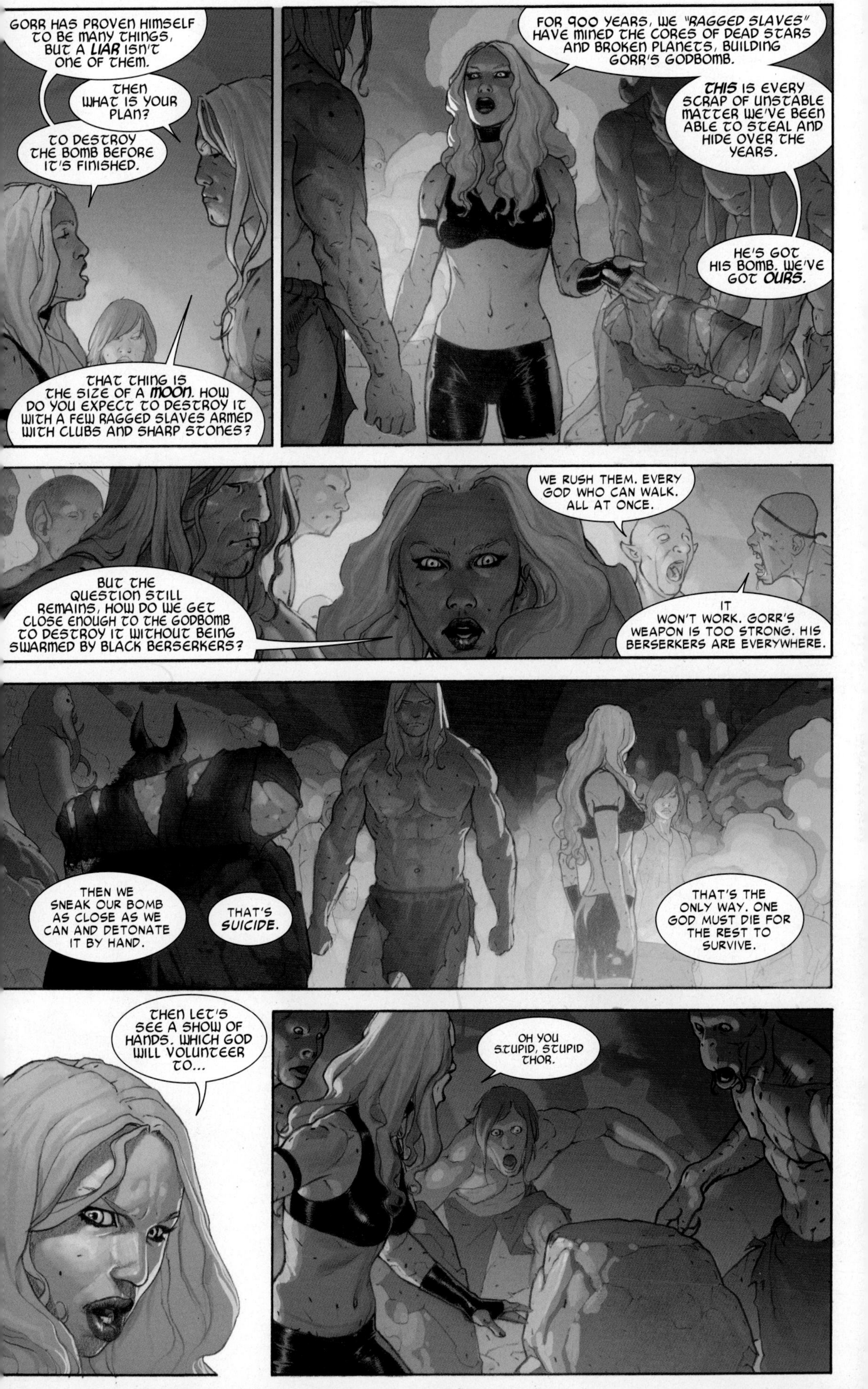
GORR HAS PROVEN HIMSELF TO BE MANY THINGS, BUT A LIAR ISN'T ONE OF THEM.
THEN WHAT IS YOUR PLAN?
TO DESTROY THE BOMB BEFORE IT'S FINISHED.
THAT THING IS THE SIZE OF A MOON. HOW DO YOU EXPECT TO DESTROY IT WITH A FEW RAGGED SLAVES ARMED WITH CLUBS AND SHARP STONES?
FOR 900 YEARS, WE "RAGGED SLAVES" HAVE MINED THE CORES OF DEAD STARS AND BROKEN PLANETS, BUILDING GORR'S GODBOMB.
THIS IS EVERY SCRAP OF UNSTABLE MATTER WE'VE BEEN ABLE TO STEAL AND HIDE OVER THE YEARS.
HE'S GOT HIS BOMB. WE'VE GOT OURS.
BUT THE QUESTION STILL REMAINS, HOW DO WE GET CLOSE ENOUGH TO THE GODBOMB TO DESTROY IT WITHOUT BEING SWARMED BY BLACK BERSERKERS?
WE RUSH THEM. EVERY GOD WHO CAN WALK. ALL AT ONCE.
IT WON'T WORK. GORR'S WEAPON IS TOO STRONG. HIS BERSERKERS ARE EVERYWHERE.
THEN WE SNEAK OUR BOMB AS CLOSE AS WE CAN AND DETONATE IT BY HAND.
THAT'S SUICIDE.
THAT'S THE ONLY WAY. ONE GOD MUST DIE FOR THE REST TO SURVIVE.
THEN LET'S SEE A SHOW OF HANDS. WHICH GOD WILL VOLUNTEER TO...
OH YOU STUPID, STUPID THOR.

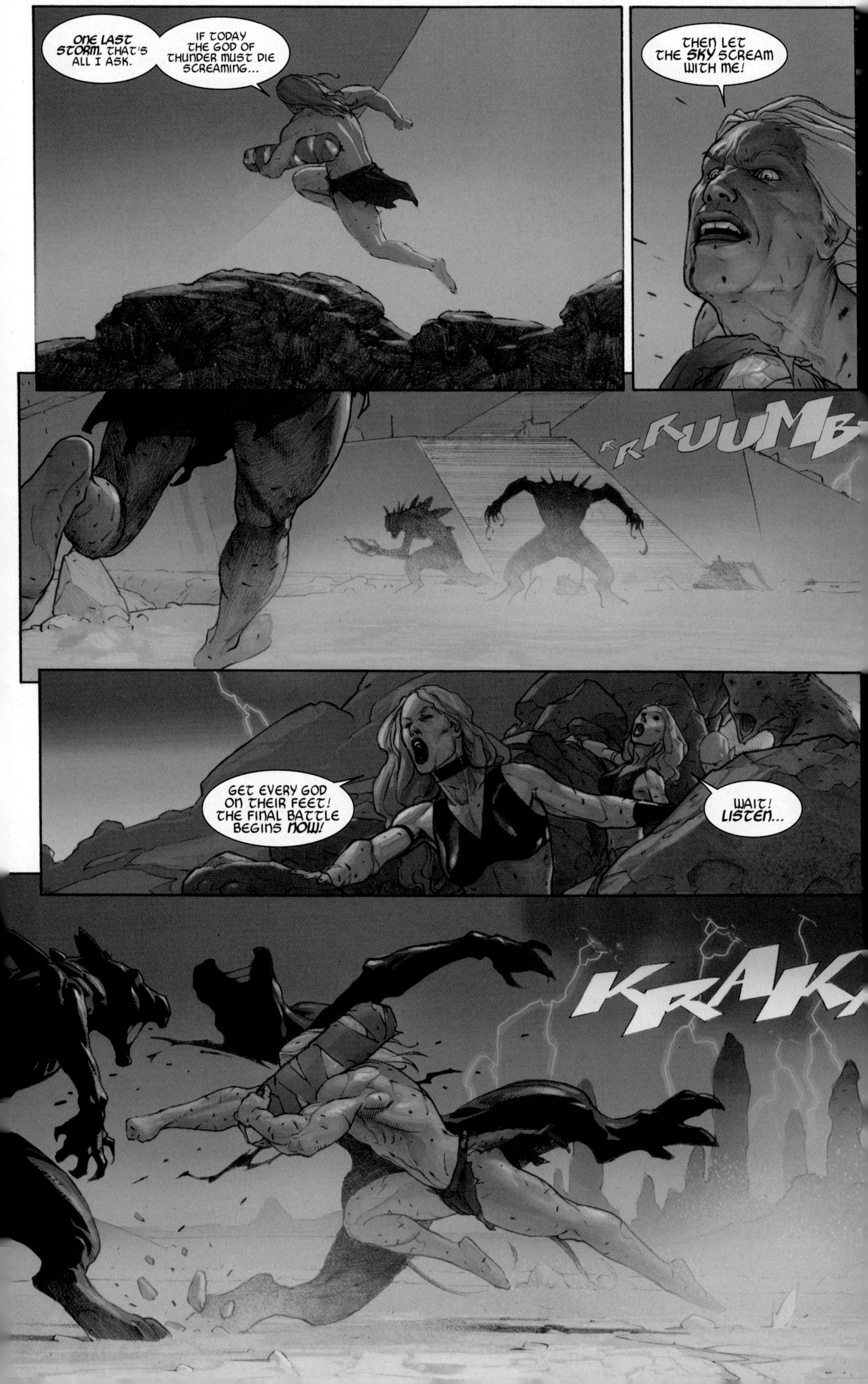
ONE LAST STORM. THAT'S ALL I ASK.
IF TODAY THE GOD OF THUNDER MUST DIE SCREAMING...
THEN LET THE SKY SCREAM WITH ME!
KRRRUUMB
GET EVERY GOD ON THEIR FEET! THE FINAL BATTLE BEGINS NOW!
WAIT! LISTEN...
KRAK

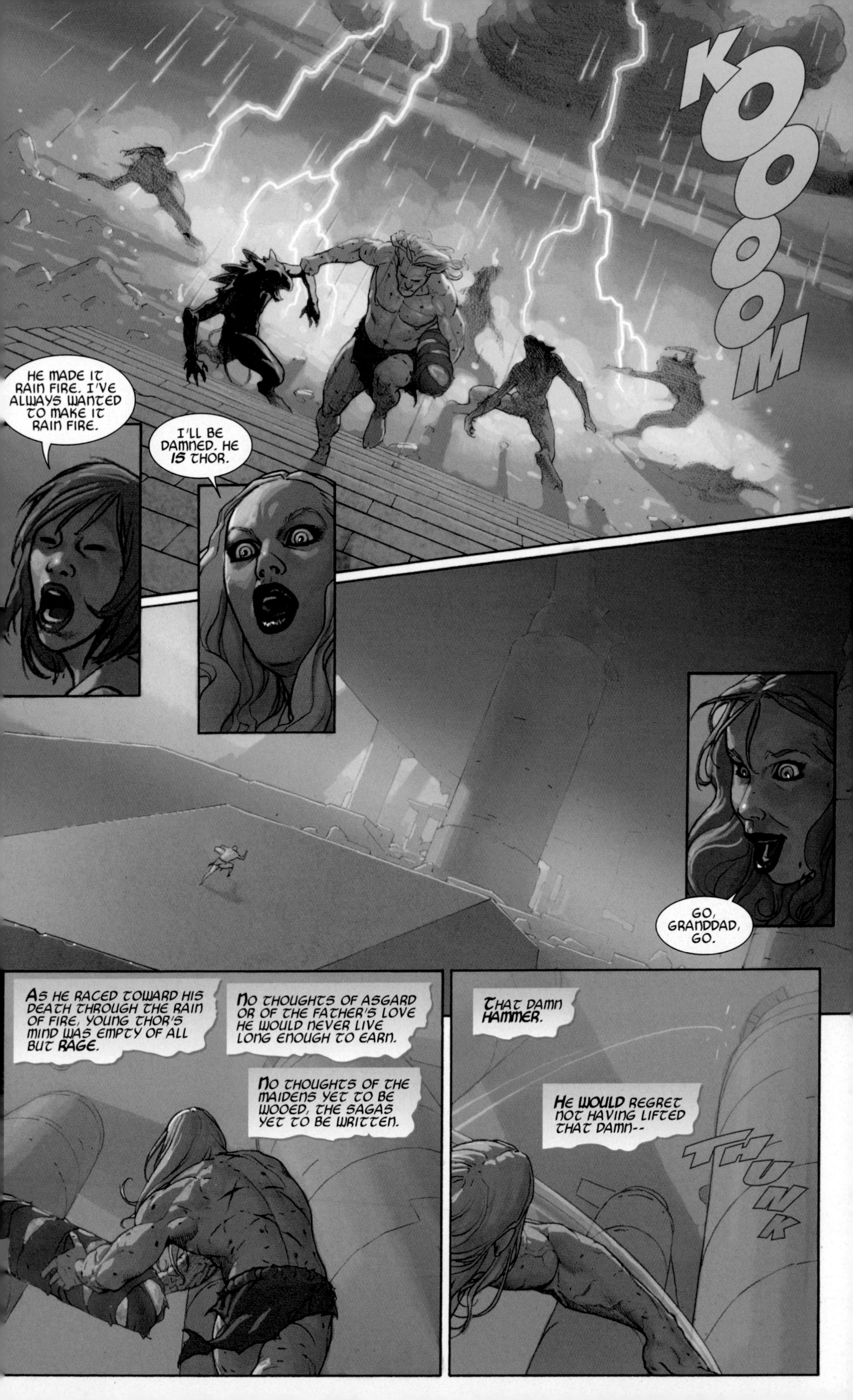
KOOOOOM
HE MADE IT RAIN FIRE. I'VE ALWAYS WANTED TO MAKE IT RAIN FIRE.
I'LL BE DAMNED. HE IS THOR.
GO, GRANDDAD, GO.
AS HE RACED TOWARD HIS DEATH THROUGH THE RAIN OF FIRE, YOUNG THOR'S MIND WAS EMPTY OF ALL BUT RAGE.
NO THOUGHTS OF ASGARD OR OF THE FATHER'S LOVE HE WOULD NEVER LIVE LONG ENOUGH TO EARN.
NO THOUGHTS OF THE MAIDENS YET TO BE WOOED, THE SAGAS YET TO BE WRITTEN.
THAT DAMN HAMMER.
HE WOULD REGRET NOT HAVING LIFTED THAT DAMN--
THUNK

BBOOOOOOMMMM
DID YOU FEEL THAT?
YES. THERE WAS A GREAT STORM IN THE DISTANCE. THOUGH IT PASSED QUICKLY. NOW ALL I FEEL IS PAIN, AND FIRE RIPPING THROUGH MY GUTS.
WE MOVE CAREFULLY FROM HERE ON OUT. OUR PREY IS NEAR.

IN ORBIT AROUND GORR'S WORLD, *STARSHARKS* FEED ON THE FLESH OF DEAD GODS, CAST INTO THE VOID OVER THE CENTURIES.

BEST FETCH YOUR *HAMMER*, BOY. I SENSE SOMETHING STIRRING. SOMETHING CLOSE. SOMETHING...

...STRANGELY FAMILIAR.

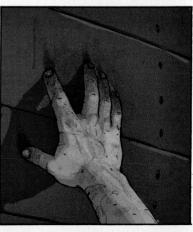

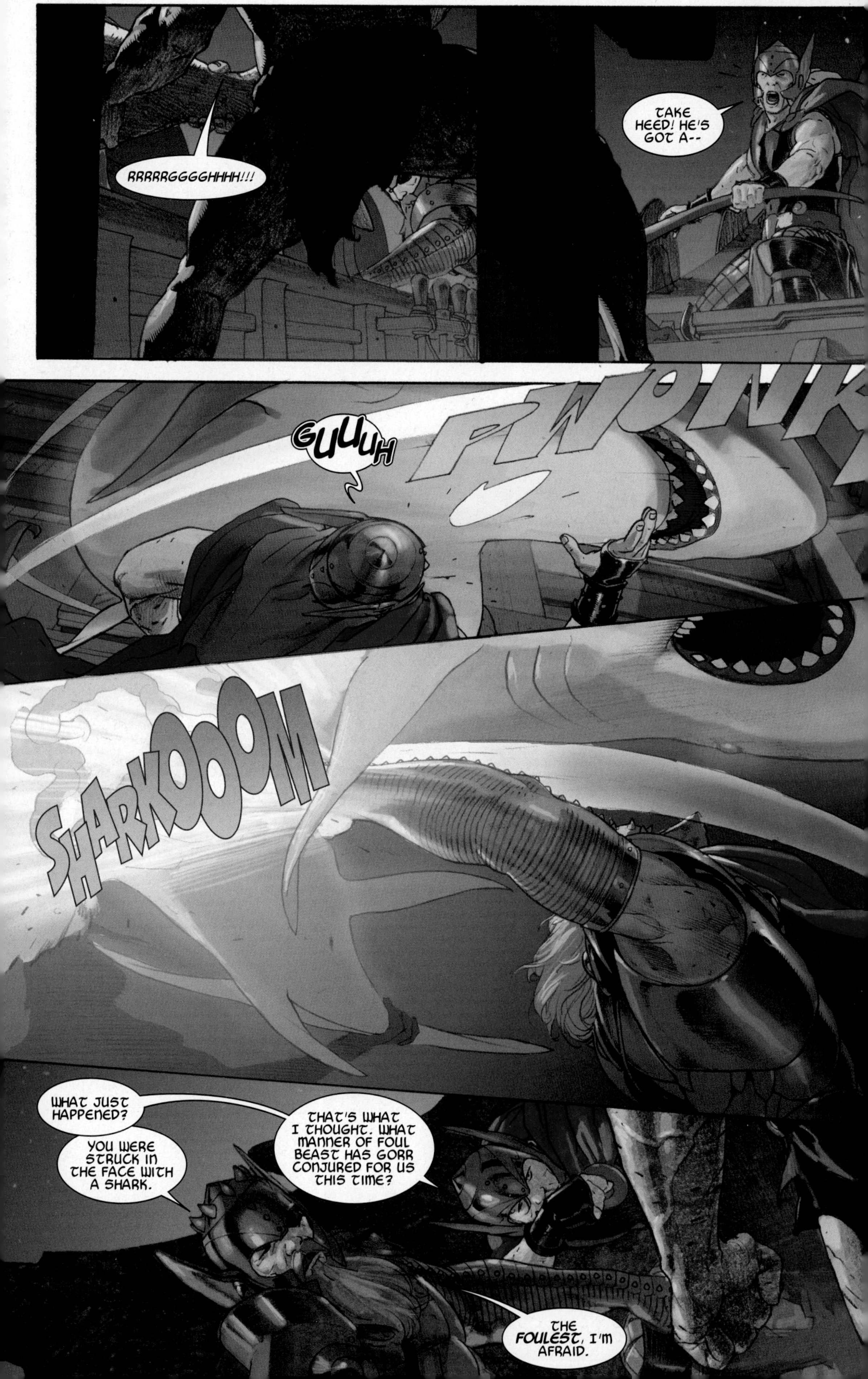
RRRRRGGGGHHHH!!!
TAKE HEED! HE'S GOT A--
GUUUH
FWONK
SHARKOOOM
WHAT JUST HAPPENED?
YOU WERE STRUCK IN THE FACE WITH A SHARK.
THAT'S WHAT I THOUGHT. WHAT MANNER OF FOUL BEAST HAS GORR CONJURED FOR US THIS TIME?
THE FOULEST, I'M AFRAID.

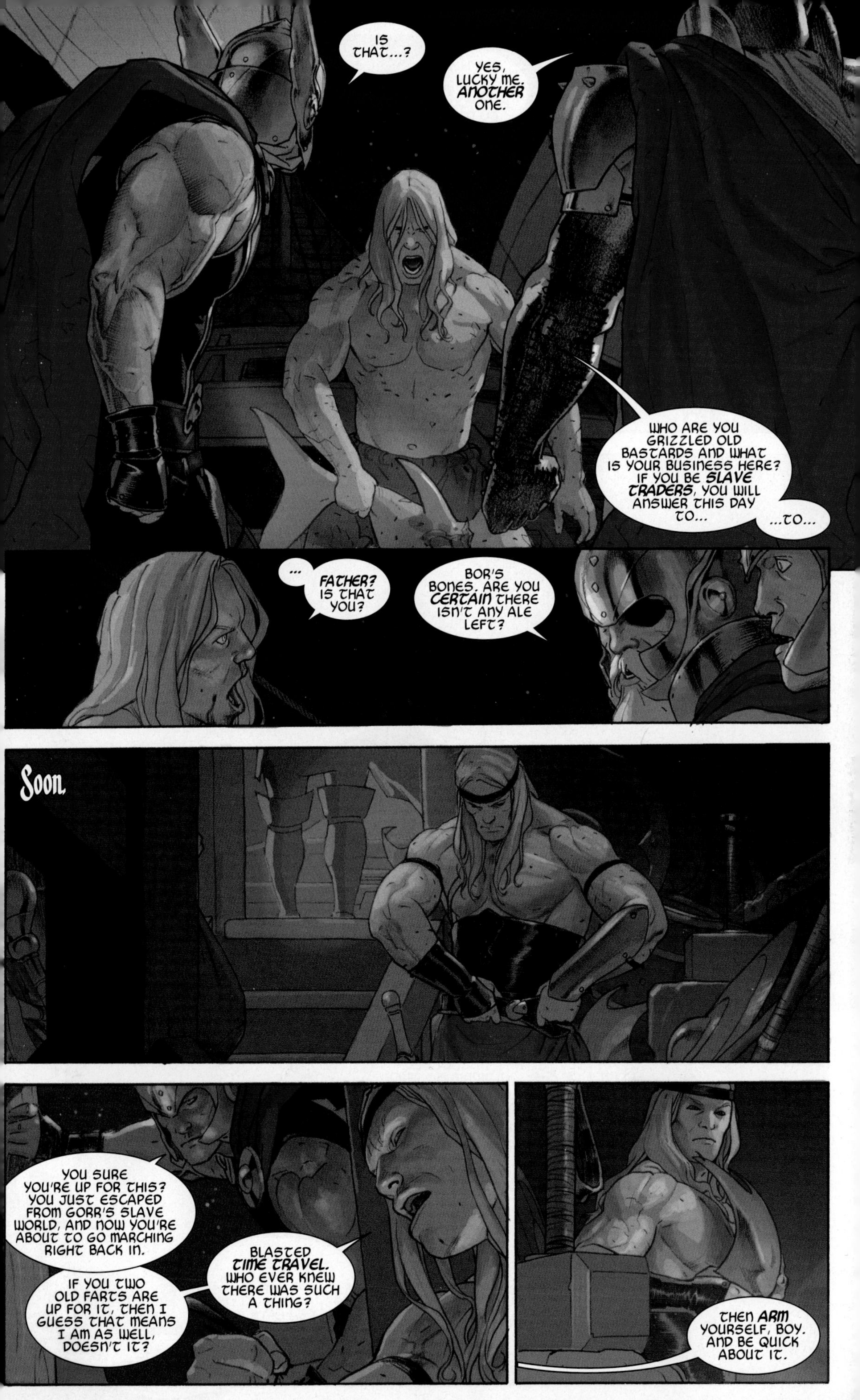
IS THAT...?
YES, LUCKY ME. ANOTHER ONE.
WHO ARE YOU GRIZZLED OLD BASTARDS AND WHAT IS YOUR BUSINESS HERE? IF YOU BE SLAVE TRADERS, YOU WILL ANSWER THIS DAY TO...
...TO...
...FATHER? IS THAT YOU?
BOR'S BONES. ARE YOU CERTAIN THERE ISN'T ANY ALE LEFT?
Soon.
YOU SURE YOU'RE UP FOR THIS? YOU JUST ESCAPED FROM GORR'S SLAVE WORLD, AND NOW YOU'RE ABOUT TO GO MARCHING RIGHT BACK IN.
BLASTED TIME TRAVEL. WHO EVER KNEW THERE WAS SUCH A THING?
IF YOU TWO OLD FARTS ARE UP FOR IT, THEN I GUESS THAT MEANS I AM AS WELL, DOESN'T IT?
THEN ARM YOURSELF, BOY. AND BE QUICK ABOUT IT.

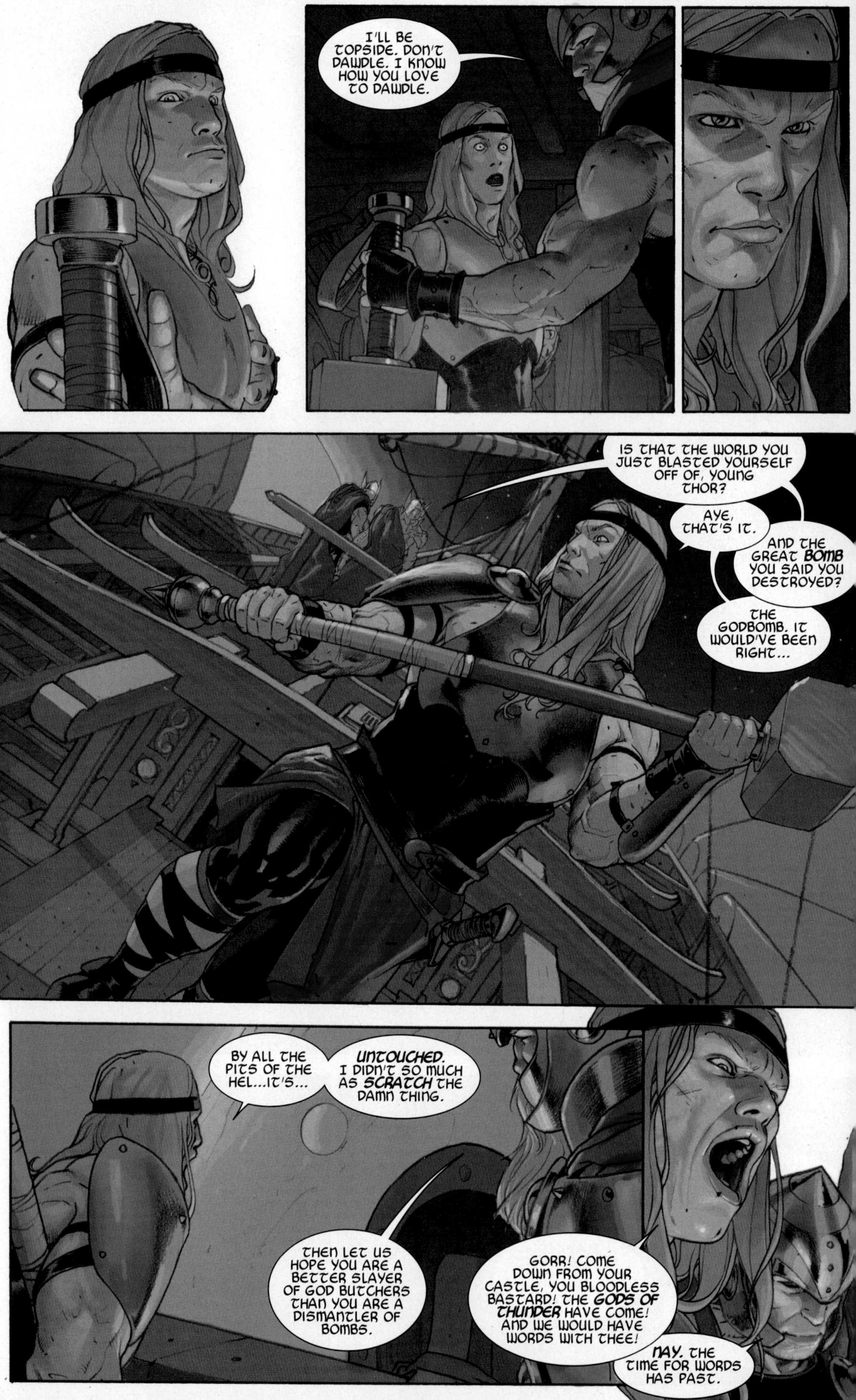

I'LL BE TOPSIDE. DON'T DAWDLE. I KNOW HOW YOU LOVE TO DAWDLE.
IS THAT THE WORLD YOU JUST BLASTED YOURSELF OFF OF, YOUNG THOR?
AYE, THAT'S IT.
AND THE GREAT **BOMB** YOU SAID YOU DESTROYED?
THE GODBOMB. IT WOULD'VE BEEN RIGHT...
BY ALL THE PITS OF THE HEL...IT'S...
UNTOUCHED. I DIDN'T SO MUCH AS *SCRATCH* THE DAMN THING.
THEN LET US HOPE YOU ARE A BETTER SLAYER OF GOD BUTCHERS THAN YOU ARE A DISMANTLER OF BOMBS.
GORR! COME DOWN FROM YOUR CASTLE, YOU BLOODLESS BASTARD! THE ***GODS OF THUNDER*** HAVE COME! AND WE WOULD HAVE WORDS WITH THEE!
NAY. THE TIME FOR WORDS HAS PAST.

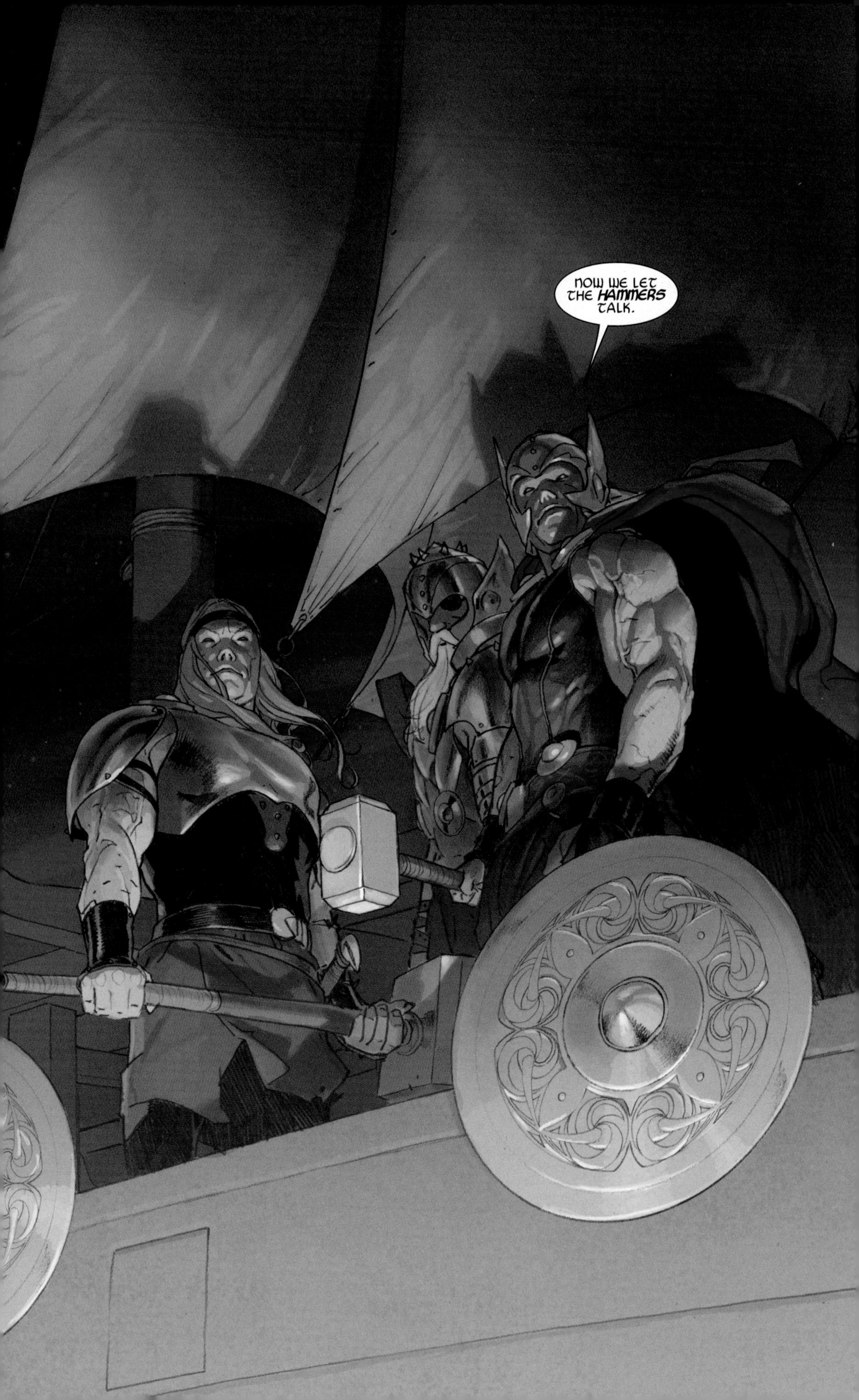
NOW WE LET THE HAMMERS TALK.

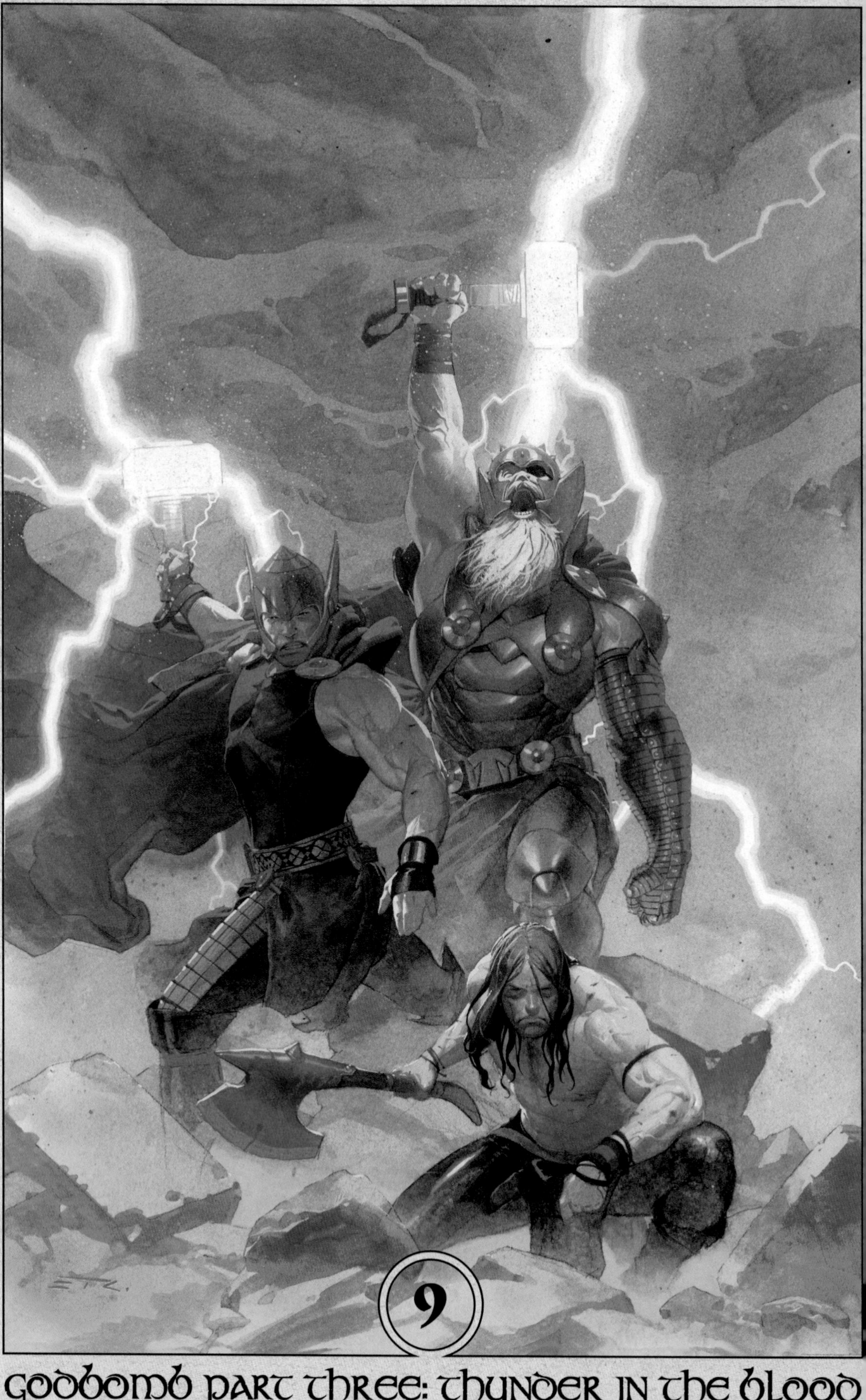
9

GODBOMB PART THREE: THUNDER IN THE BLOOD

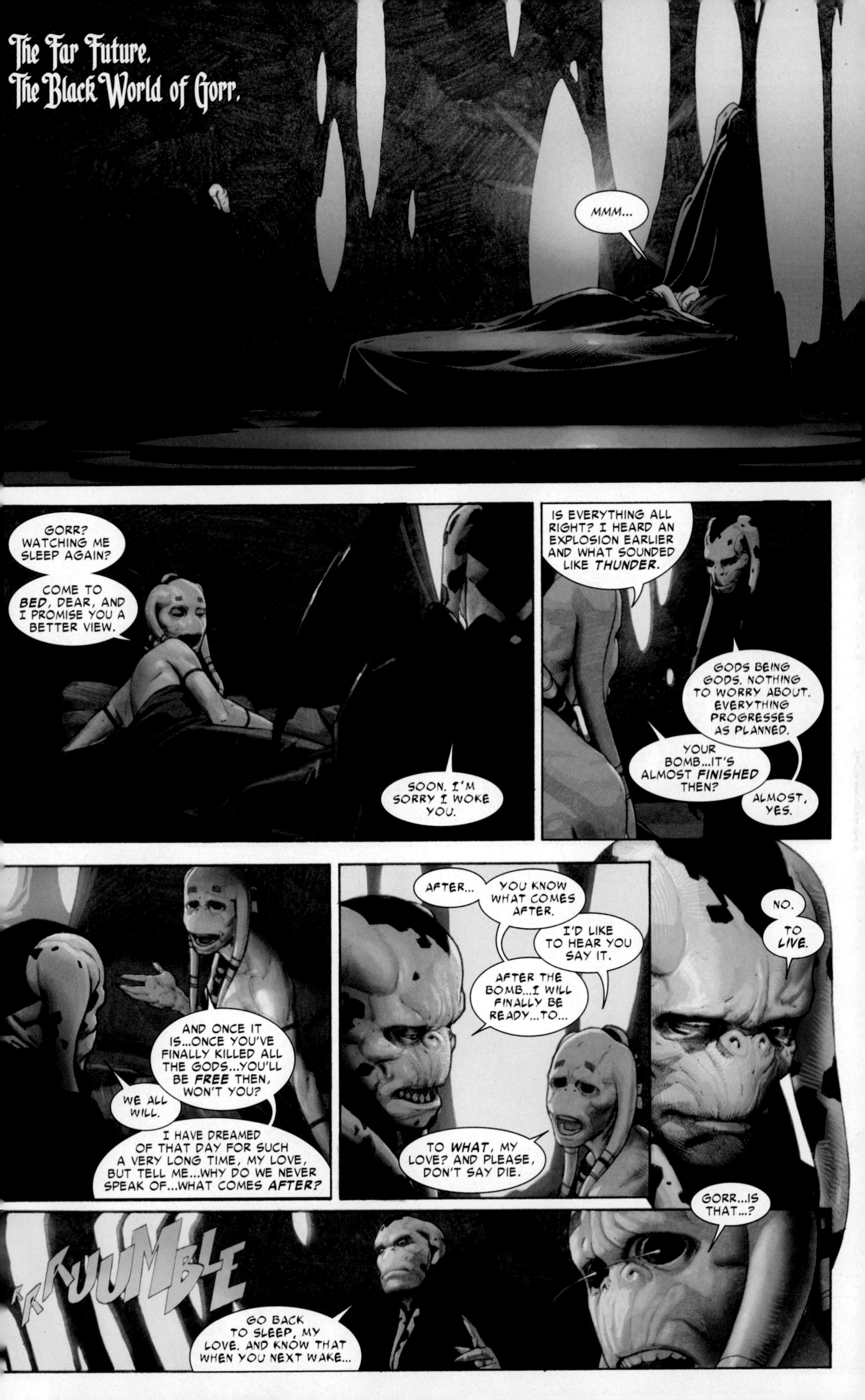
The Far Future.
The Black World of Gorr.
MMM...
GORR? WATCHING ME SLEEP AGAIN?
COME TO BED, DEAR, AND I PROMISE YOU A BETTER VIEW.
SOON. I'M SORRY I WOKE YOU.
IS EVERYTHING ALL RIGHT? I HEARD AN EXPLOSION EARLIER AND WHAT SOUNDED LIKE THUNDER.
GODS BEING GODS. NOTHING TO WORRY ABOUT. EVERYTHING PROGRESSES AS PLANNED.
YOUR BOMB...IT'S ALMOST FINISHED THEN?
ALMOST, YES.
AND ONCE IT IS...ONCE YOU'VE FINALLY KILLED ALL THE GODS...YOU'LL BE FREE THEN, WON'T YOU?
WE ALL WILL.
I HAVE DREAMED OF THAT DAY FOR SUCH A VERY LONG TIME, MY LOVE, BUT TELL ME...WHY DO WE NEVER SPEAK OF...WHAT COMES AFTER?
AFTER...
YOU KNOW WHAT COMES AFTER.
I'D LIKE TO HEAR YOU SAY IT.
AFTER THE BOMB...I WILL FINALLY BE READY...TO...
TO WHAT, MY LOVE? AND PLEASE, DON'T SAY DIE.
NO.
TO LIVE.
KRRUUMBLE
GORR...IS THAT...?
GO BACK TO SLEEP, MY LOVE. AND KNOW THAT WHEN YOU NEXT WAKE...

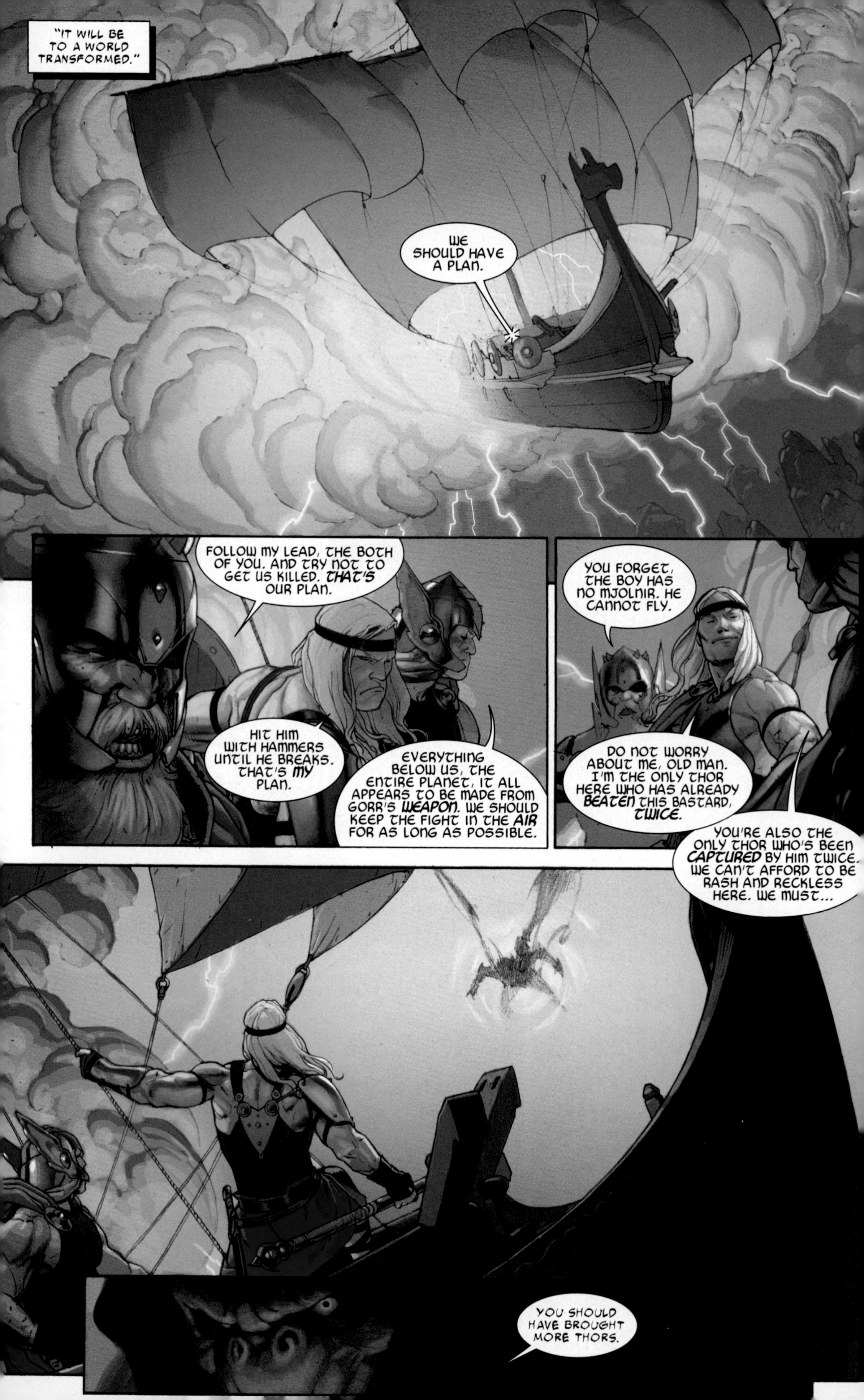
"IT WILL BE TO A WORLD TRANSFORMED."
WE SHOULD HAVE A PLAN.
FOLLOW MY LEAD, THE BOTH OF YOU. AND TRY NOT TO GET US KILLED. THAT'S OUR PLAN.
HIT HIM WITH HAMMERS UNTIL HE BREAKS. THAT'S MY PLAN.
EVERYTHING BELOW US, THE ENTIRE PLANET, IT ALL APPEARS TO BE MADE FROM GORR'S WEAPON. WE SHOULD KEEP THE FIGHT IN THE AIR FOR AS LONG AS POSSIBLE.
YOU FORGET, THE BOY HAS NO MJOLNIR. HE CANNOT FLY.
DO NOT WORRY ABOUT ME, OLD MAN. I'M THE ONLY THOR HERE WHO HAS ALREADY BEATEN THIS BASTARD, TWICE.
YOU'RE ALSO THE ONLY THOR WHO'S BEEN CAPTURED BY HIM TWICE. WE CAN'T AFFORD TO BE RASH AND RECKLESS HERE. WE MUST...
YOU SHOULD HAVE BROUGHT MORE THORS.

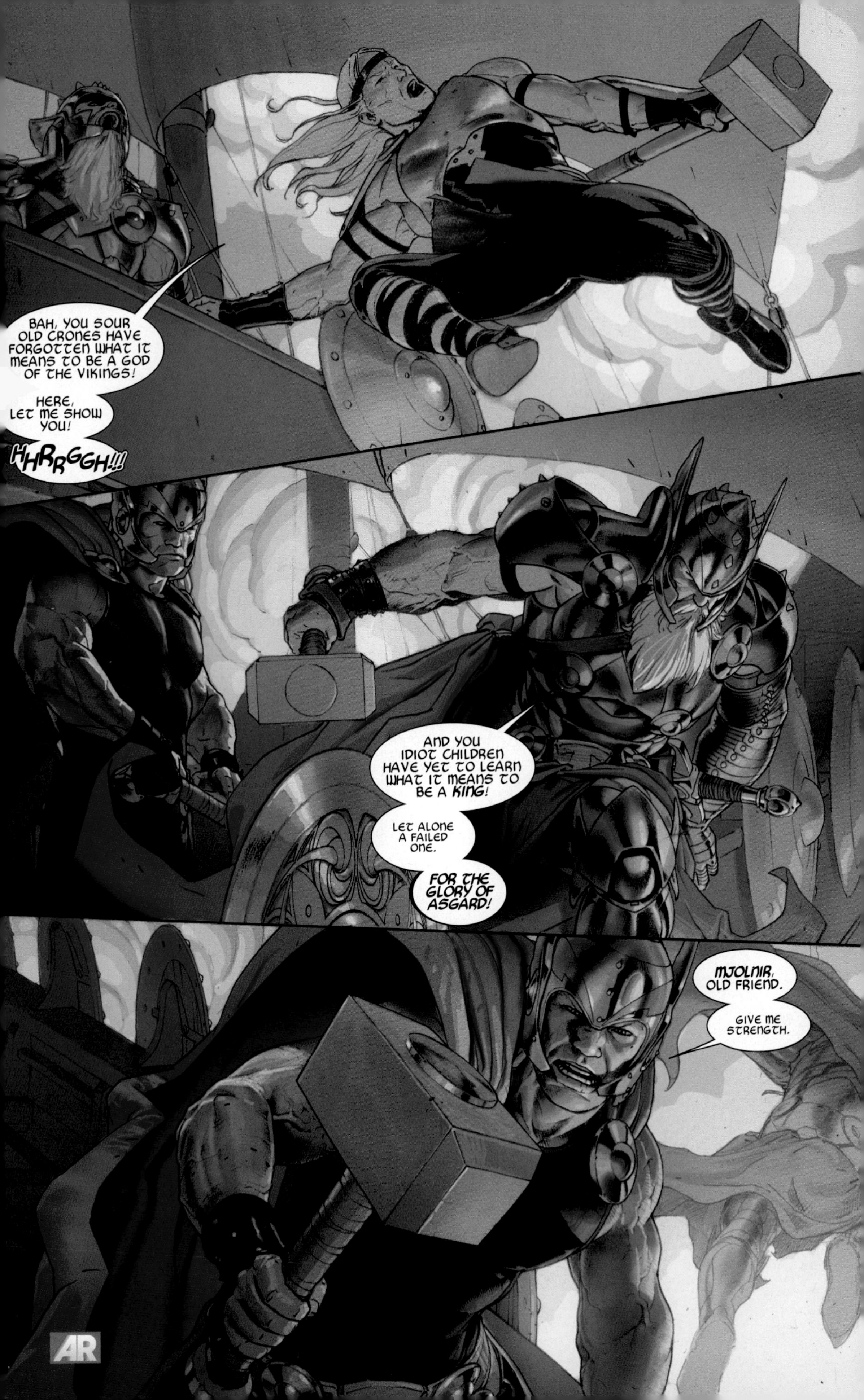
BAH, YOU SOUR OLD CRONES HAVE FORGOTTEN WHAT IT MEANS TO BE A GOD OF THE VIKINGS!
HERE, LET ME SHOW YOU!
HHRRGGH!!!
AND YOU IDIOT CHILDREN HAVE YET TO LEARN WHAT IT MEANS TO BE A KING!
LET ALONE A FAILED ONE.
FOR THE GLORY OF ASGARD!
MJOLNIR, OLD FRIEND.
GIVE ME STRENGTH.
AR

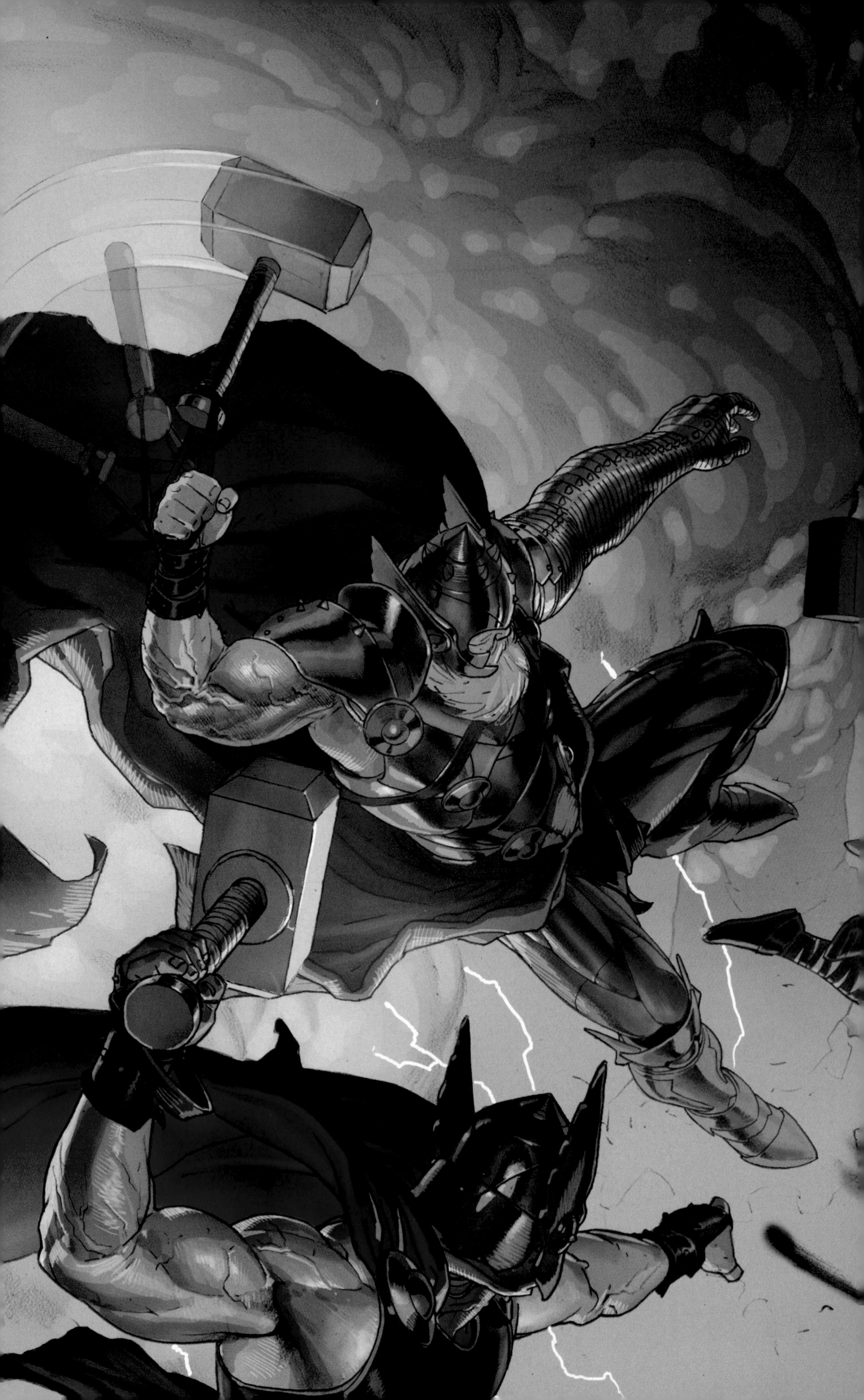

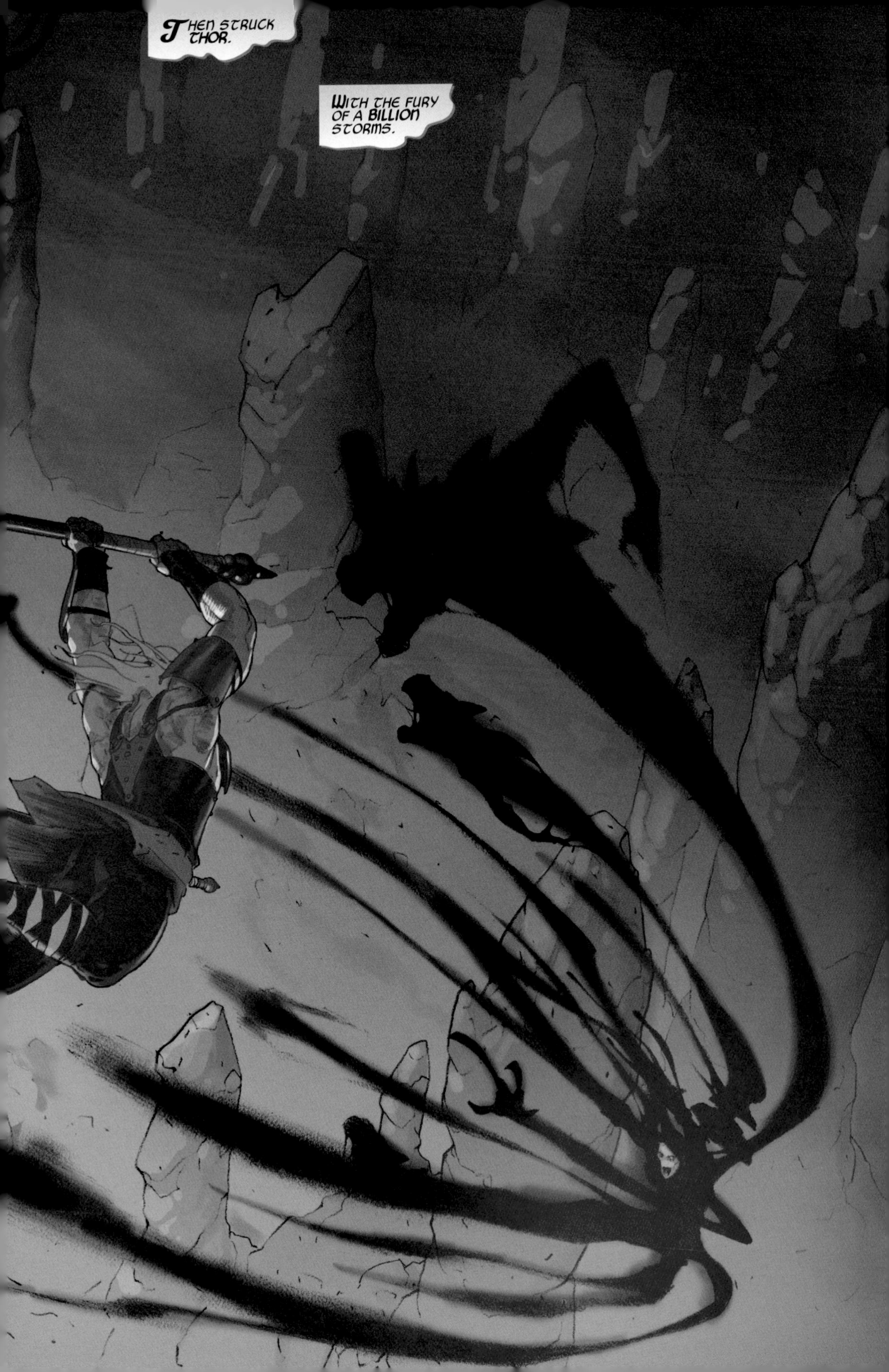
THEN STRUCK THOR.
WITH THE FURY OF A BILLION STORMS.

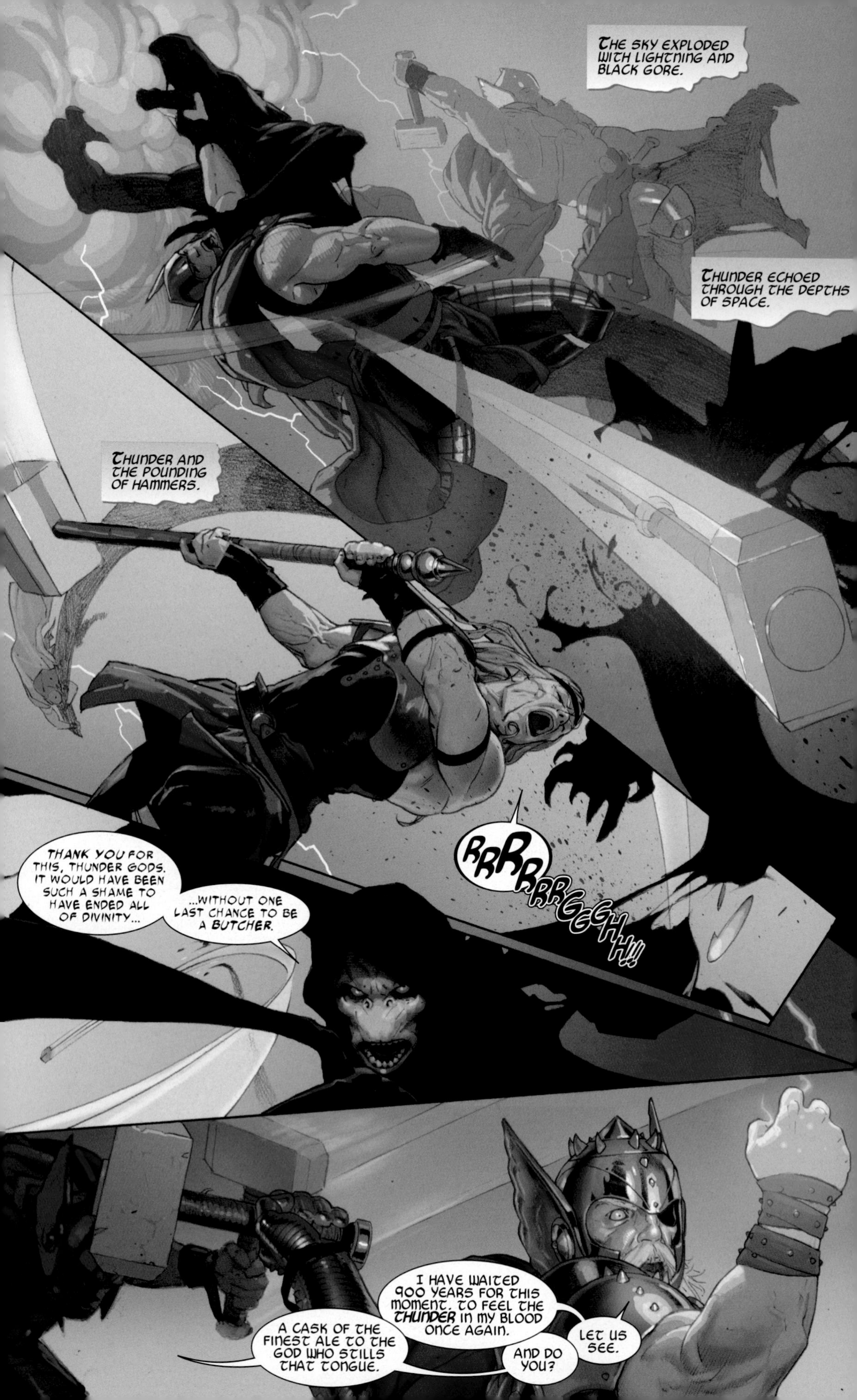

THE SKY EXPLODED WITH LIGHTNING AND BLACK GORE.
THUNDER ECHOED THROUGH THE DEPTHS OF SPACE.
THUNDER AND THE POUNDING OF HAMMERS.
RRRRRRGGGHH!!
THANK YOU FOR THIS, THUNDER GODS. IT WOULD HAVE BEEN SUCH A SHAME TO HAVE ENDED ALL OF DIVINITY...
...WITHOUT ONE LAST CHANCE TO BE A BUTCHER.
I HAVE WAITED 900 YEARS FOR THIS MOMENT. TO FEEL THE THUNDER IN MY BLOOD ONCE AGAIN.
LET US SEE.
A CASK OF THE FINEST ALE TO THE GOD WHO STILLS THAT TONGUE.
AND DO YOU?

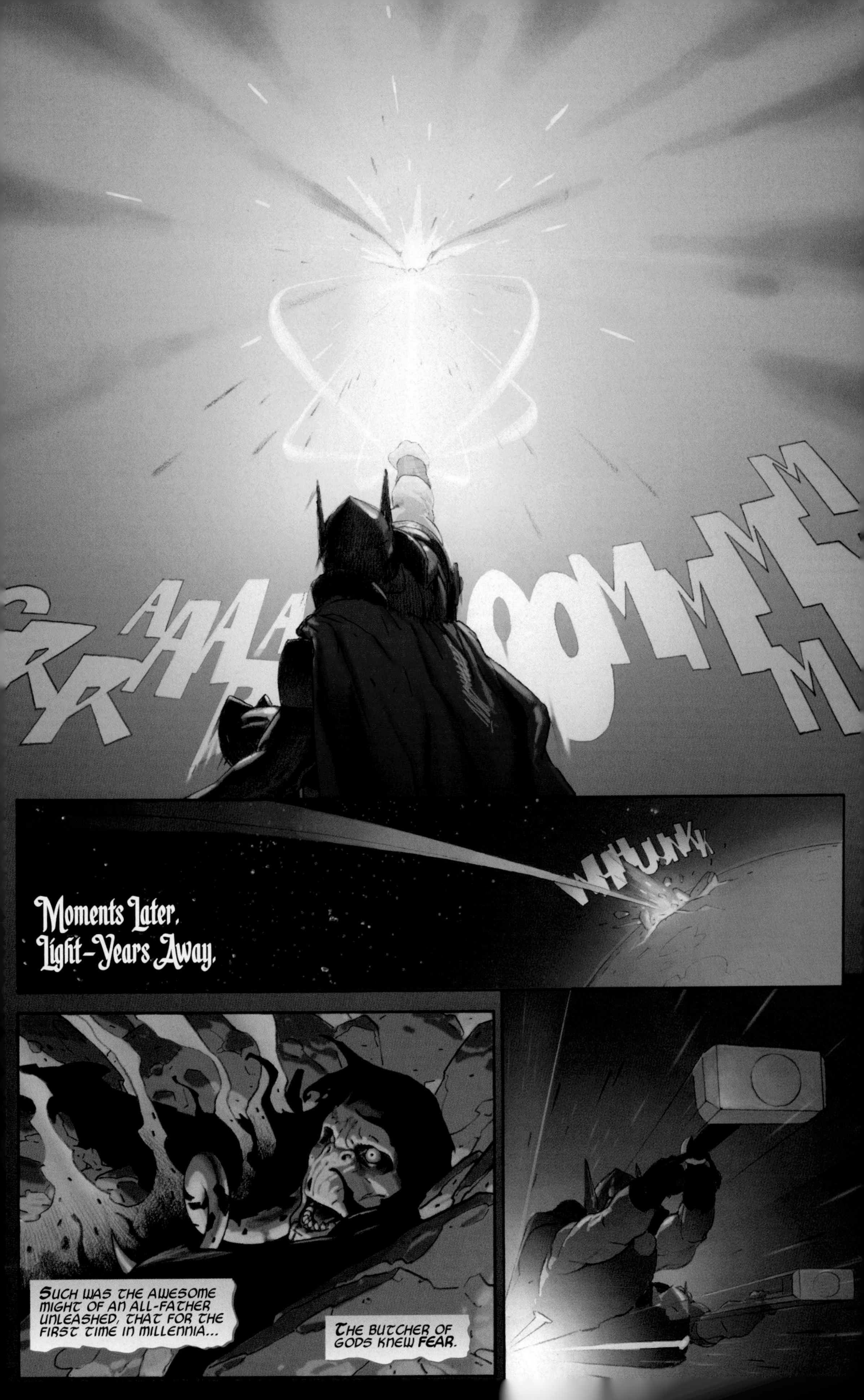
KRRAAAAAKA-BOOOOMMMM
WHUNK
Moments Later, Light-Years Away,
SUCH WAS THE AWESOME MIGHT OF AN ALL-FATHER UNLEASHED, THAT FOR THE FIRST TIME IN MILLENNIA...
THE BUTCHER OF GODS KNEW FEAR.

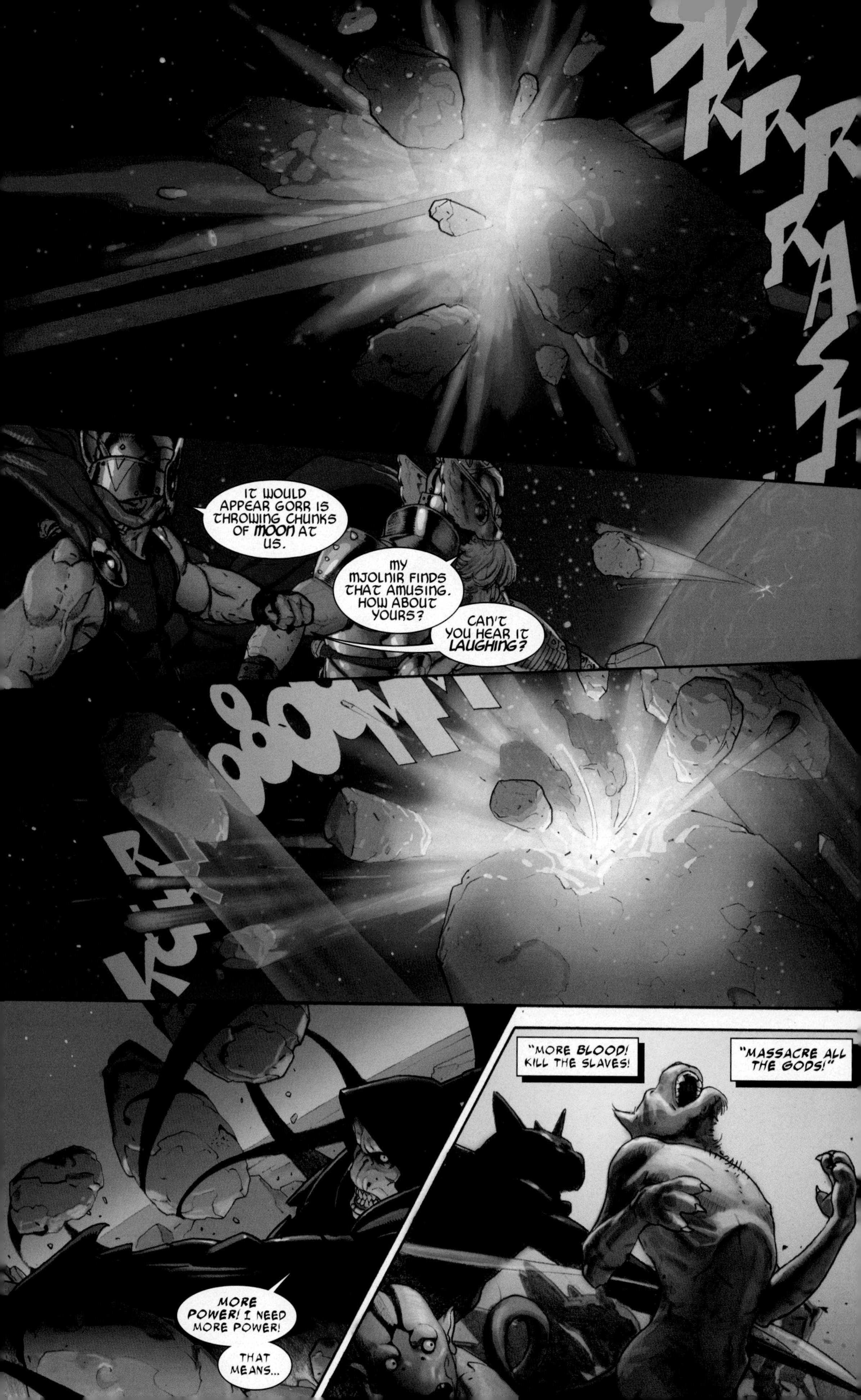
SKRRRASH
IT WOULD APPEAR GORR IS THROWING CHUNKS OF MOON AT US.
MY MJOLNIR FINDS THAT AMUSING. HOW ABOUT YOURS?
CAN'T YOU HEAR IT LAUGHING?
MORE POWER! I NEED MORE POWER!
THAT MEANS...
"MORE BLOOD! KILL THE SLAVES!
"MASSACRE ALL THE GODS!"

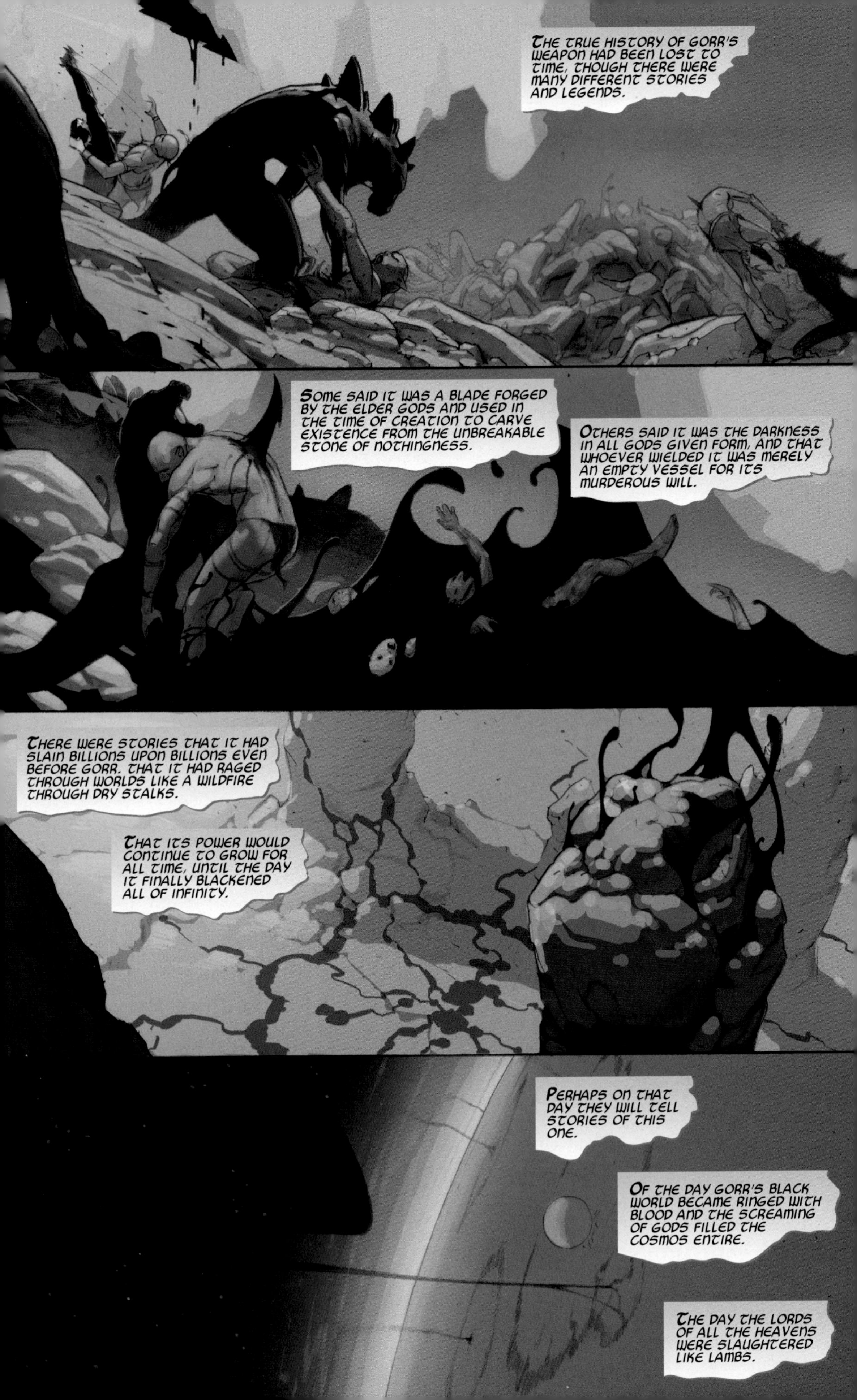
THE TRUE HISTORY OF GORR'S WEAPON HAD BEEN LOST TO TIME, THOUGH THERE WERE MANY DIFFERENT STORIES AND LEGENDS.
SOME SAID IT WAS A BLADE FORGED BY THE ELDER GODS AND USED IN THE TIME OF CREATION TO CARVE EXISTENCE FROM THE UNBREAKABLE STONE OF NOTHINGNESS.
OTHERS SAID IT WAS THE DARKNESS IN ALL GODS GIVEN FORM, AND THAT WHOEVER WIELDED IT WAS MERELY AN EMPTY VESSEL FOR ITS MURDEROUS WILL.
THERE WERE STORIES THAT IT HAD SLAIN BILLIONS UPON BILLIONS EVEN BEFORE GORR. THAT IT HAD RAGED THROUGH WORLDS LIKE A WILDFIRE THROUGH DRY STALKS.
THAT ITS POWER WOULD CONTINUE TO GROW FOR ALL TIME, UNTIL THE DAY IT FINALLY BLACKENED ALL OF INFINITY.
PERHAPS ON THAT DAY THEY WILL TELL STORIES OF THIS ONE.
OF THE DAY GORR'S BLACK WORLD BECAME RINGED WITH BLOOD AND THE SCREAMING OF GODS FILLED THE COSMOS ENTIRE.
THE DAY THE LORDS OF ALL THE HEAVENS WERE SLAUGHTERED LIKE LAMBS.

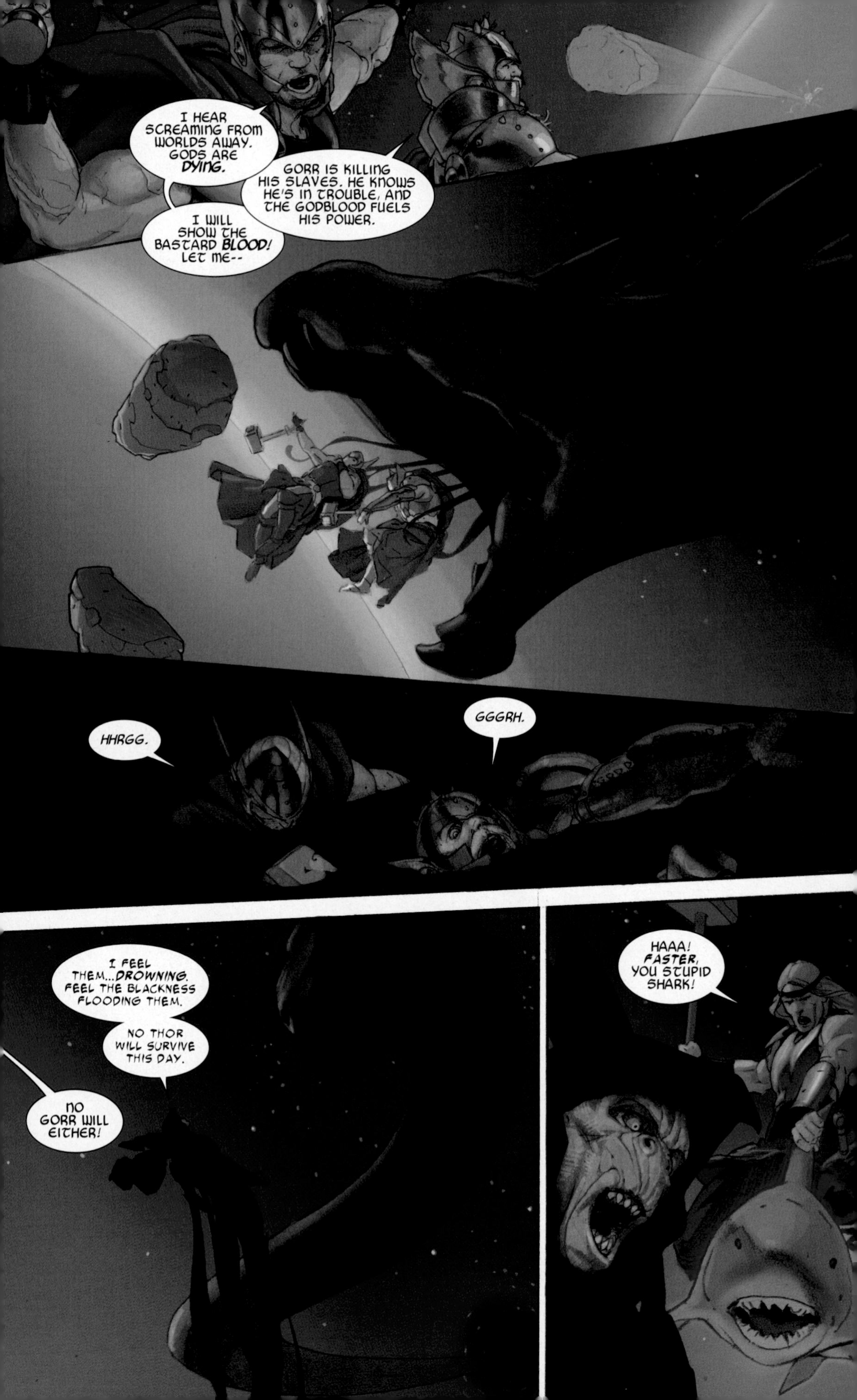
I HEAR SCREAMING FROM WORLDS AWAY. GODS ARE **DYING.**
I WILL SHOW THE BASTARD **BLOOD!** LET ME--
GORR IS KILLING HIS SLAVES. HE KNOWS HE'S IN TROUBLE, AND THE GODBLOOD FUELS HIS POWER.
HHRGG.
GGGRH.
I FEEL THEM...**DROWNING.** FEEL THE BLACKNESS FLOODING THEM.
NO THOR WILL SURVIVE THIS DAY.
NO GORR WILL EITHER!
HAAA! **FASTER,** YOU STUPID SHARK!

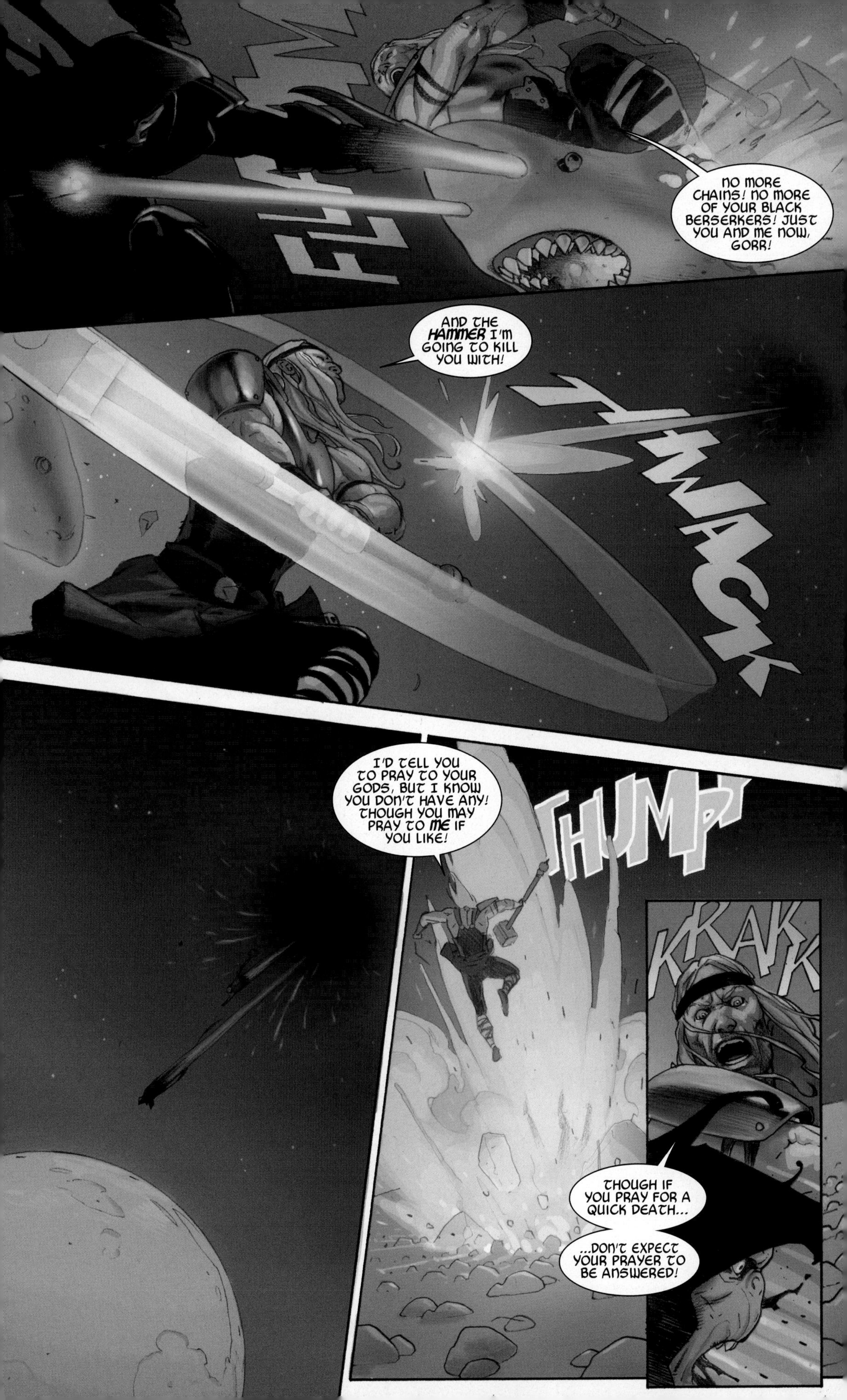
NO MORE CHAINS! NO MORE OF YOUR BLACK BERSERKERS! JUST YOU AND ME NOW, GORR!
AND THE HAMMER I'M GOING TO KILL YOU WITH!
THWACK
I'D TELL YOU TO PRAY TO YOUR GODS, BUT I KNOW YOU DON'T HAVE ANY! THOUGH YOU MAY PRAY TO ME IF YOU LIKE!
THUMP
KRAKK
THOUGH IF YOU PRAY FOR A QUICK DEATH...
...DON'T EXPECT YOUR PRAYER TO BE ANSWERED!

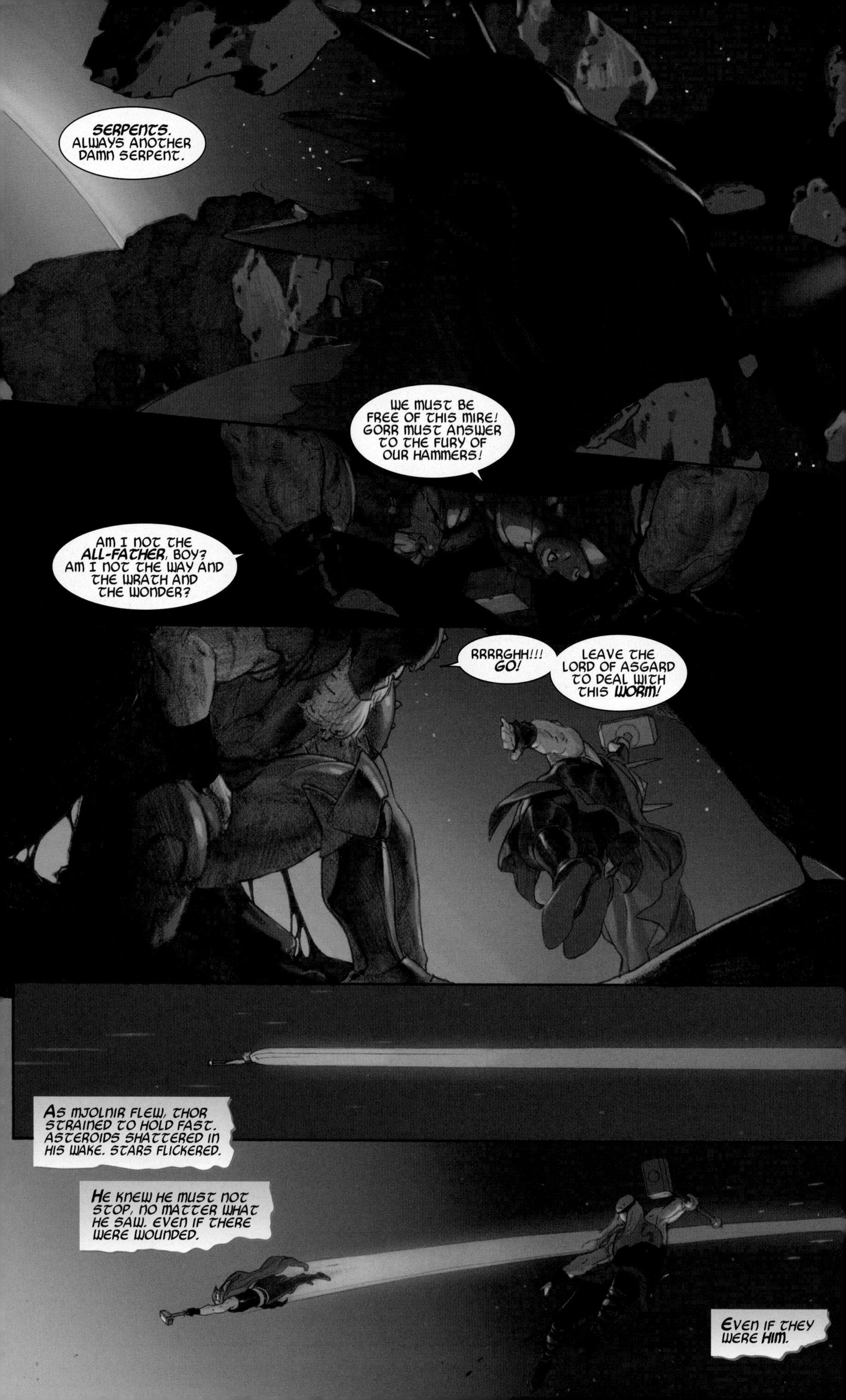
SERPENTS. ALWAYS ANOTHER DAMN SERPENT.
WE MUST BE FREE OF THIS MIRE! GORR MUST ANSWER TO THE FURY OF OUR HAMMERS!
AM I NOT THE ALL-FATHER, BOY? AM I NOT THE WAY AND THE WRATH AND THE WONDER?
RRRRGHH!!! GO!
LEAVE THE LORD OF ASGARD TO DEAL WITH THIS WORM!
AS MJOLNIR FLEW, THOR STRAINED TO HOLD FAST. ASTEROIDS SHATTERED IN HIS WAKE. STARS FLICKERED.
HE KNEW HE MUST NOT STOP, NO MATTER WHAT HE SAW. EVEN IF THERE WERE WOUNDED.
EVEN IF THEY WERE HIM.

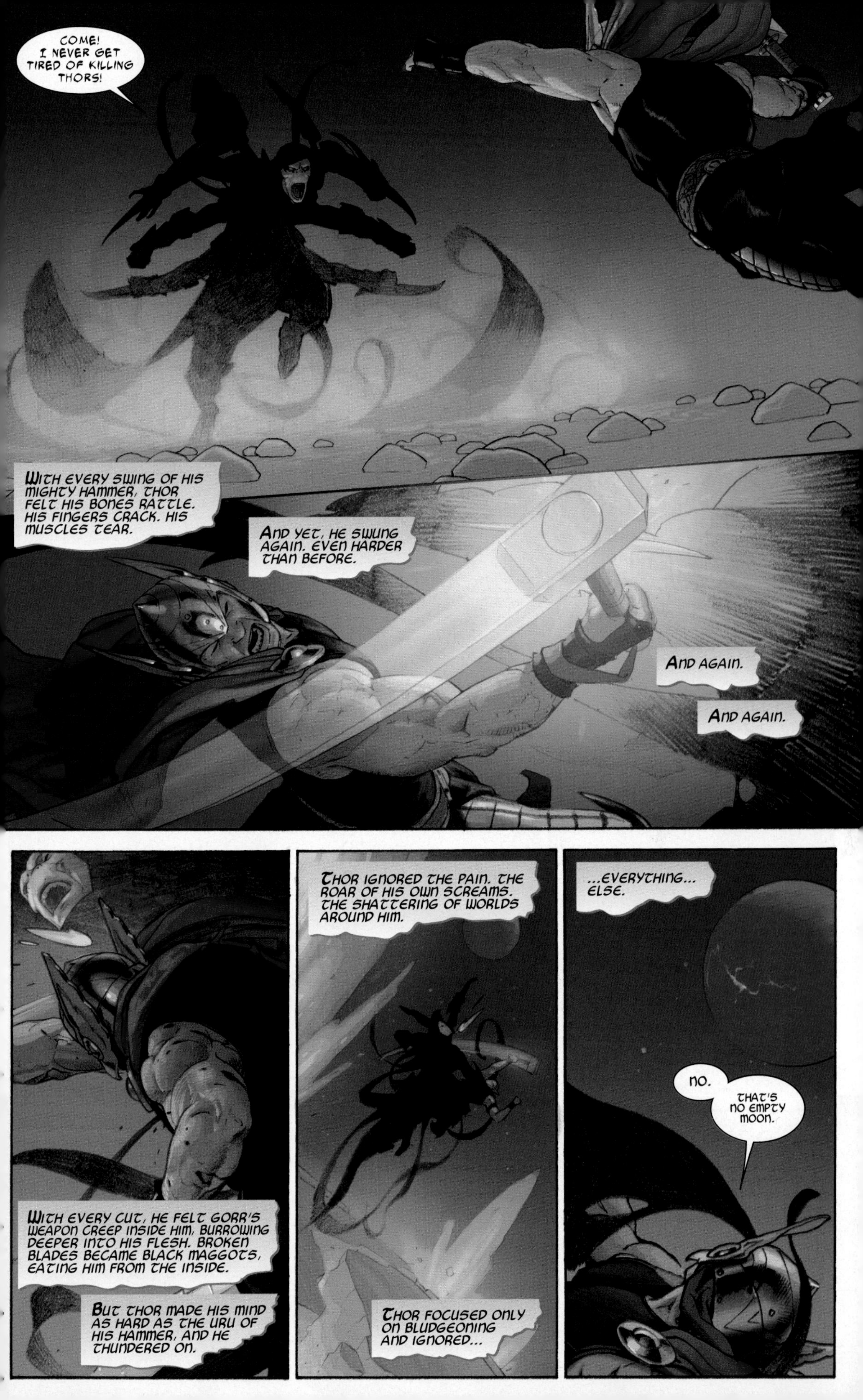
COME! I NEVER GET TIRED OF KILLING THORS!
WITH EVERY SWING OF HIS MIGHTY HAMMER, THOR FELT HIS BONES RATTLE. HIS FINGERS CRACK. HIS MUSCLES TEAR.
AND YET, HE SWUNG AGAIN. EVEN HARDER THAN BEFORE.
AND AGAIN.
AND AGAIN.
WITH EVERY CUT, HE FELT GORR'S WEAPON CREEP INSIDE HIM, BURROWING DEEPER INTO HIS FLESH. BROKEN BLADES BECAME BLACK MAGGOTS, EATING HIM FROM THE INSIDE.
BUT THOR MADE HIS MIND AS HARD AS THE URU OF HIS HAMMER, AND HE THUNDERED ON.
THOR IGNORED THE PAIN. THE ROAR OF HIS OWN SCREAMS. THE SHATTERING OF WORLDS AROUND HIM.
THOR FOCUSED ONLY ON BLUDGEONING AND IGNORED...
...EVERYTHING... ELSE.
NO.
THAT'S NO EMPTY MOON.

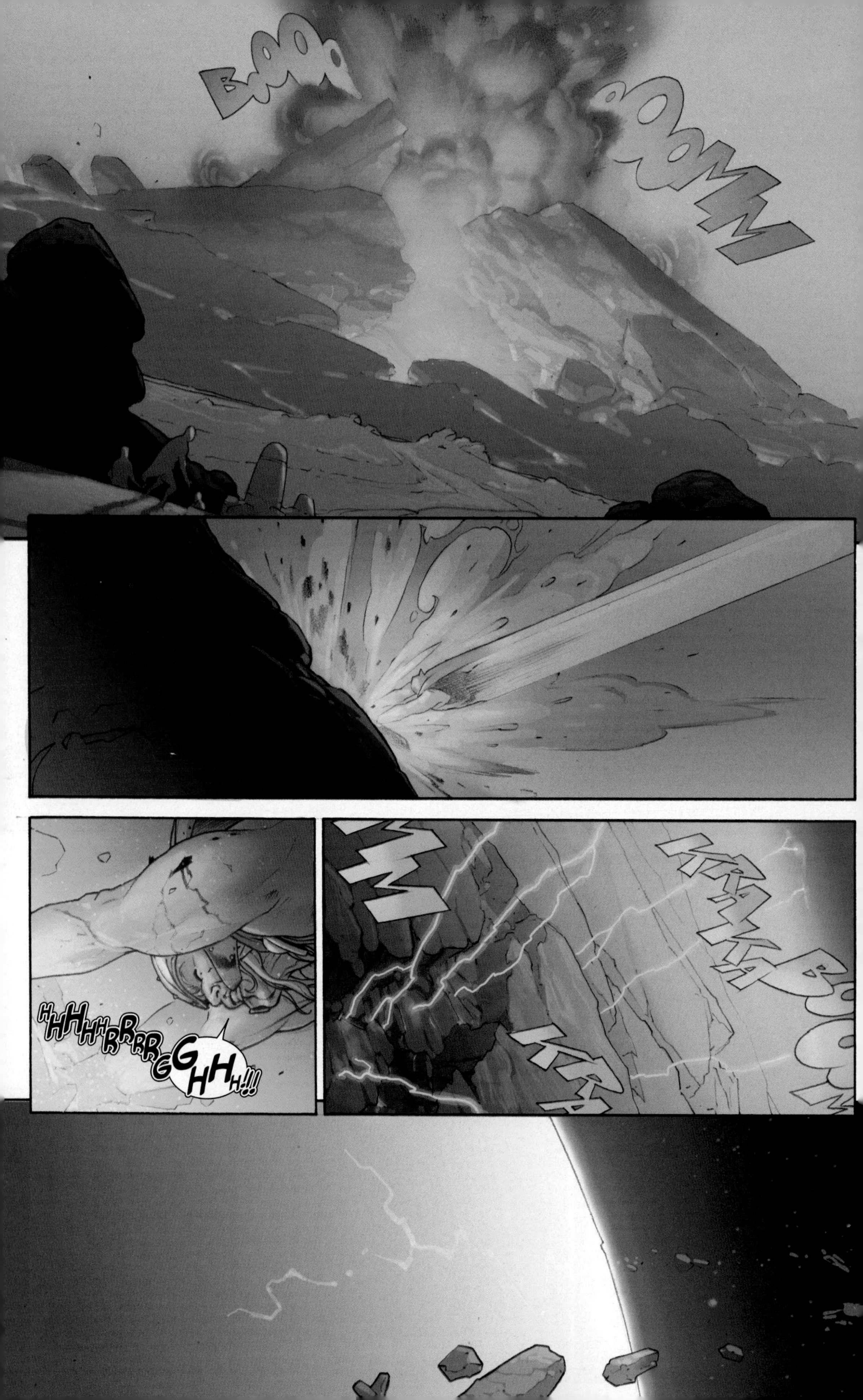
BOOOOOOOMM
HHHHHRRRRRGGHHH!!!
MMM
KRAKABOOM
KRA

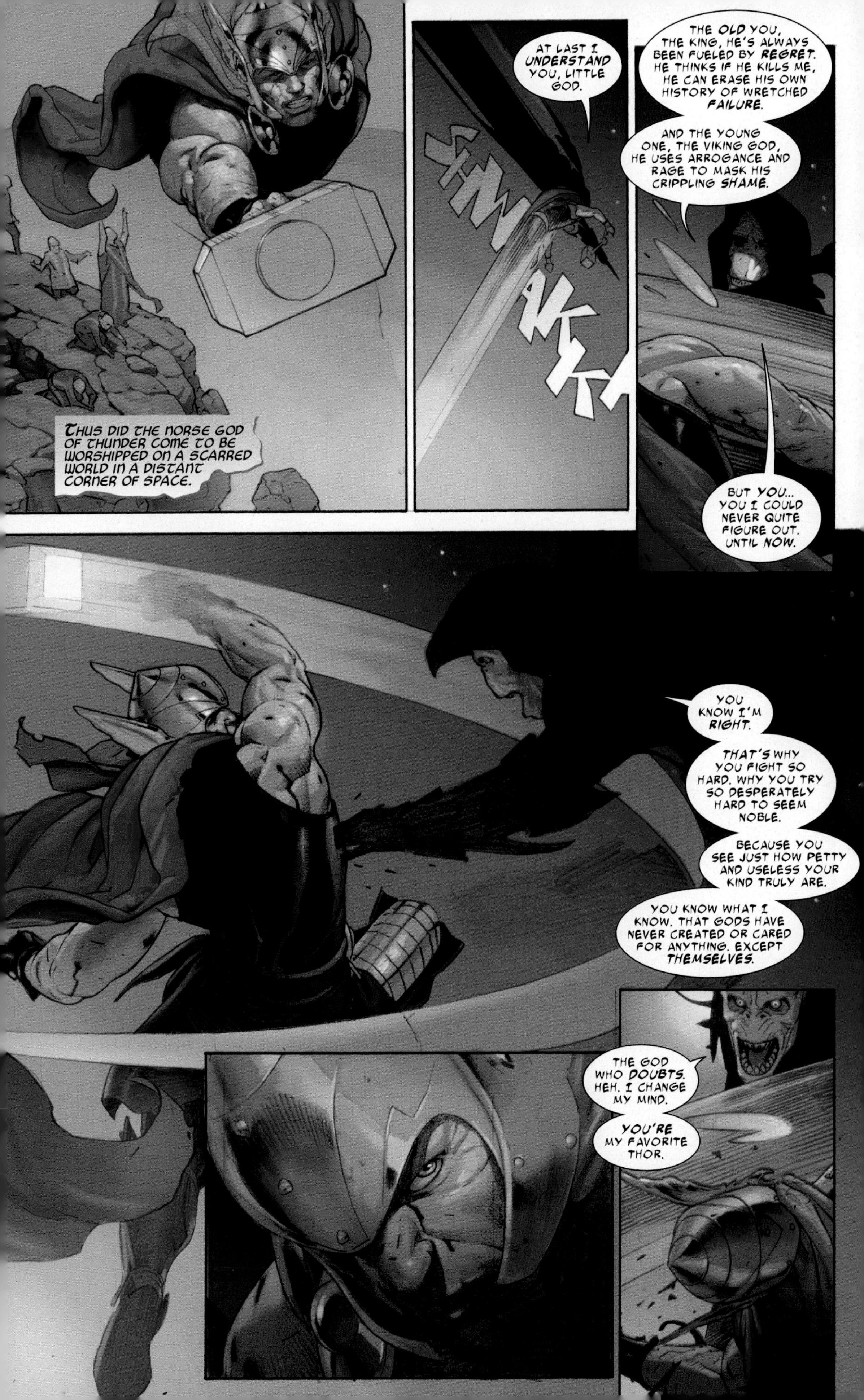
THUS DID THE NORSE GOD OF THUNDER COME TO BE WORSHIPPED ON A SCARRED WORLD IN A DISTANT CORNER OF SPACE.
AT LAST I UNDERSTAND YOU, LITTLE GOD.
SHWAKKK
THE OLD YOU, THE KING, HE'S ALWAYS BEEN FUELED BY REGRET. HE THINKS IF HE KILLS ME, HE CAN ERASE HIS OWN HISTORY OF WRETCHED FAILURE.
AND THE YOUNG ONE, THE VIKING GOD, HE USES ARROGANCE AND RAGE TO MASK HIS CRIPPLING SHAME.
BUT YOU... YOU I COULD NEVER QUITE FIGURE OUT. UNTIL NOW.
YOU KNOW I'M RIGHT.
THAT'S WHY YOU FIGHT SO HARD. WHY YOU TRY SO DESPERATELY HARD TO SEEM NOBLE.
BECAUSE YOU SEE JUST HOW PETTY AND USELESS YOUR KIND TRULY ARE.
YOU KNOW WHAT I KNOW. THAT GODS HAVE NEVER CREATED OR CARED FOR ANYTHING. EXCEPT THEMSELVES.
THE GOD WHO DOUBTS. HEH. I CHANGE MY MIND.
YOU'RE MY FAVORITE THOR.

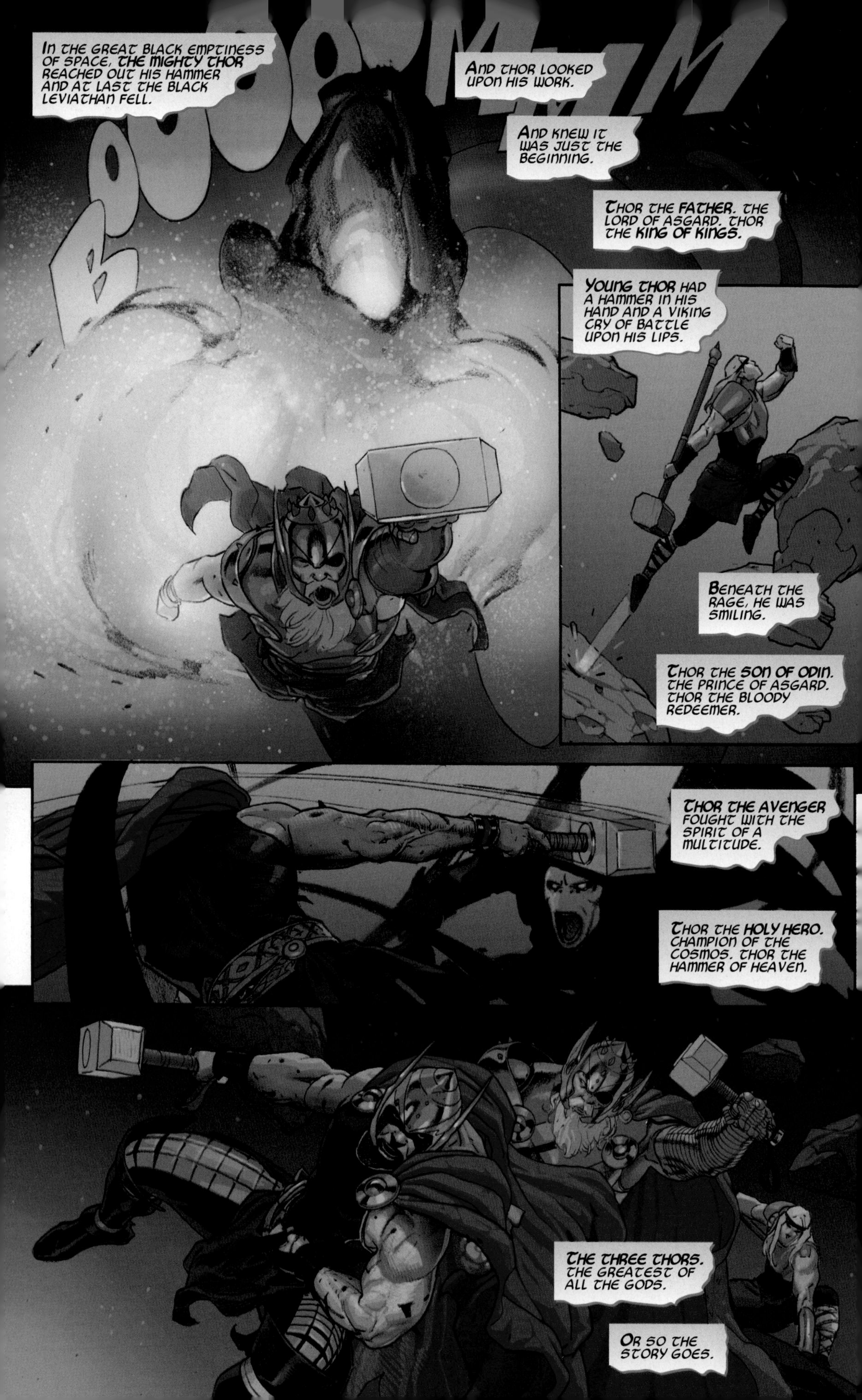
In the great black emptiness of space, THE MIGHTY THOR reached out his hammer and at last the black Leviathan fell.
And Thor looked upon his work.
And knew it was just the beginning.
Thor the FATHER. The Lord of Asgard. Thor the KING OF KINGS.
YOUNG THOR had a hammer in his hand and a Viking cry of battle upon his lips.
Beneath the rage, he was smiling.
Thor the SON OF ODIN. The Prince of Asgard. Thor the Bloody Redeemer.
THOR THE AVENGER fought with the spirit of a multitude.
Thor the HOLY HERO. Champion of the cosmos. Thor the Hammer of Heaven.
THE THREE THORS. The greatest of all the gods.
Or so the story goes.

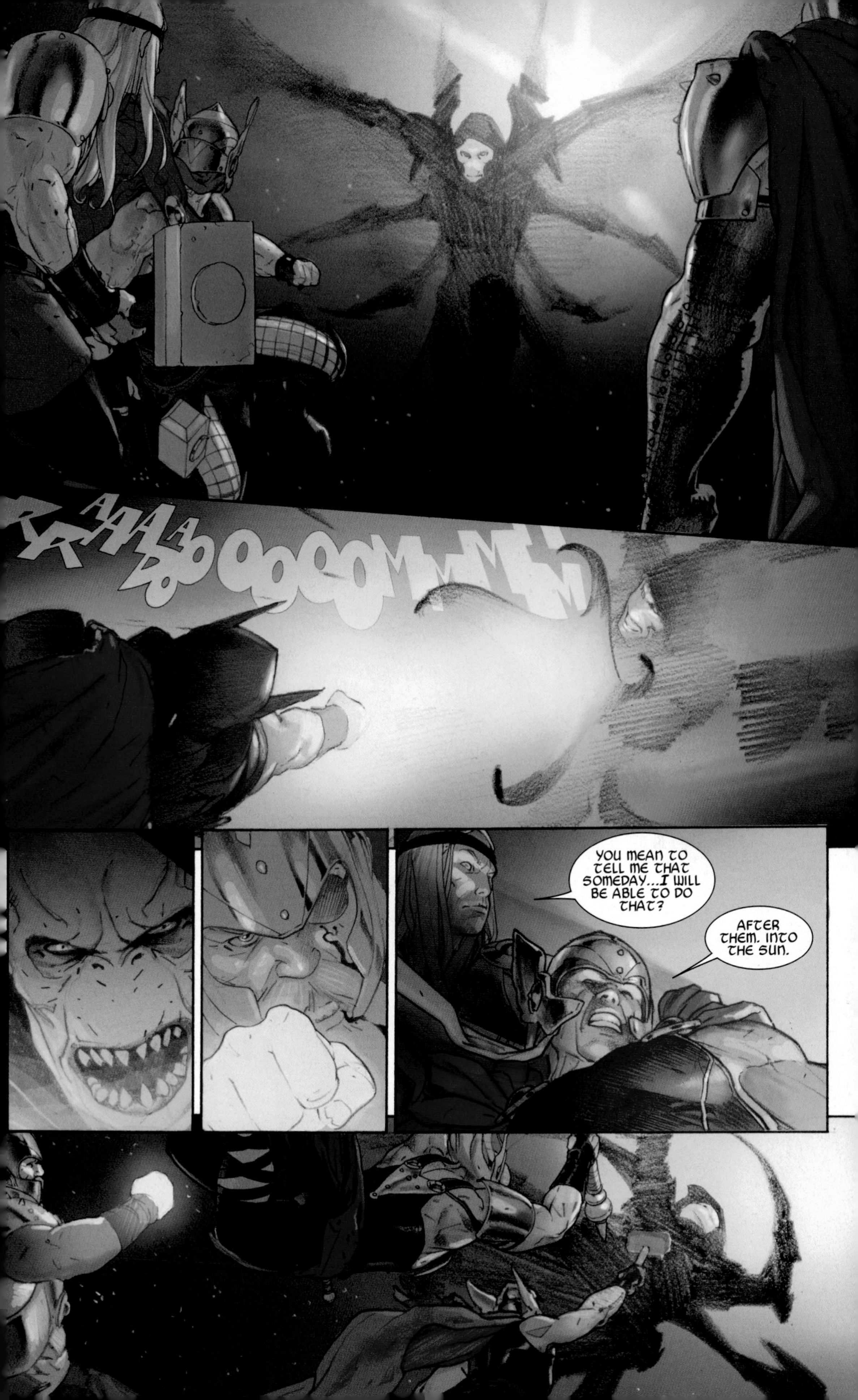
RRAAAABOOOOOMMMM!
YOU MEAN TO TELL ME THAT SOMEDAY...I WILL BE ABLE TO DO THAT?
AFTER THEM. INTO THE SUN.

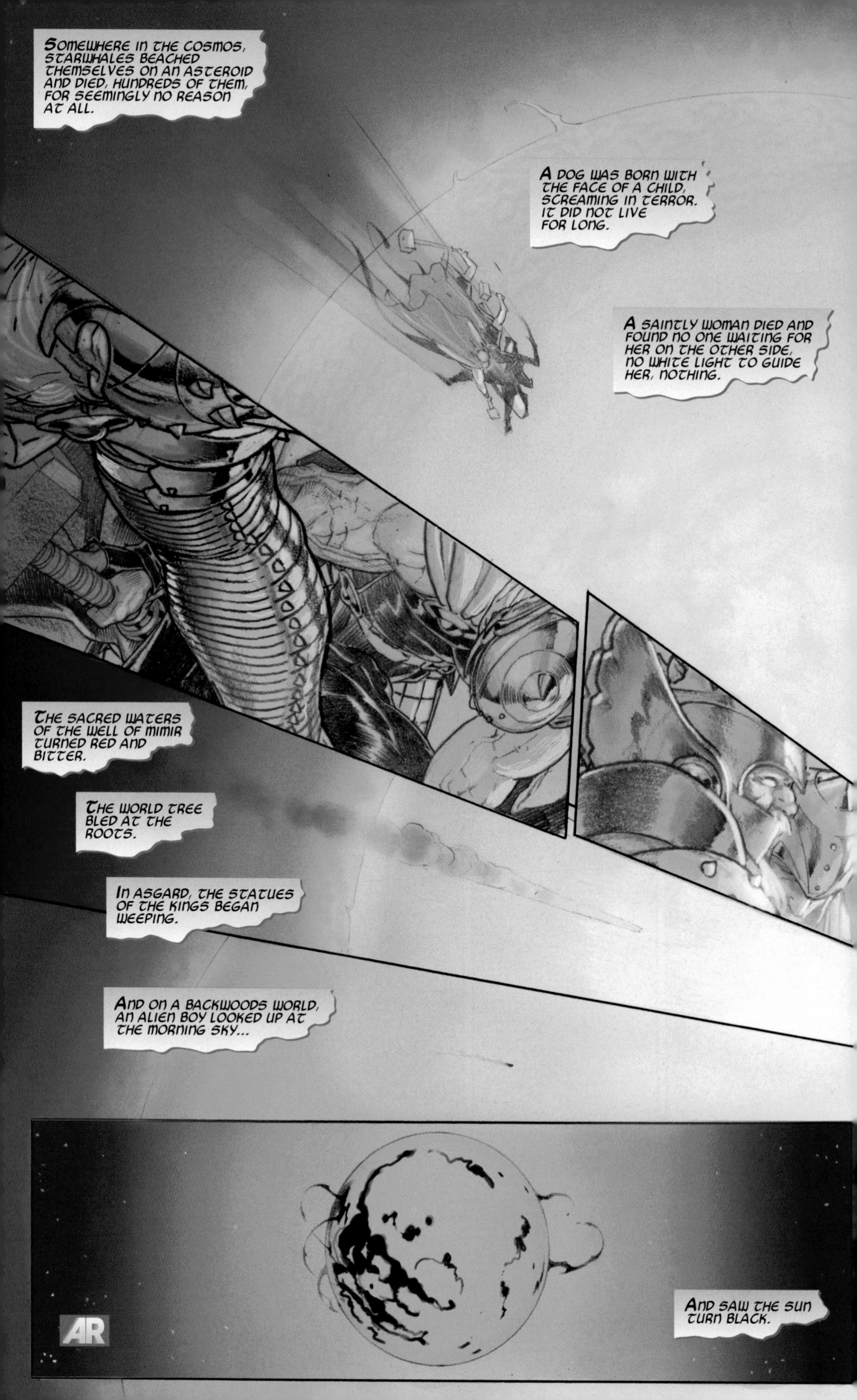
Somewhere in the cosmos, starwhales beached themselves on an asteroid and died, hundreds of them, for seemingly no reason at all.
A dog was born with the face of a child, screaming in terror. It did not live for long.
A saintly woman died and found no one waiting for her on the other side, no white light to guide her, nothing.
The sacred waters of the well of mimir turned red and bitter.
The world tree bled at the roots.
In Asgard, the statues of the kings began weeping.
And on a backwoods world, an alien boy looked up at the morning sky...
And saw the sun turn black.
AR

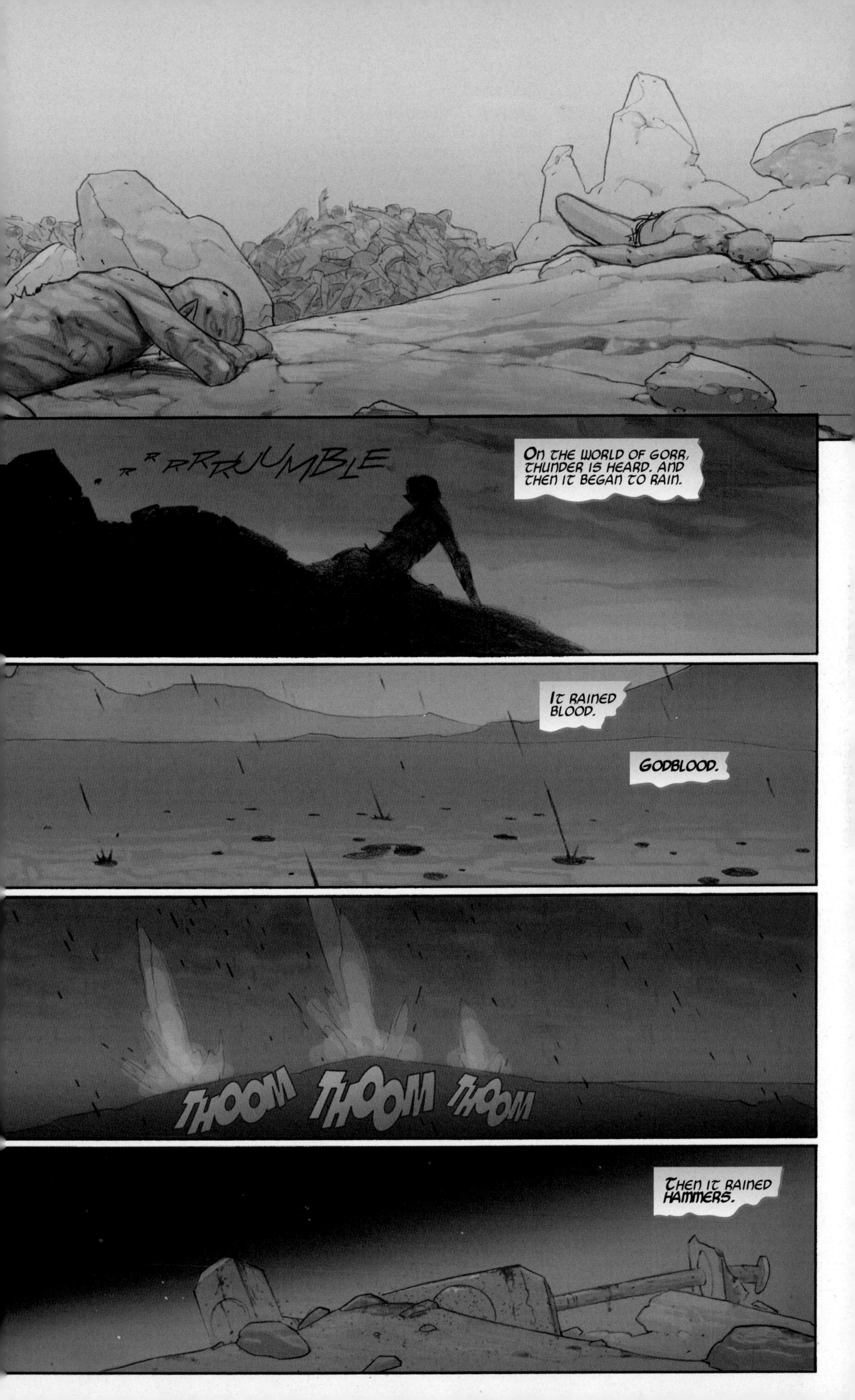
R R RRRUUMBLE
ON THE WORLD OF GORR, THUNDER IS HEARD. AND THEN IT BEGAN TO RAIN.
IT RAINED BLOOD.
GODBLOOD.
THOOM THOOM THOOM
THEN IT RAINED HAMMERS.

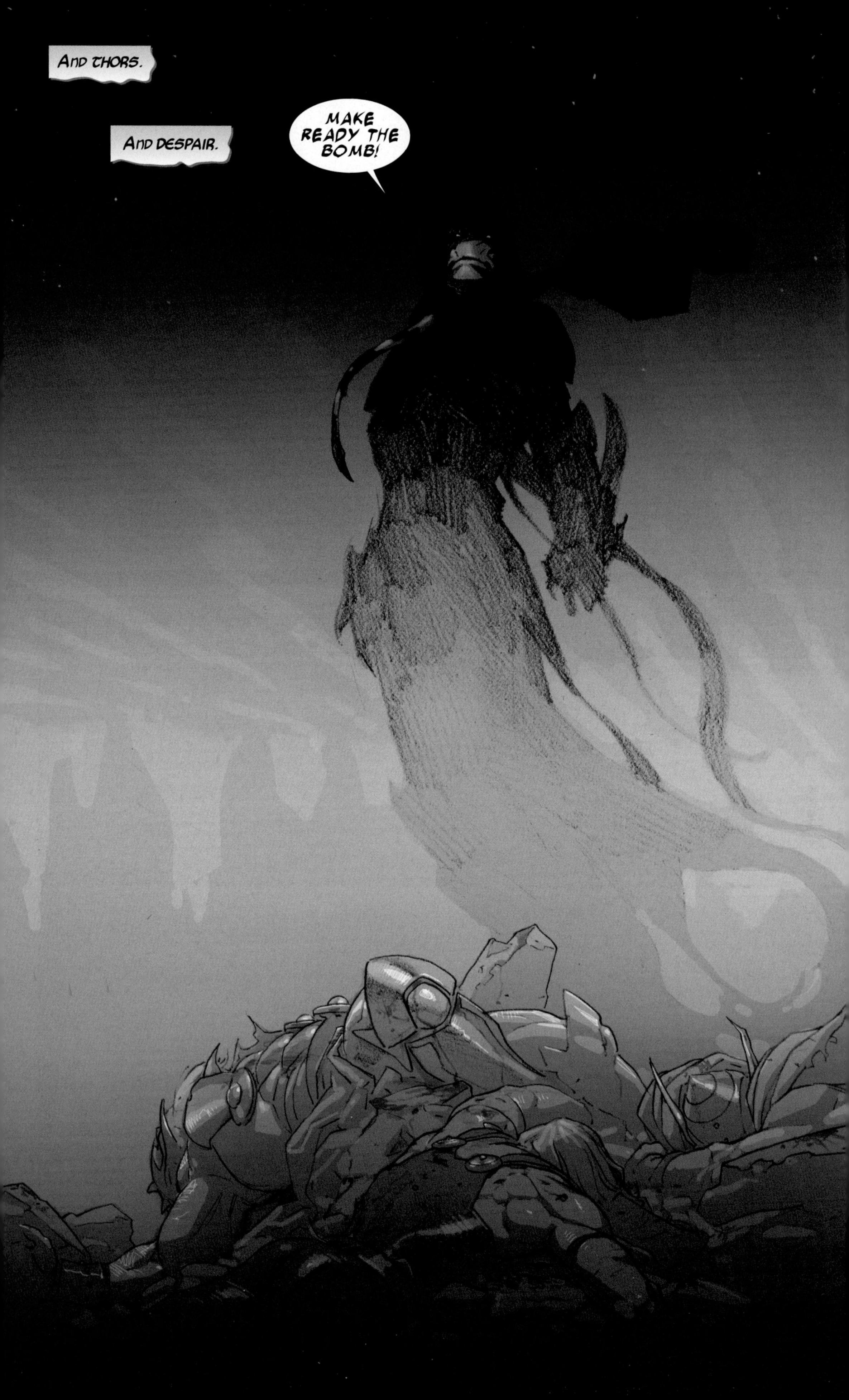
And thors.
And despair.
MAKE READY THE BOMB!

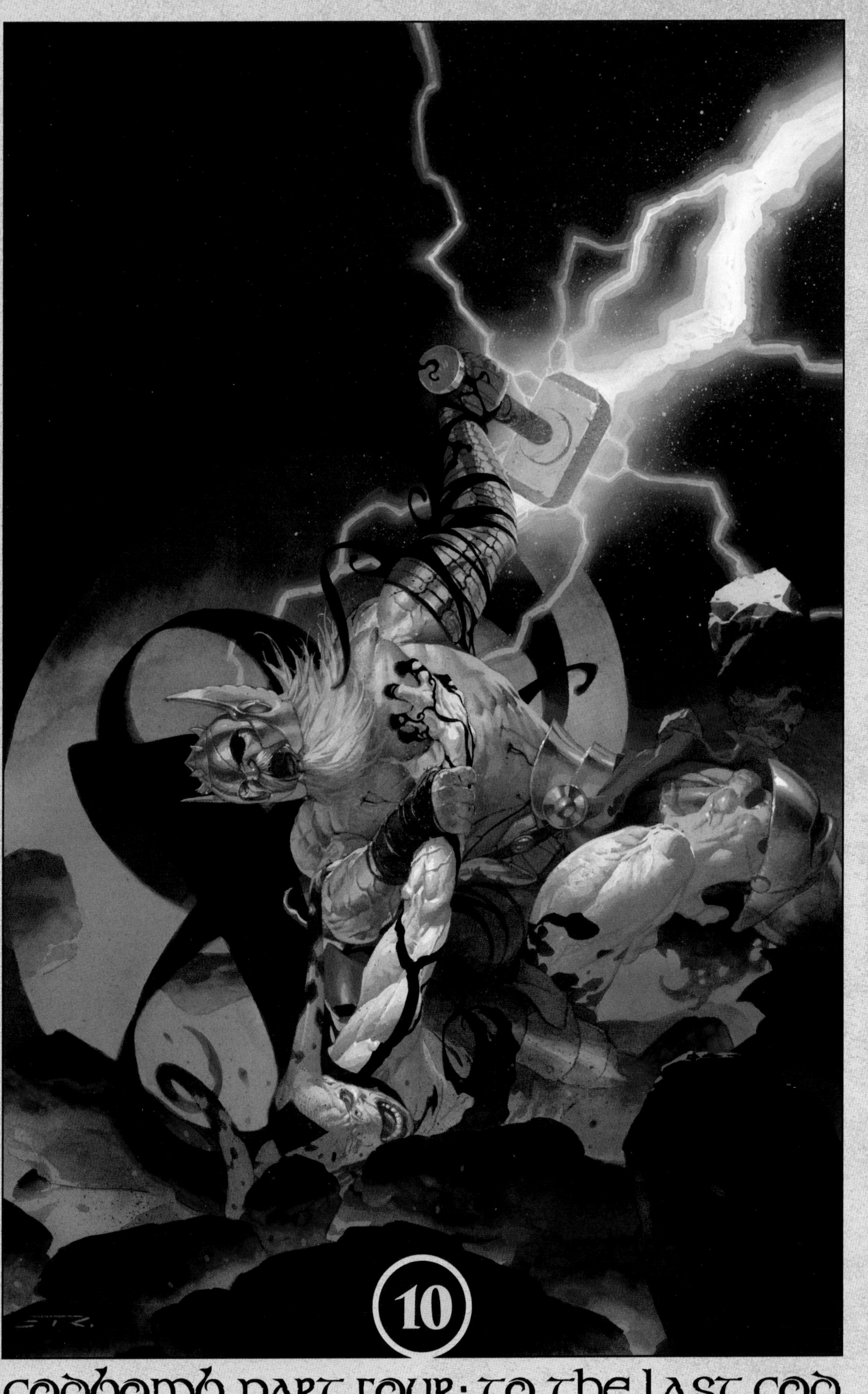
10

GODBOMB PART FOUR: TO THE LAST GOD

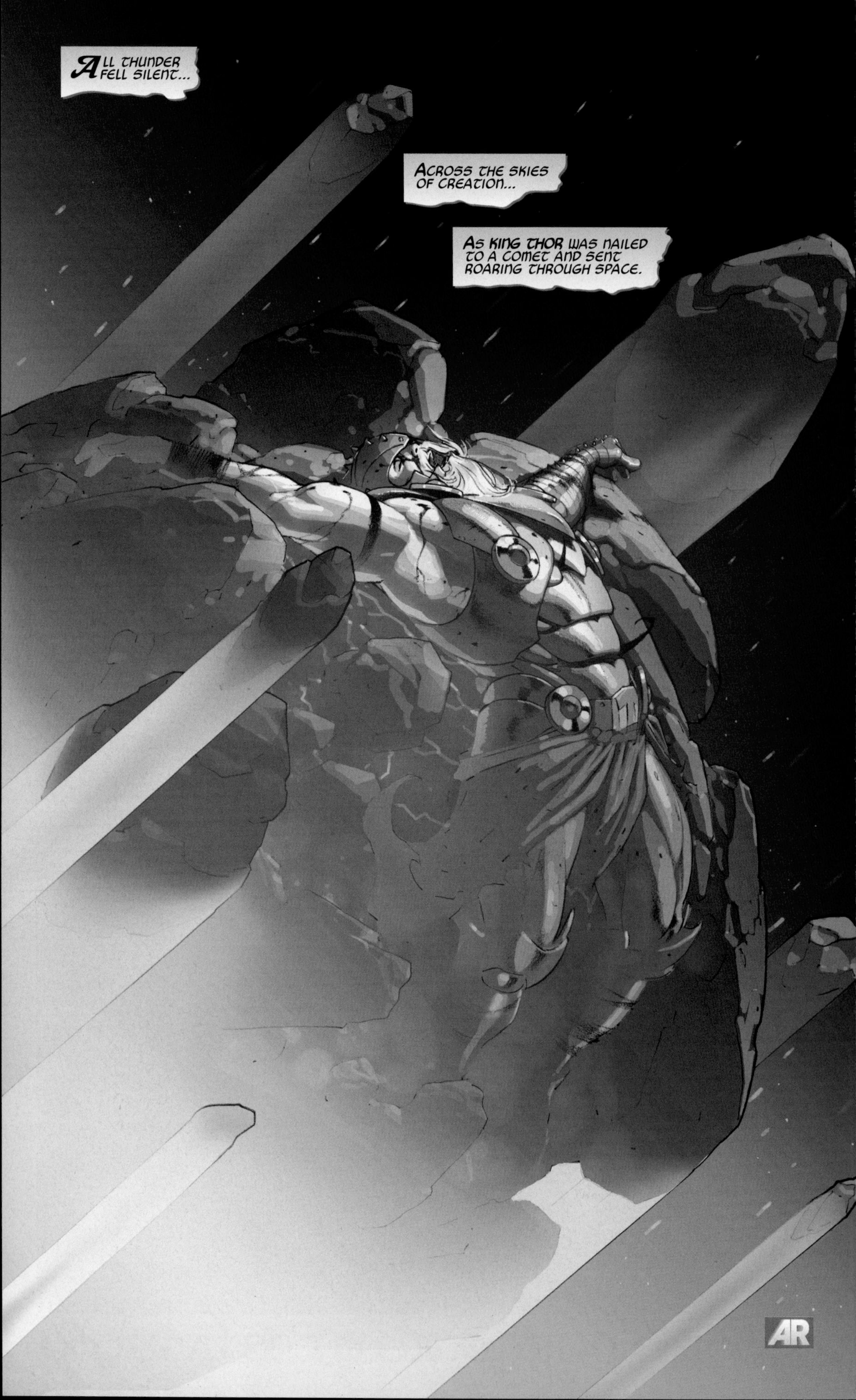
ALL THUNDER FELL SILENT...
ACROSS THE SKIES OF CREATION...
AS KING THOR WAS NAILED TO A COMET AND SENT ROARING THROUGH SPACE.
AR

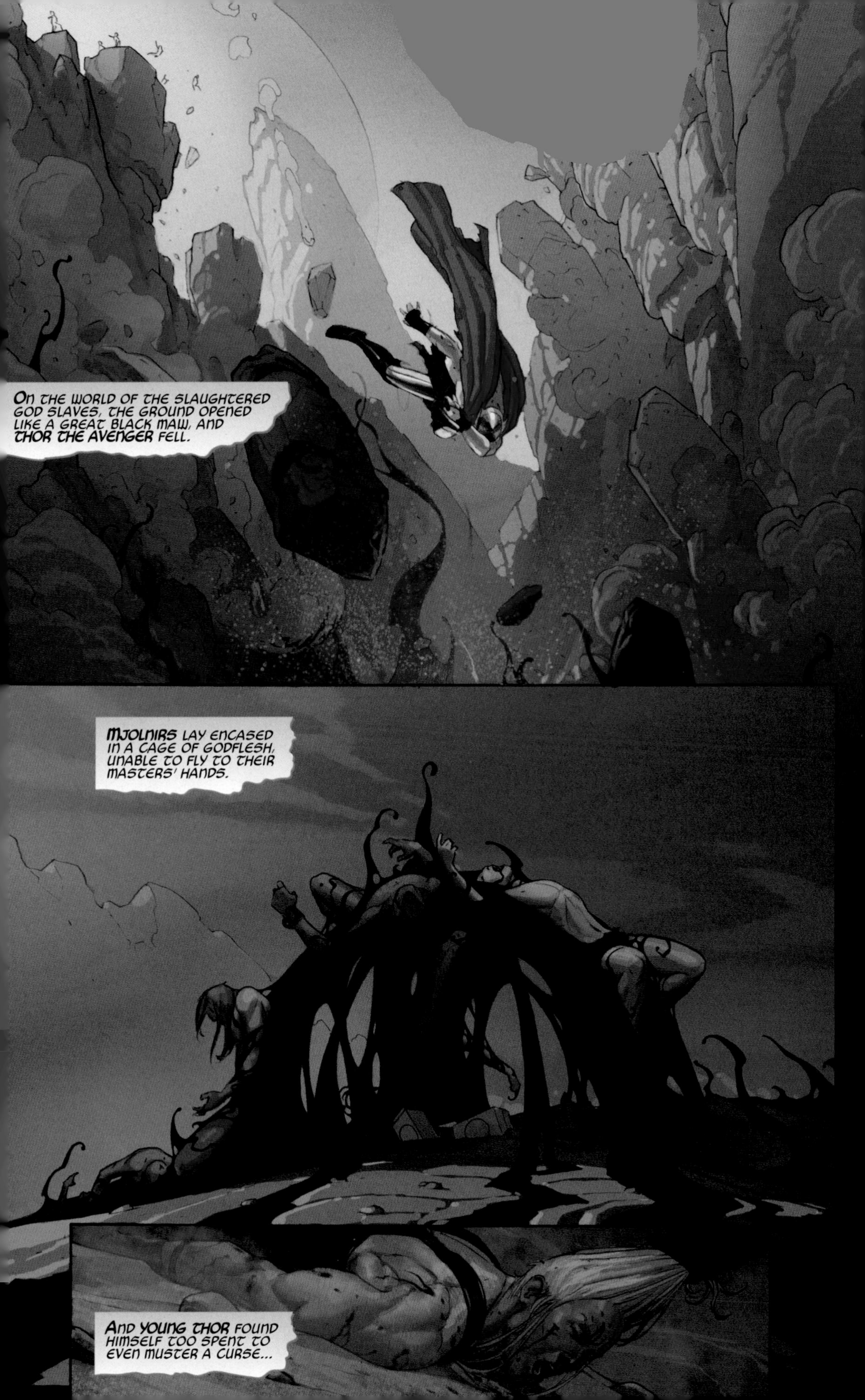
On the world of the slaughtered god slaves, the ground opened like a great black maw, and **Thor the Avenger** fell.
Mjolnirs lay encased in a cage of godflesh, unable to fly to their masters' hands.
And **young Thor** found himself too spent to even muster a curse...

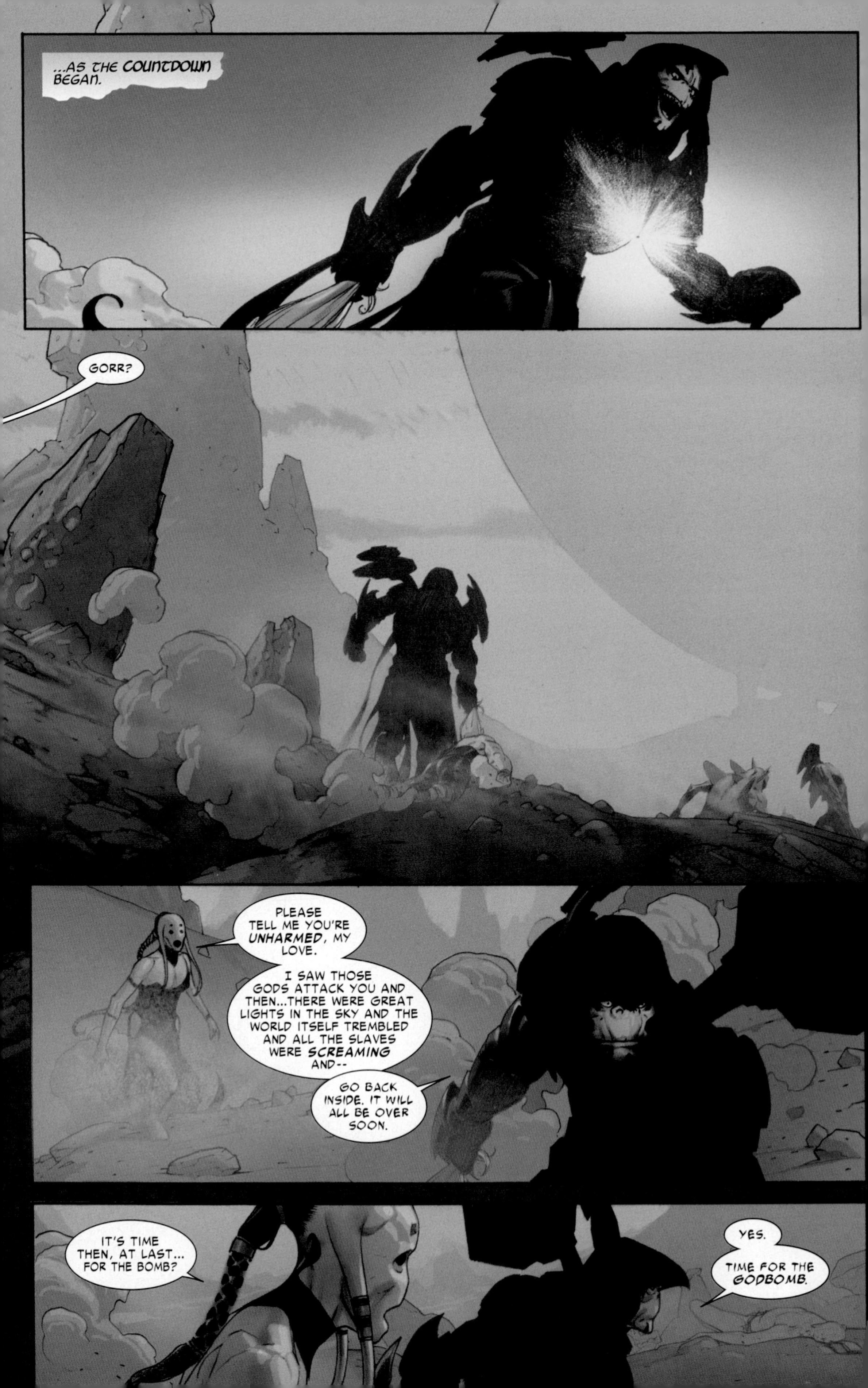
...AS THE COUNTDOWN BEGAN.
GORR?
PLEASE TELL ME YOU'RE UNHARMED, MY LOVE.
I SAW THOSE GODS ATTACK YOU AND THEN...THERE WERE GREAT LIGHTS IN THE SKY AND THE WORLD ITSELF TREMBLED AND ALL THE SLAVES WERE SCREAMING AND--
GO BACK INSIDE. IT WILL ALL BE OVER SOON.
IT'S TIME THEN, AT LAST... FOR THE BOMB?
YES.
TIME FOR THE GODBOMB.

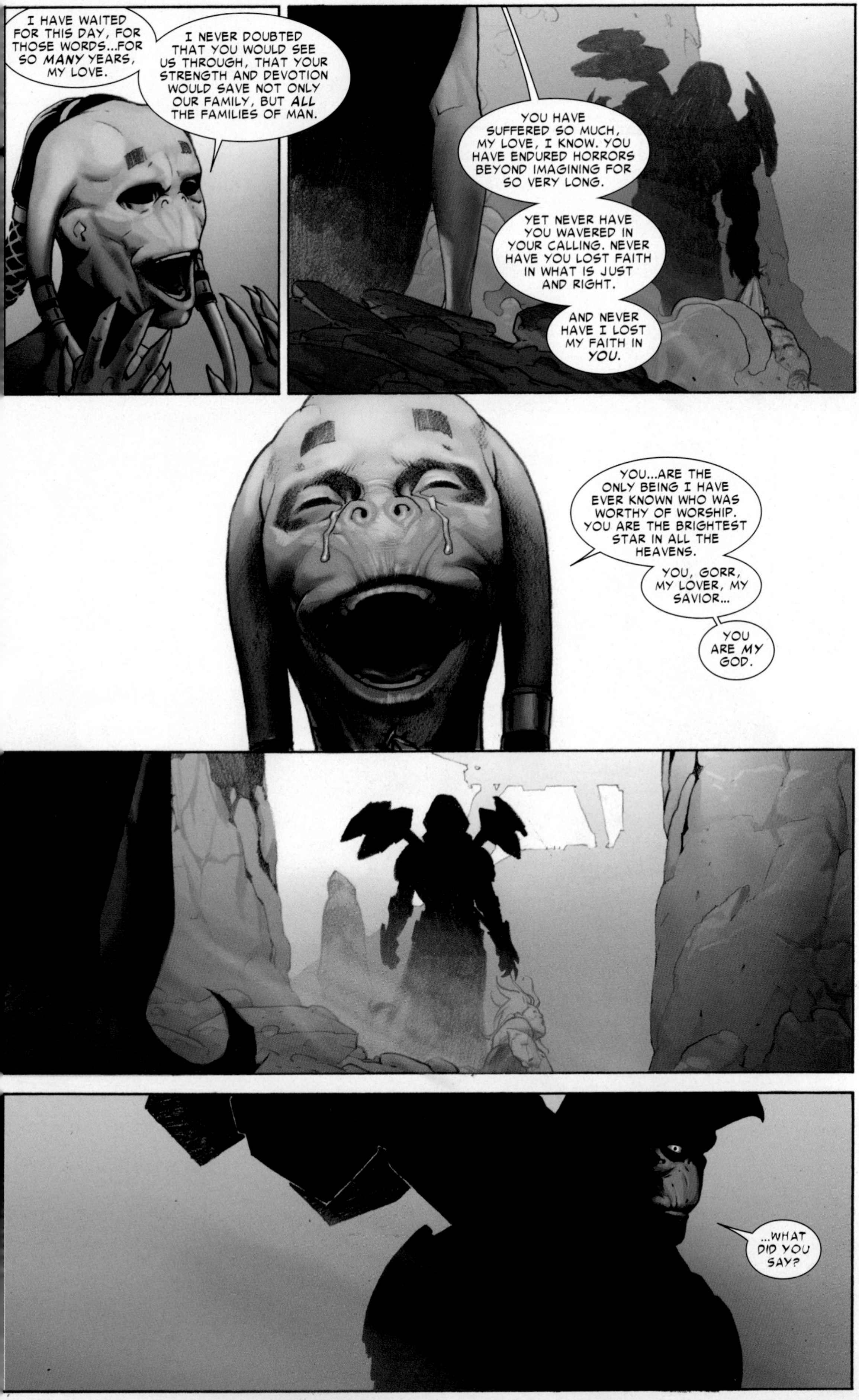
I HAVE WAITED FOR THIS DAY, FOR THOSE WORDS...FOR SO MANY YEARS, MY LOVE.
I NEVER DOUBTED THAT YOU WOULD SEE US THROUGH, THAT YOUR STRENGTH AND DEVOTION WOULD SAVE NOT ONLY OUR FAMILY, BUT ALL THE FAMILIES OF MAN.
YOU HAVE SUFFERED SO MUCH, MY LOVE, I KNOW. YOU HAVE ENDURED HORRORS BEYOND IMAGINING FOR SO VERY LONG.
YET NEVER HAVE YOU WAVERED IN YOUR CALLING. NEVER HAVE YOU LOST FAITH IN WHAT IS JUST AND RIGHT.
AND NEVER HAVE I LOST MY FAITH IN YOU.
YOU...ARE THE ONLY BEING I HAVE EVER KNOWN WHO WAS WORTHY OF WORSHIP. YOU ARE THE BRIGHTEST STAR IN ALL THE HEAVENS.
YOU, GORR, MY LOVER, MY SAVIOR...
YOU ARE MY GOD.
...WHAT DID YOU SAY?

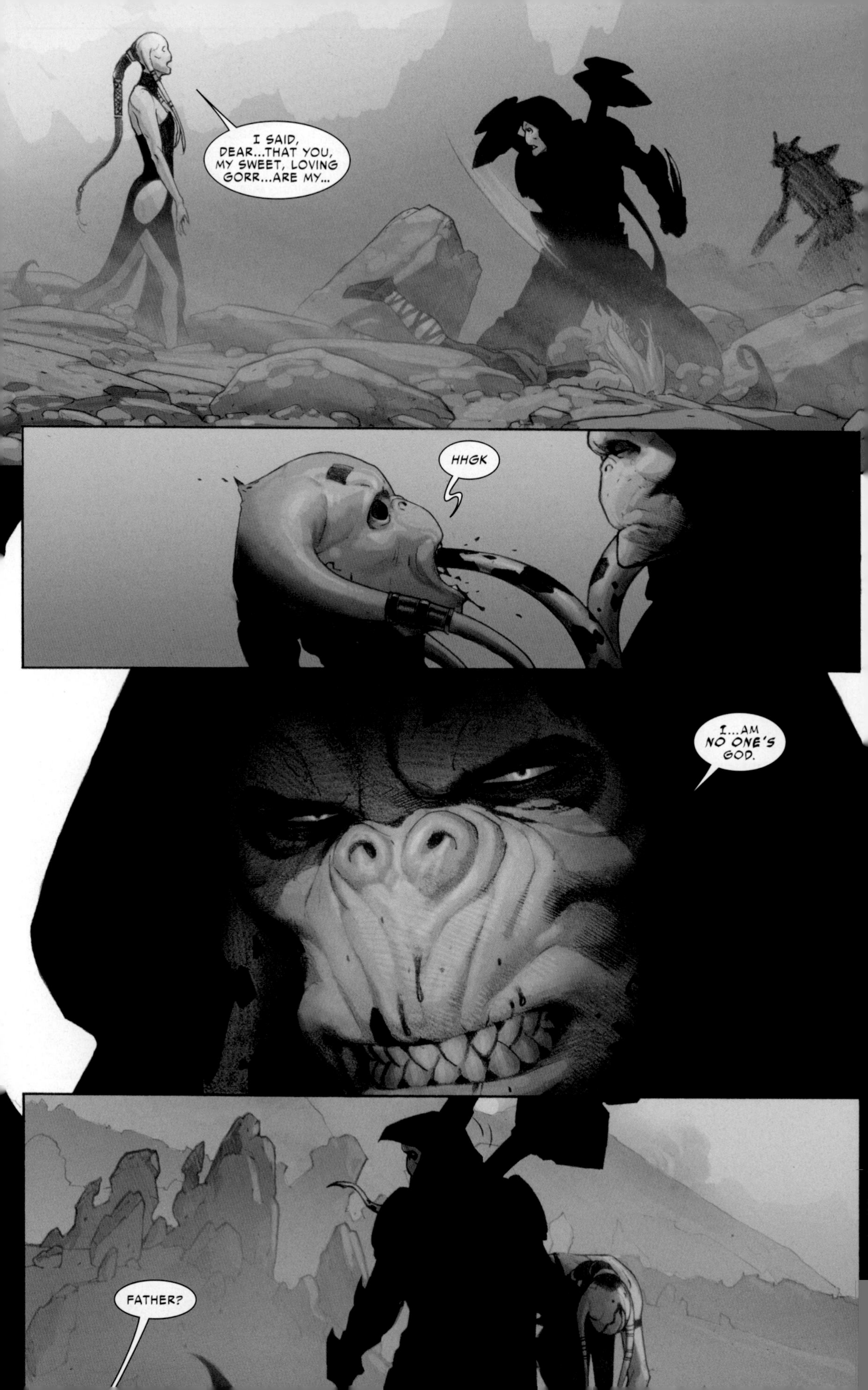
I SAID, DEAR...THAT YOU, MY SWEET, LOVING GORR...ARE MY...
HHGK
I...AM NO ONE'S GOD.
FATHER?

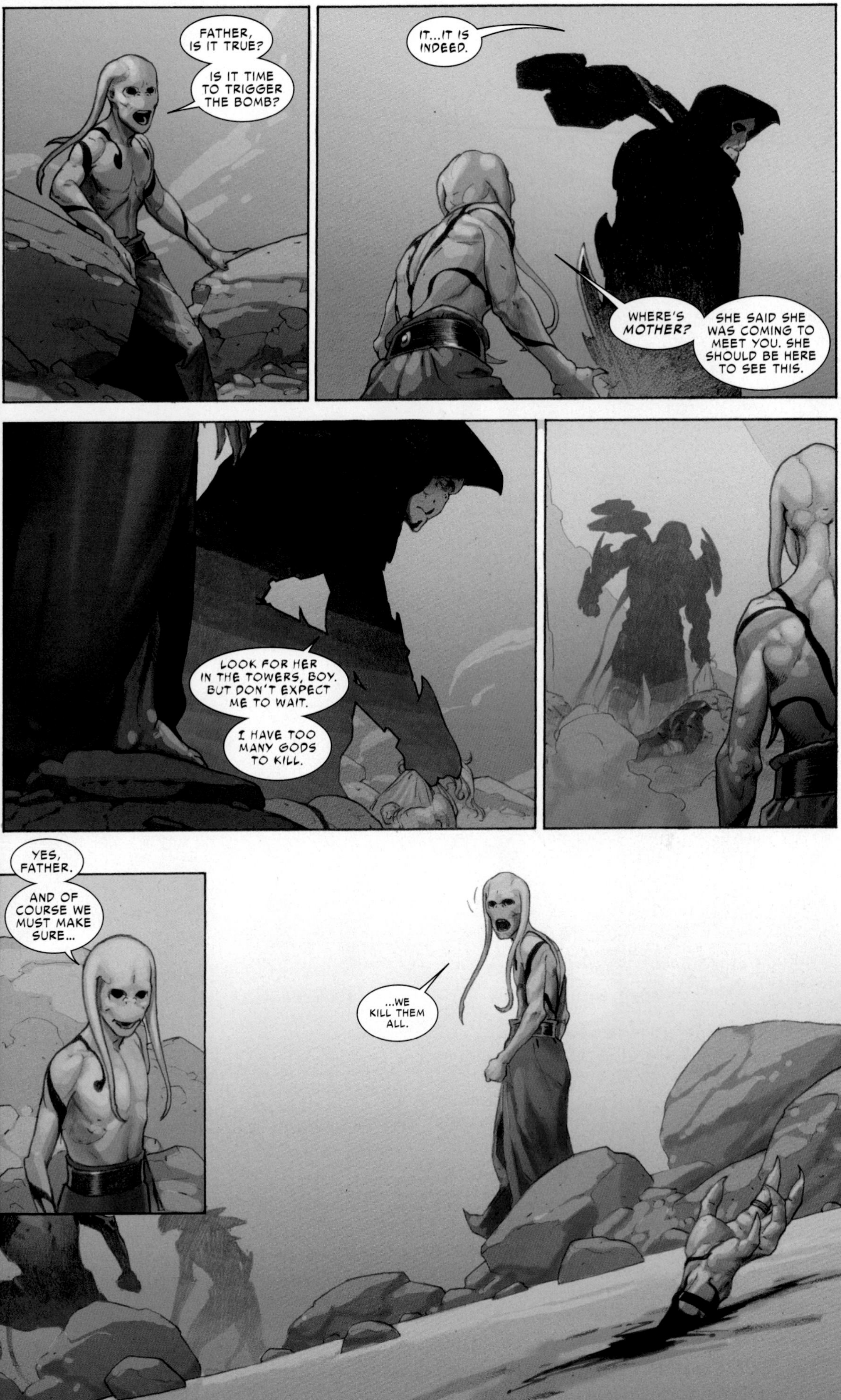
FATHER, IS IT TRUE?
IS IT TIME TO TRIGGER THE BOMB?
IT...IT IS INDEED.
WHERE'S *MOTHER?*
SHE SAID SHE WAS COMING TO MEET YOU. SHE SHOULD BE HERE TO SEE THIS.
LOOK FOR HER IN THE TOWERS, BOY. BUT DON'T EXPECT ME TO WAIT.
I HAVE TOO MANY GODS TO KILL.
YES, FATHER.
AND OF COURSE WE MUST MAKE SURE...
...WE KILL THEM ALL.

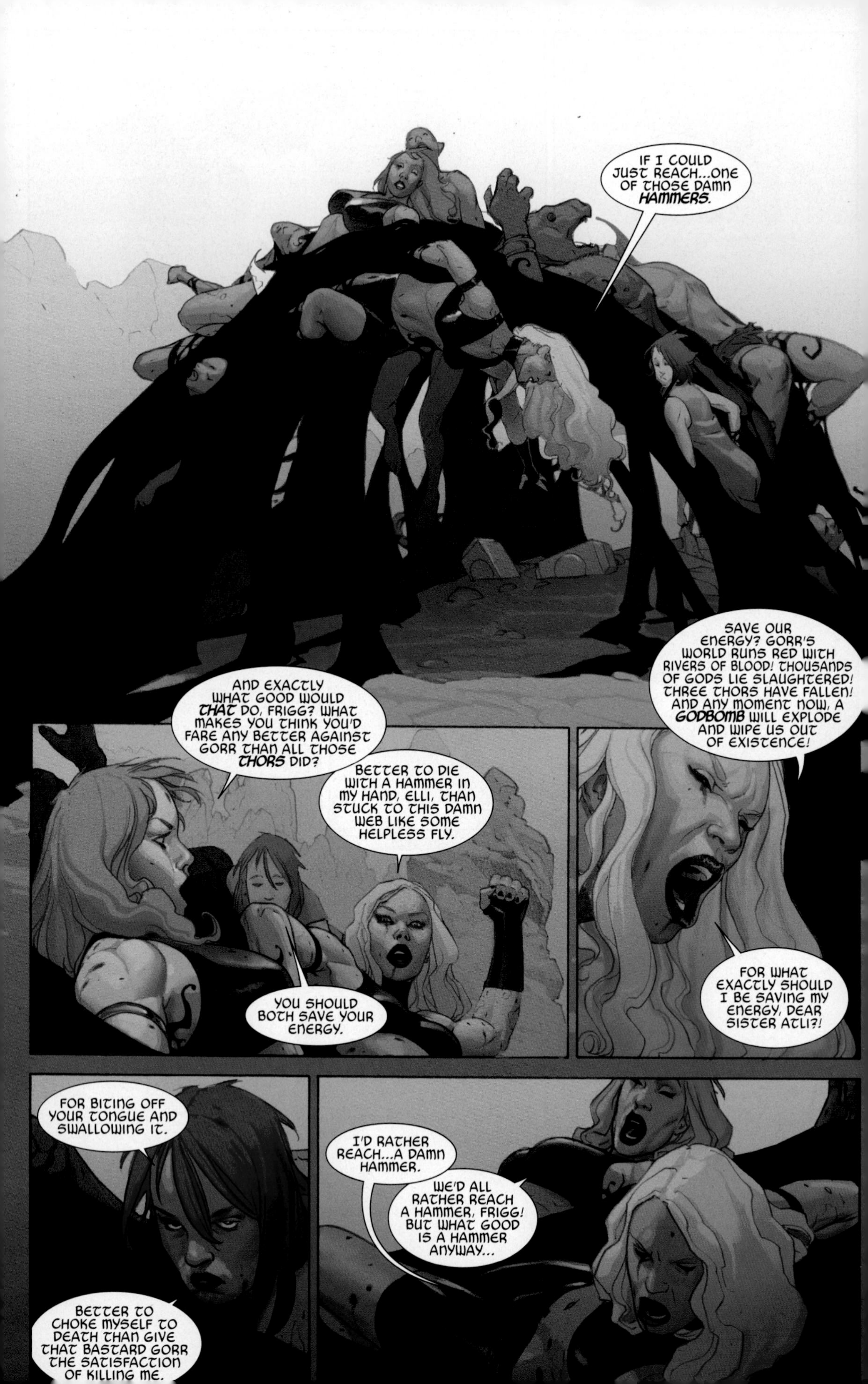
IF I COULD JUST REACH...ONE OF THOSE DAMN HAMMERS.
AND EXACTLY WHAT GOOD WOULD THAT DO, FRIGG? WHAT MAKES YOU THINK YOU'D FARE ANY BETTER AGAINST GORR THAN ALL THOSE THORS DID?
BETTER TO DIE WITH A HAMMER IN MY HAND, ELLI, THAN STUCK TO THIS DAMN WEB LIKE SOME HELPLESS FLY.
YOU SHOULD BOTH SAVE YOUR ENERGY.
SAVE OUR ENERGY? GORR'S WORLD RUNS RED WITH RIVERS OF BLOOD! THOUSANDS OF GODS LIE SLAUGHTERED! THREE THORS HAVE FALLEN! AND ANY MOMENT NOW, A GODBOMB WILL EXPLODE AND WIPE US OUT OF EXISTENCE!
FOR WHAT EXACTLY SHOULD I BE SAVING MY ENERGY, DEAR SISTER ATLI?!
FOR BITING OFF YOUR TONGUE AND SWALLOWING IT.
BETTER TO CHOKE MYSELF TO DEATH THAN GIVE THAT BASTARD GORR THE SATISFACTION OF KILLING ME.
I'D RATHER REACH...A DAMN HAMMER.
WE'D ALL RATHER REACH A HAMMER, FRIGG! BUT WHAT GOOD IS A HAMMER ANYWAY...

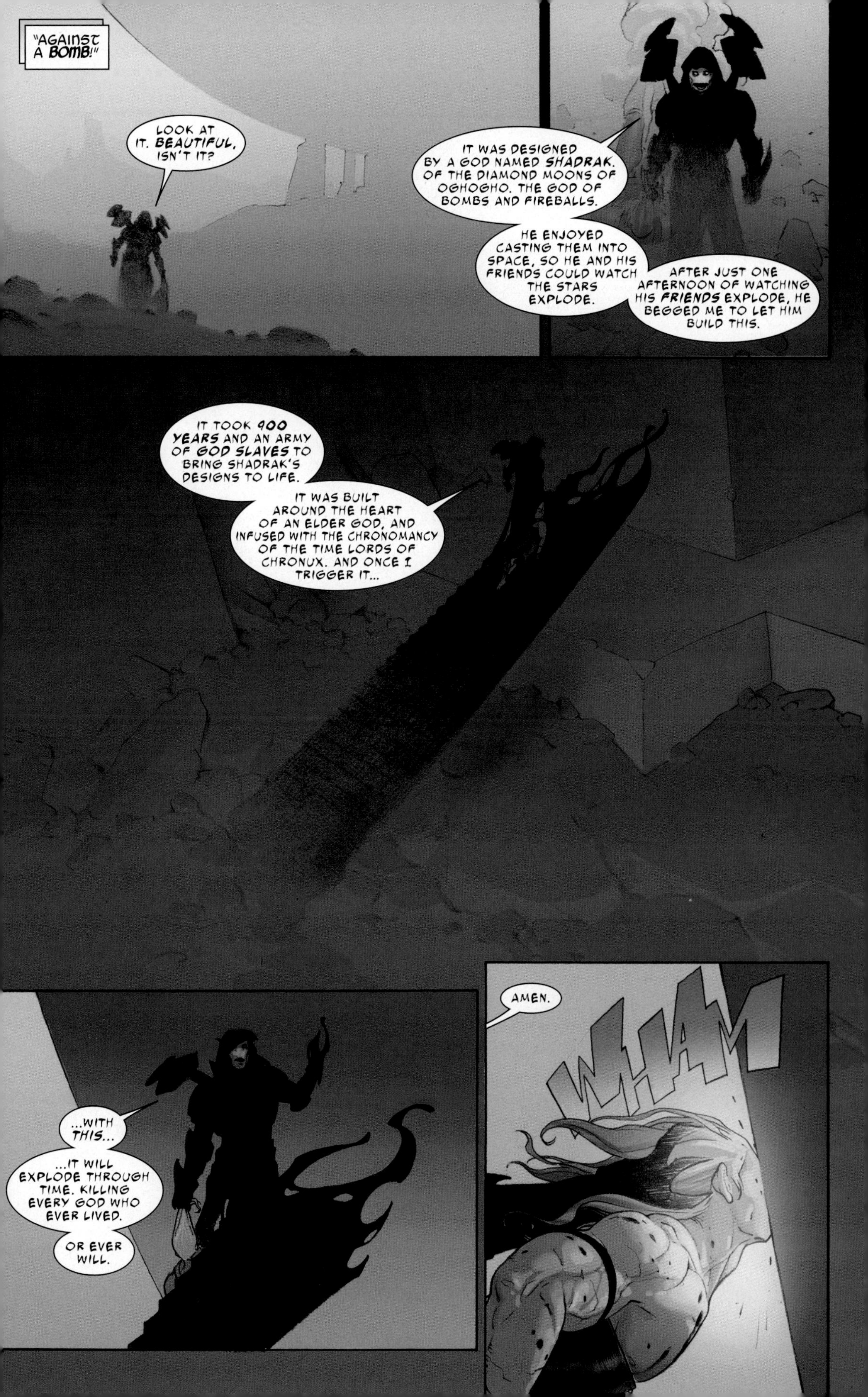
"AGAINST A BOMB!"
LOOK AT IT. BEAUTIFUL, ISN'T IT?
IT WAS DESIGNED BY A GOD NAMED SHADRAK. OF THE DIAMOND MOONS OF OGHOGHO. THE GOD OF BOMBS AND FIREBALLS.
HE ENJOYED CASTING THEM INTO SPACE, SO HE AND HIS FRIENDS COULD WATCH THE STARS EXPLODE.
AFTER JUST ONE AFTERNOON OF WATCHING HIS FRIENDS EXPLODE, HE BEGGED ME TO LET HIM BUILD THIS.
IT TOOK 900 YEARS AND AN ARMY OF GOD SLAVES TO BRING SHADRAK'S DESIGNS TO LIFE.
IT WAS BUILT AROUND THE HEART OF AN ELDER GOD, AND INFUSED WITH THE CHRONOMANCY OF THE TIME LORDS OF CHRONUX. AND ONCE I TRIGGER IT...
...WITH THIS...
...IT WILL EXPLODE THROUGH TIME. KILLING EVERY GOD WHO EVER LIVED.
OR EVER WILL.
AMEN.
WHAM

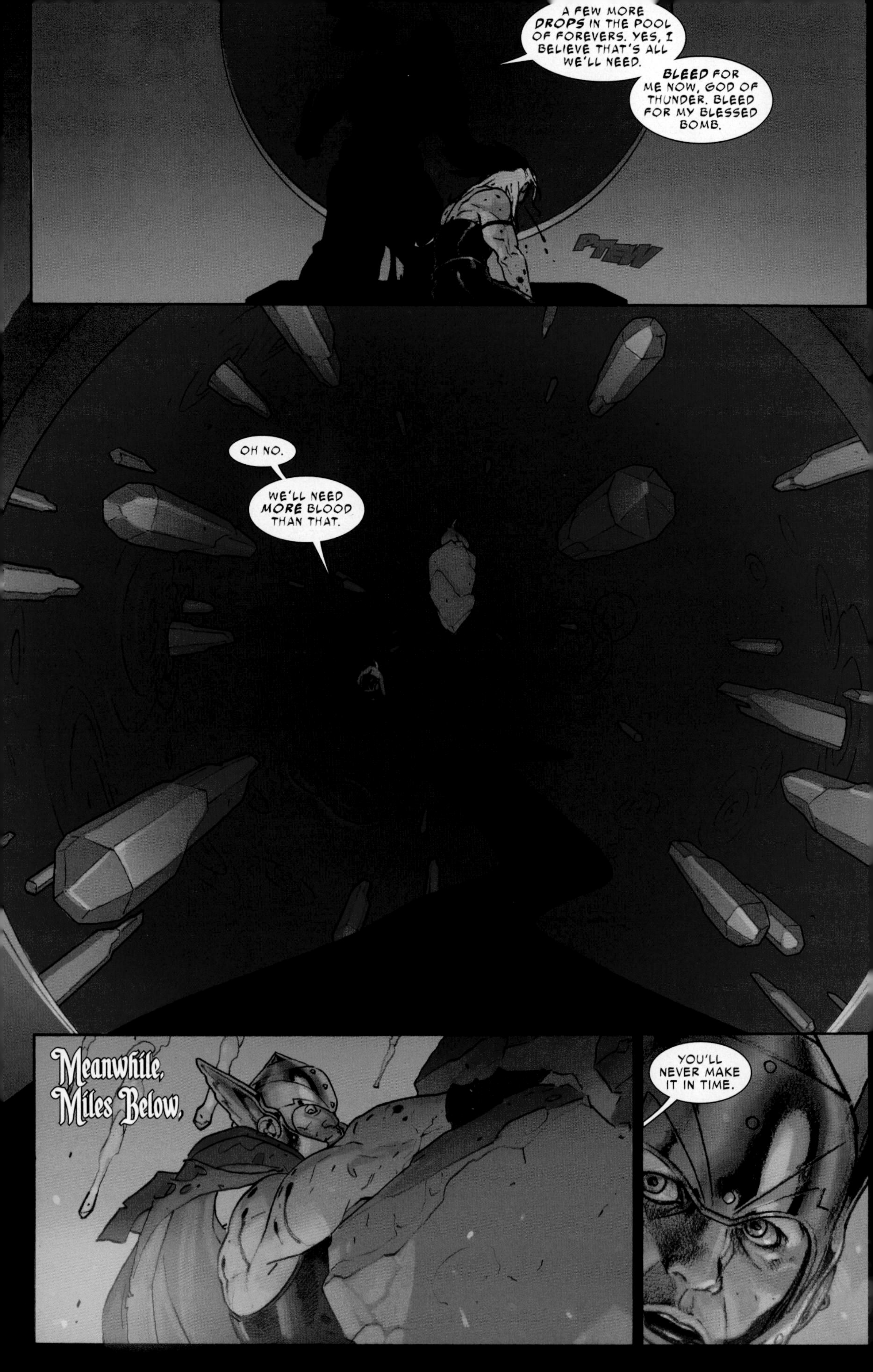
A FEW MORE DROPS IN THE POOL OF FOREVERS. YES, I BELIEVE THAT'S ALL WE'LL NEED.
BLEED FOR ME NOW, GOD OF THUNDER. BLEED FOR MY BLESSED BOMB.
PTEW
OH NO.
WE'LL NEED MORE BLOOD THAN THAT.
Meanwhile, Miles Below,
YOU'LL NEVER MAKE IT IN TIME.

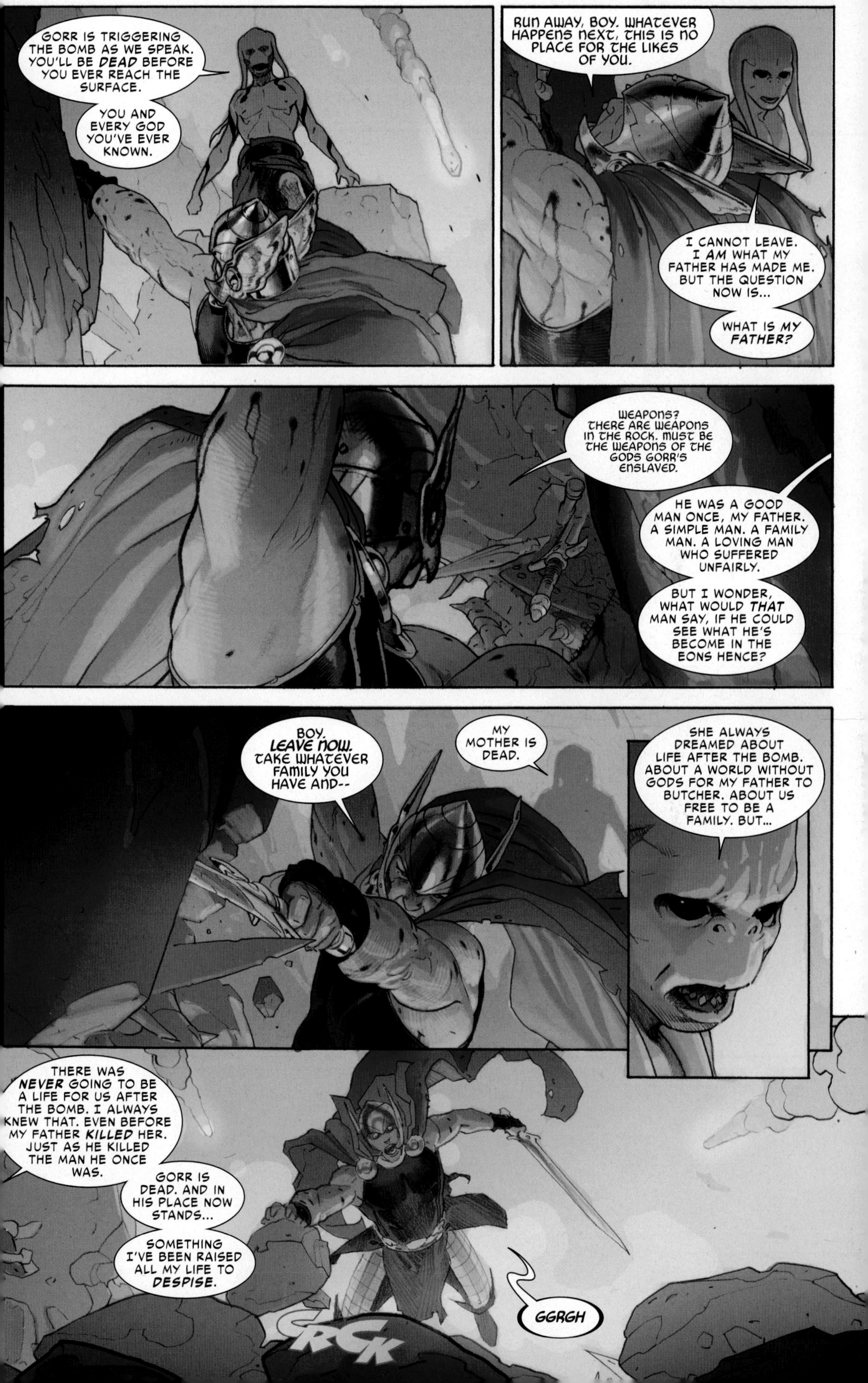
GORR IS TRIGGERING THE BOMB AS WE SPEAK. YOU'LL BE *DEAD* BEFORE YOU EVER REACH THE SURFACE.
YOU AND EVERY GOD YOU'VE EVER KNOWN.
RUN AWAY, BOY. WHATEVER HAPPENS NEXT, THIS IS NO PLACE FOR THE LIKES OF YOU.
I CANNOT LEAVE. I *AM* WHAT MY FATHER HAS MADE ME. BUT THE QUESTION NOW IS...
WHAT IS *MY FATHER?*
WEAPONS? THERE ARE WEAPONS IN THE ROCK. MUST BE THE WEAPONS OF THE GODS GORR'S ENSLAVED.
HE WAS A GOOD MAN ONCE, MY FATHER. A SIMPLE MAN. A FAMILY MAN. A LOVING MAN WHO SUFFERED UNFAIRLY.
BUT I WONDER, WHAT WOULD *THAT* MAN SAY, IF HE COULD SEE WHAT HE'S BECOME IN THE EONS HENCE?
BOY. *LEAVE NOW.* TAKE WHATEVER FAMILY YOU HAVE AND--
MY MOTHER IS DEAD.
SHE ALWAYS DREAMED ABOUT LIFE AFTER THE BOMB. ABOUT A WORLD WITHOUT GODS FOR MY FATHER TO BUTCHER. ABOUT US FREE TO BE A FAMILY. BUT...
THERE WAS *NEVER* GOING TO BE A LIFE FOR US AFTER THE BOMB. I ALWAYS KNEW THAT. EVEN BEFORE MY FATHER *KILLED* HER. JUST AS HE KILLED THE MAN HE ONCE WAS.
GORR IS DEAD. AND IN HIS PLACE NOW STANDS...
SOMETHING I'VE BEEN RAISED ALL MY LIFE TO *DESPISE*.
CRCK
GGRGH

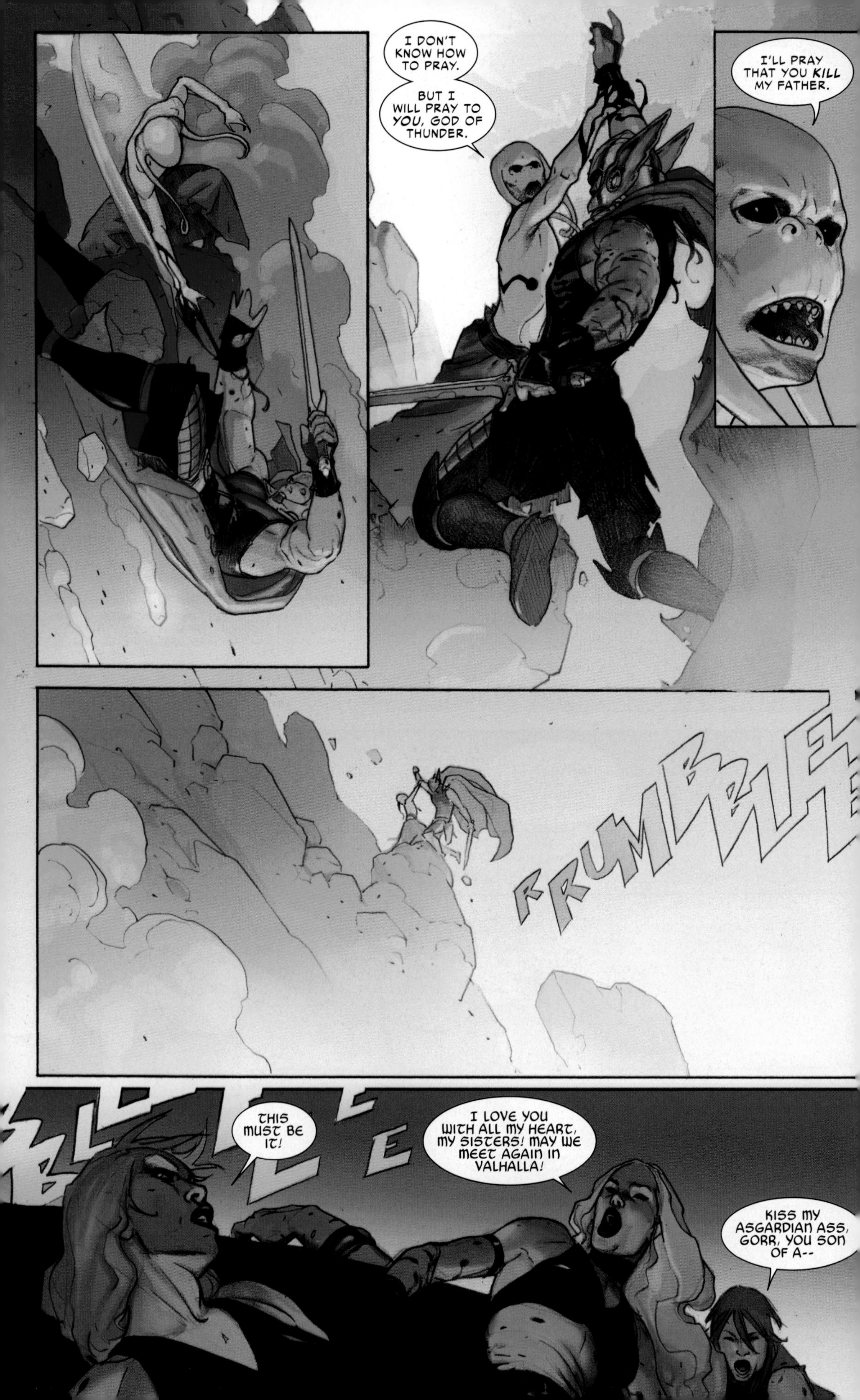

I DON'T KNOW HOW TO PRAY.
BUT I WILL PRAY TO YOU, GOD OF THUNDER.
I'LL PRAY THAT YOU KILL MY FATHER.
RUMBLE
THIS MUST BE IT!
I LOVE YOU WITH ALL MY HEART, MY SISTERS! MAY WE MEET AGAIN IN VALHALLA!
KISS MY ASGARDIAN ASS, GORR, YOU SON OF A--

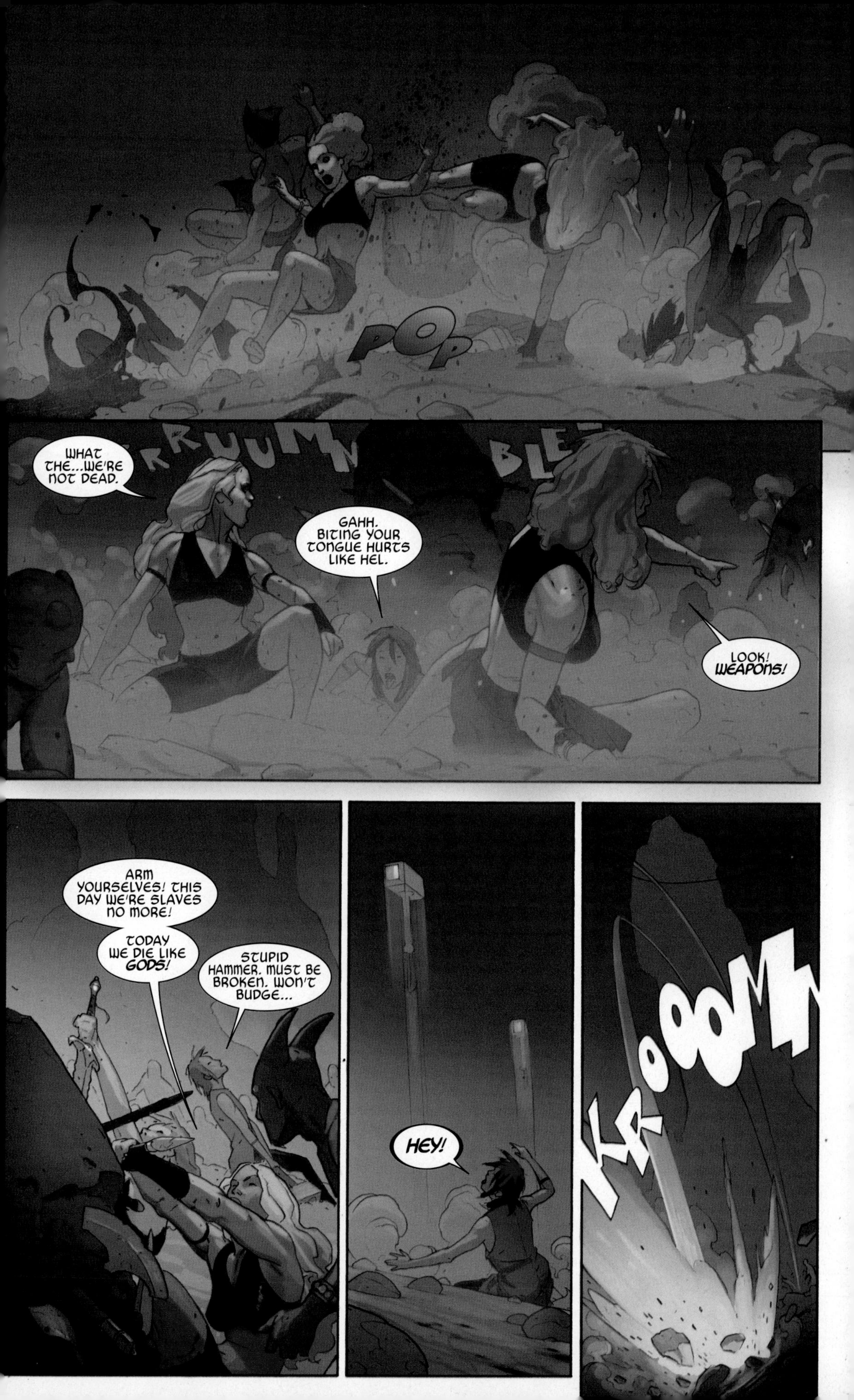
POP
RRUUMBLE
WHAT THE...WE'RE NOT DEAD.
GAHH. BITING YOUR TONGUE HURTS LIKE HEL.
LOOK! WEAPONS!
ARM YOURSELVES! THIS DAY WE'RE SLAVES NO MORE!
TODAY WE DIE LIKE GODS!
STUPID HAMMER. MUST BE BROKEN. WON'T BUDGE...
HEY!
KROOOM

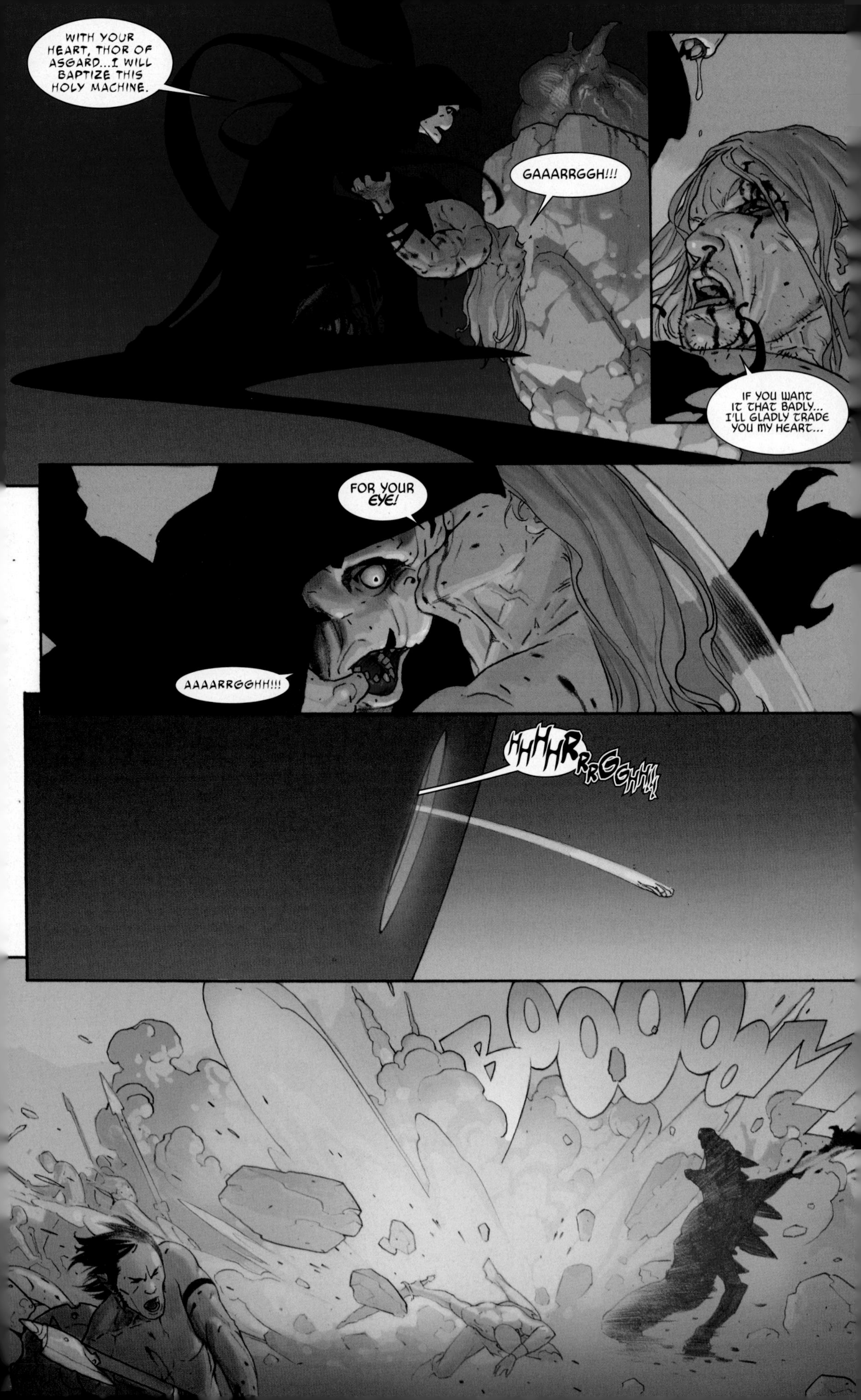
WITH YOUR HEART, THOR OF ASGARD...I WILL BAPTIZE THIS HOLY MACHINE.
GAAARRGGH!!!
IF YOU WANT IT THAT BADLY... I'LL GLADLY TRADE YOU MY HEART...
FOR YOUR EYE!
AAAARRGGHH!!!
HHHHRRRGGHH!!!
BOOOOOM

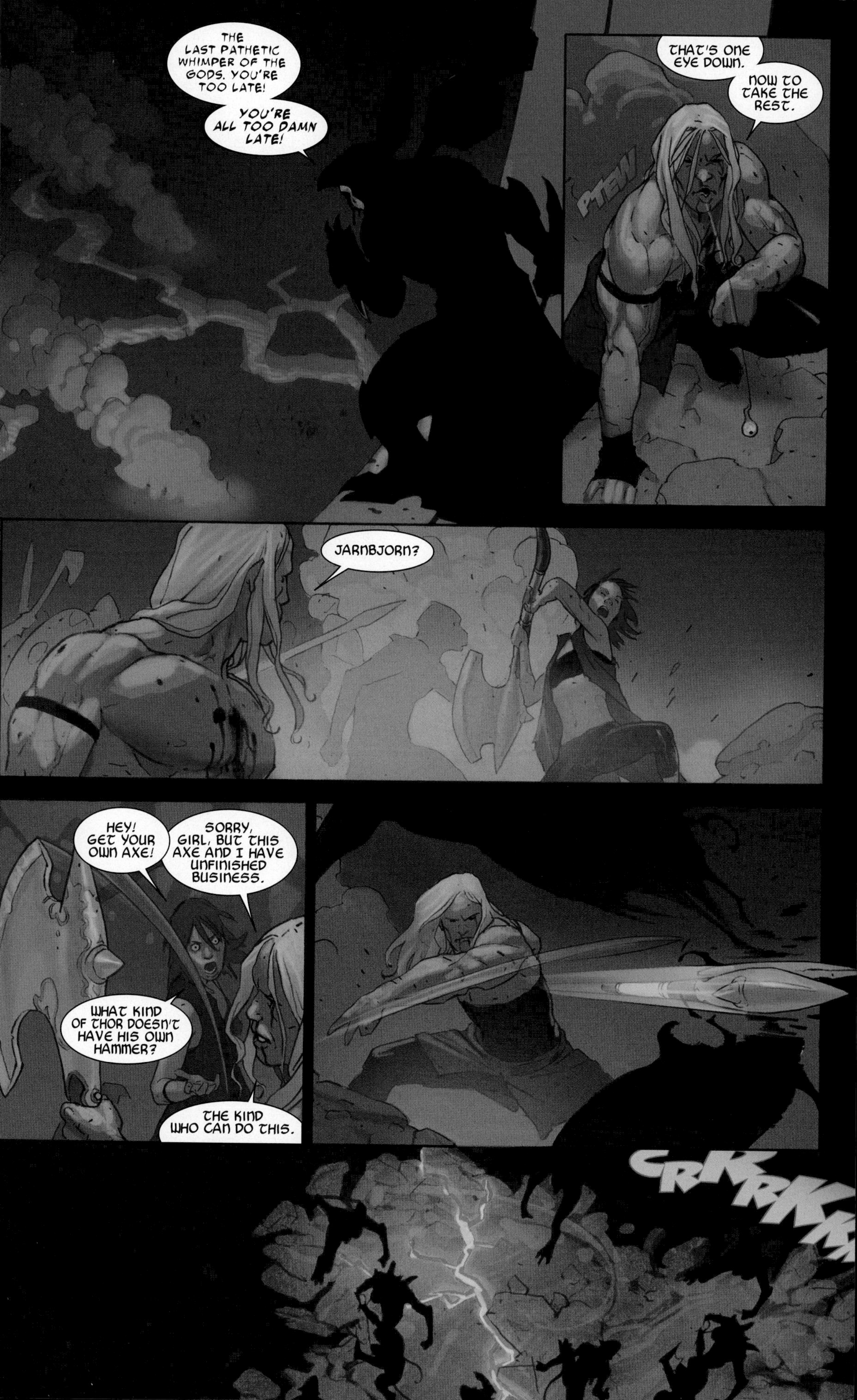
THE LAST PATHETIC WHIMPER OF THE GODS. YOU'RE TOO LATE!
YOU'RE ALL TOO DAMN LATE!
THAT'S ONE EYE DOWN.
PTEW
NOW TO TAKE THE REST.
JARNBJORN?
HEY! GET YOUR OWN AXE!
SORRY, GIRL, BUT THIS AXE AND I HAVE UNFINISHED BUSINESS.
WHAT KIND OF THOR DOESN'T HAVE HIS OWN HAMMER?
THE KIND WHO CAN DO THIS.
CRKRKKK

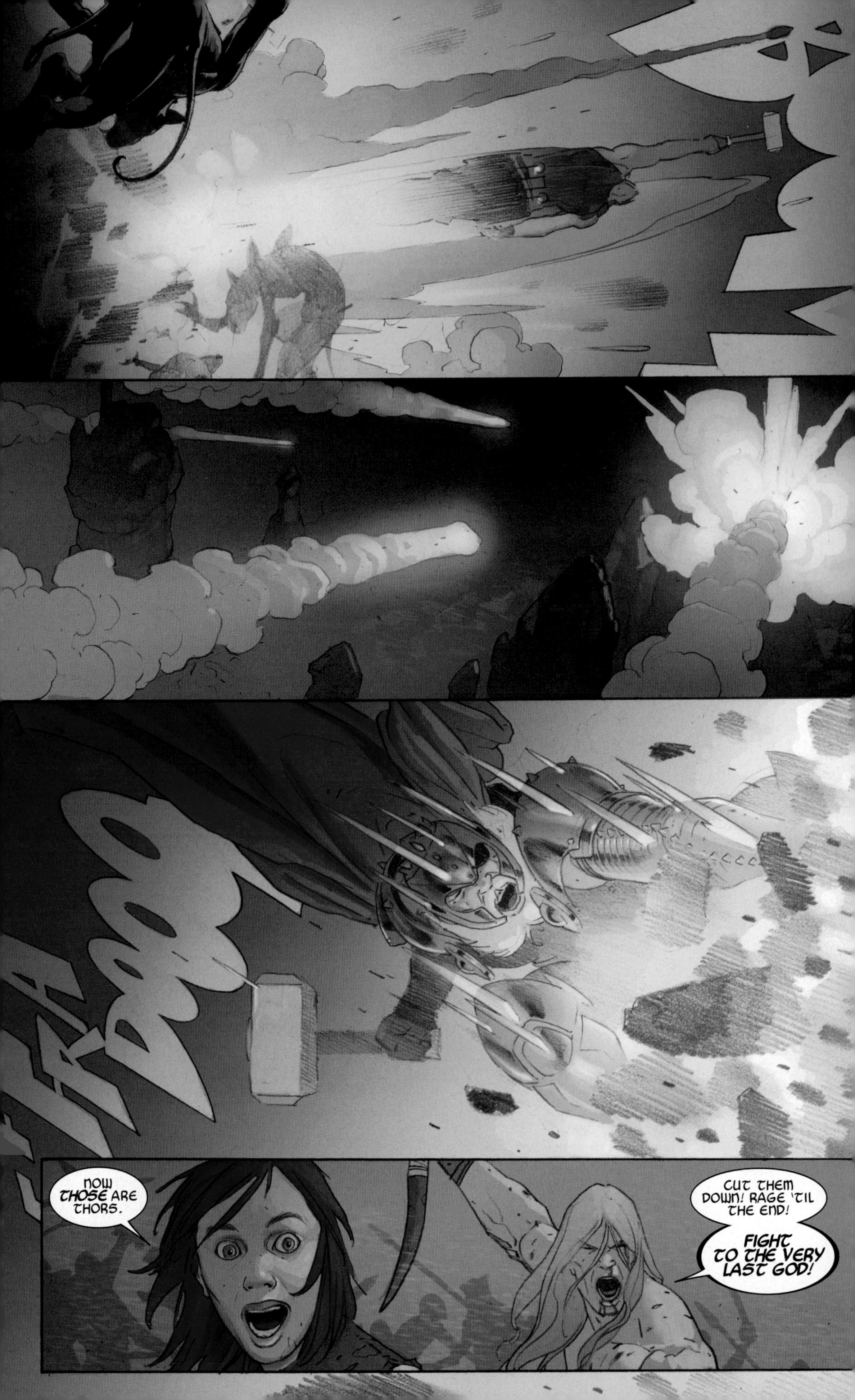

NOW *THOSE* ARE THORS.
CUT THEM DOWN! RAGE 'TIL THE END!
FIGHT TO THE VERY LAST GOD!

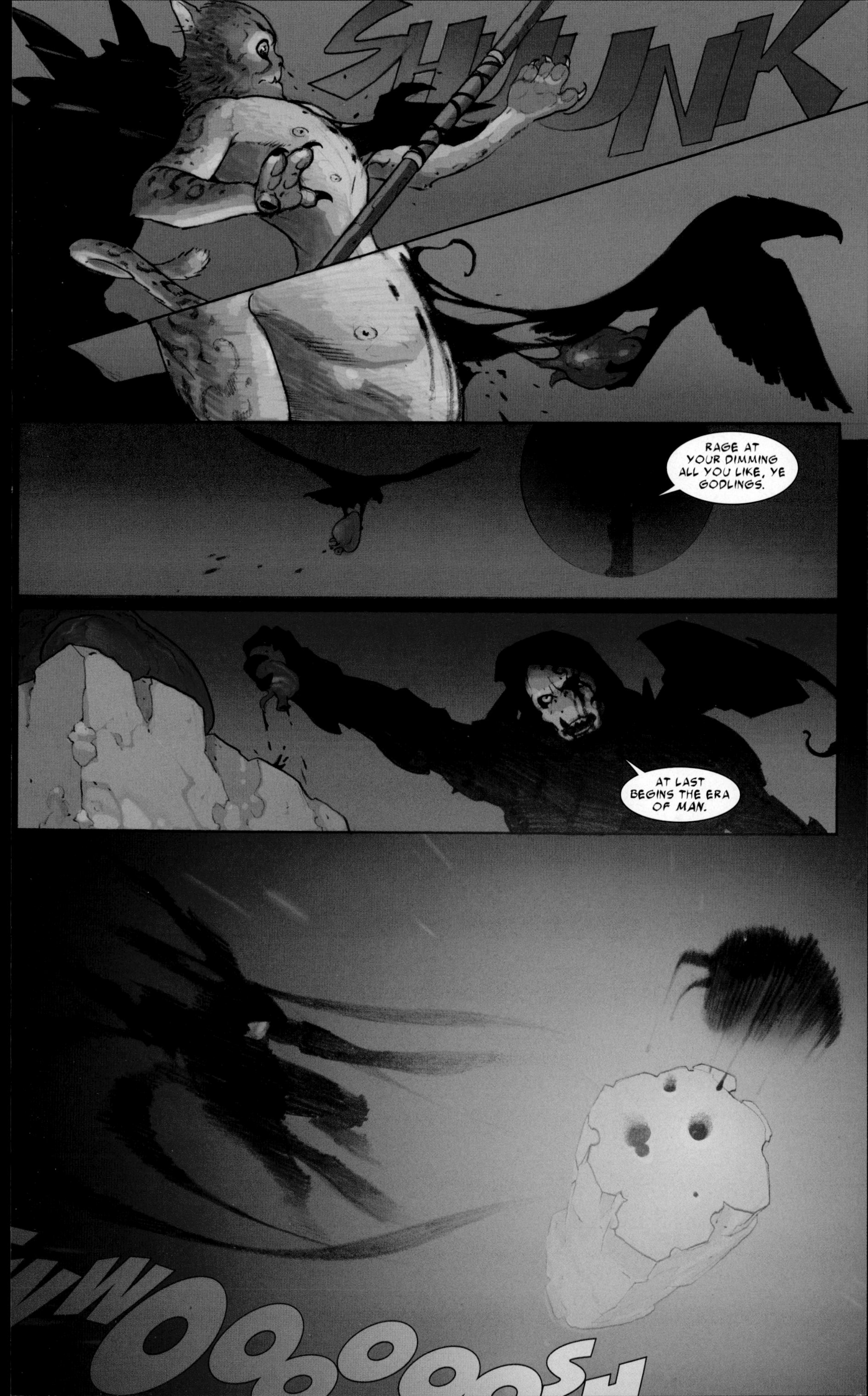
SHUNK
RAGE AT YOUR DIMMING ALL YOU LIKE, YE GODLINGS.
AT LAST BEGINS THE ERA OF MAN.
WOOOOOOSH

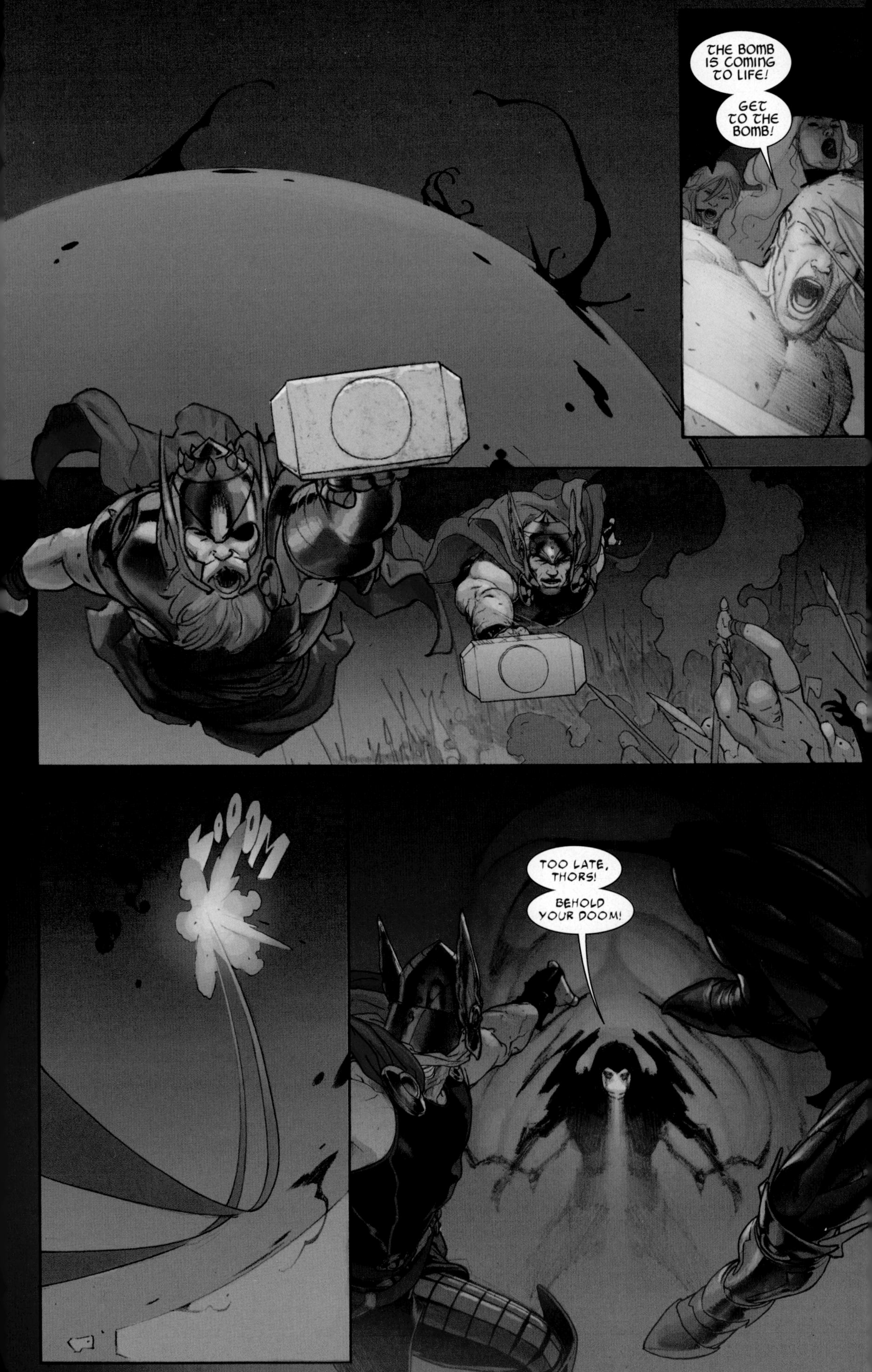
THE BOMB IS COMING TO LIFE!
GET TO THE BOMB!
KA-DOOM
TOO LATE, THORS!
BEHOLD YOUR DOOM!

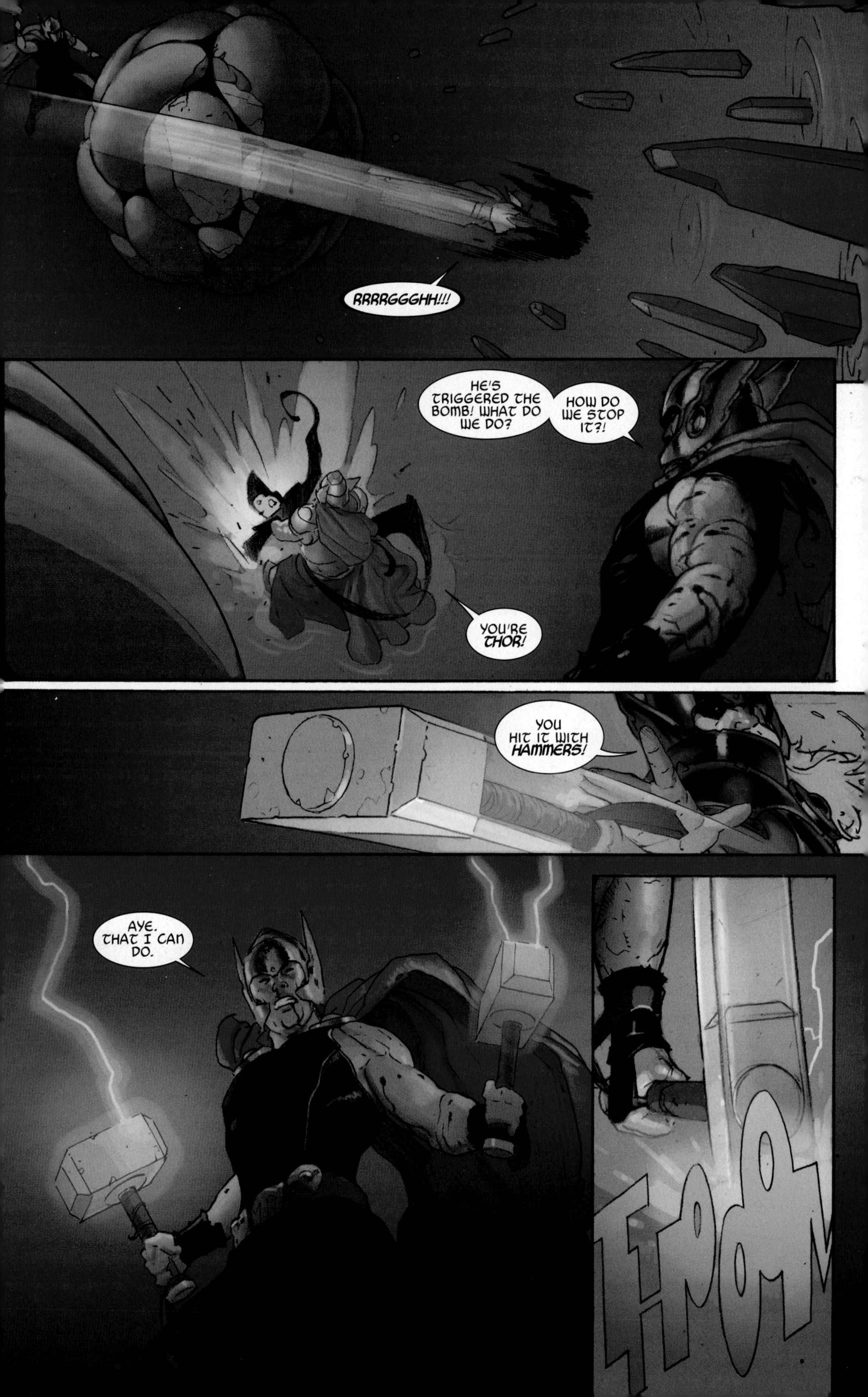

RRRRGGGHH!!!
HE'S TRIGGERED THE BOMB! WHAT DO WE DO?
HOW DO WE STOP IT?!
YOU'RE **THOR!**
YOU HIT IT WITH **HAMMERS!**
AYE. THAT I CAN DO.
TTOOM

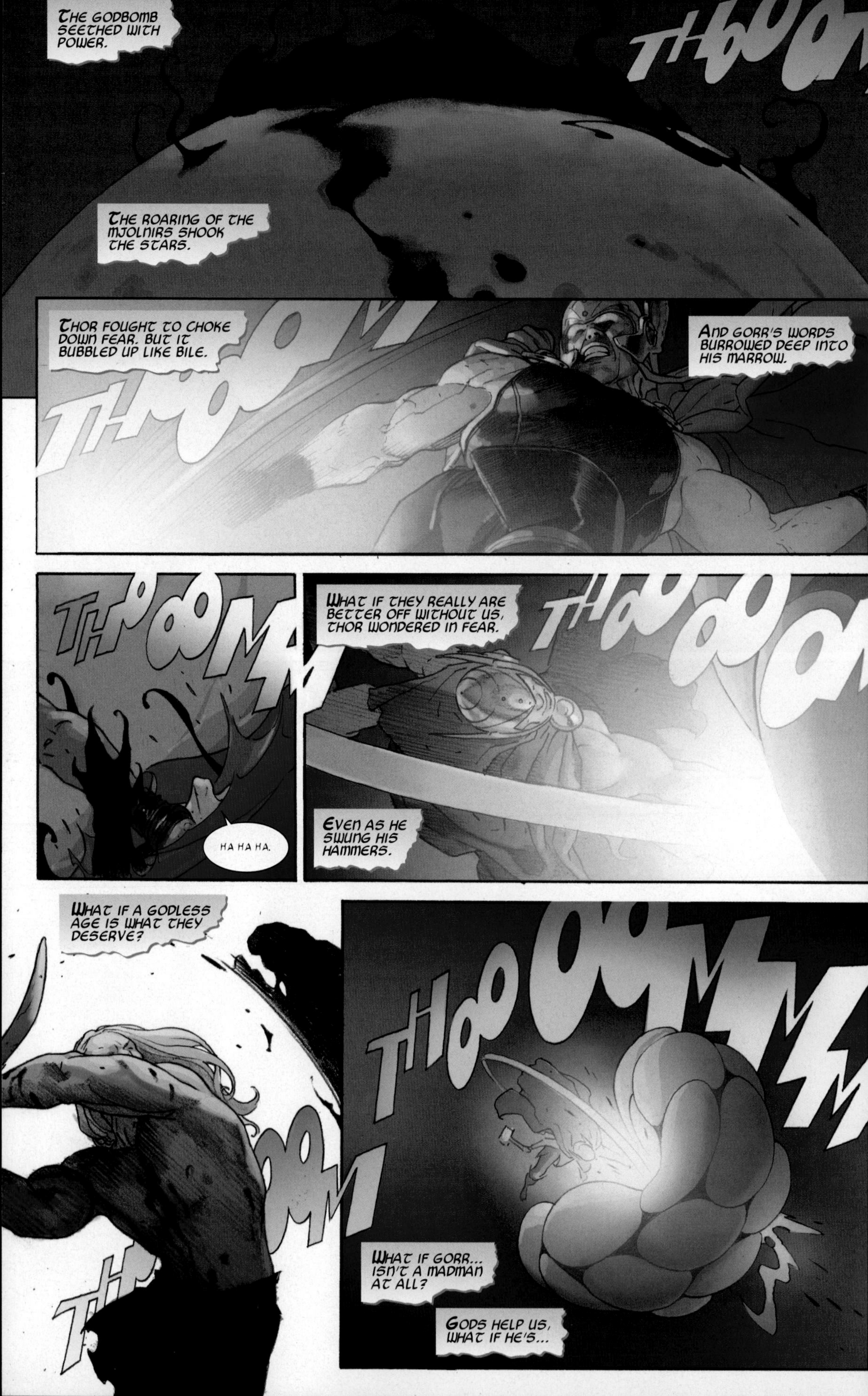
THE GODBOMB SEETHED WITH POWER.
THOOOM
THE ROARING OF THE MJOLNIRS SHOOK THE STARS.
THOR FOUGHT TO CHOKE DOWN FEAR. BUT IT BUBBLED UP LIKE BILE.
THOOOM
AND GORR'S WORDS BURROWED DEEP INTO HIS MARROW.
THOOOM
HA HA HA.
WHAT IF THEY REALLY ARE BETTER OFF WITHOUT US, THOR WONDERED IN FEAR.
THOOOOOM
EVEN AS HE SWUNG HIS HAMMERS.
WHAT IF A GODLESS AGE IS WHAT THEY DESERVE?
THOOOM
THOOOOMMM
WHAT IF GORR... ISN'T A MADMAN AT ALL?
GODS HELP US, WHAT IF HE'S...

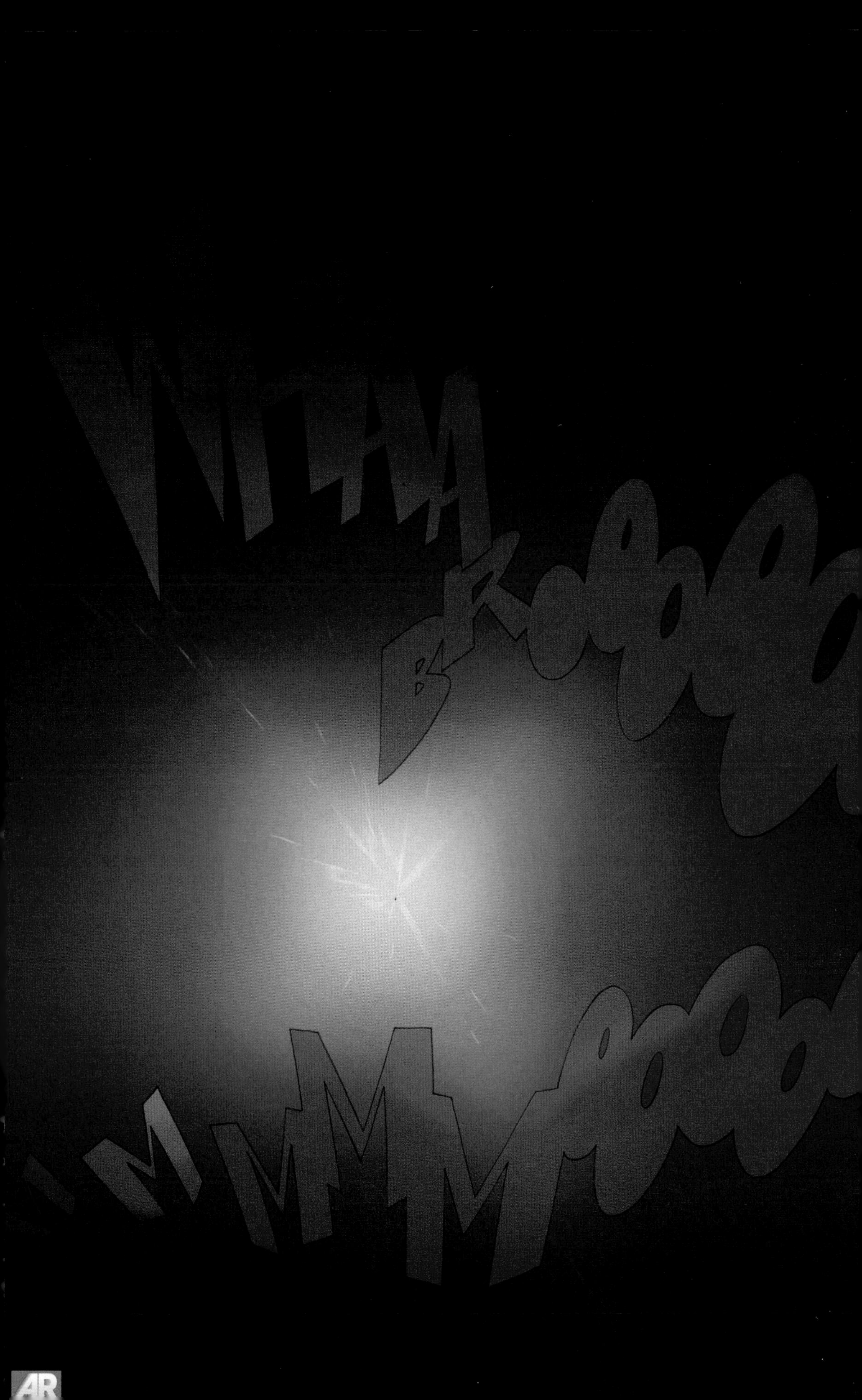

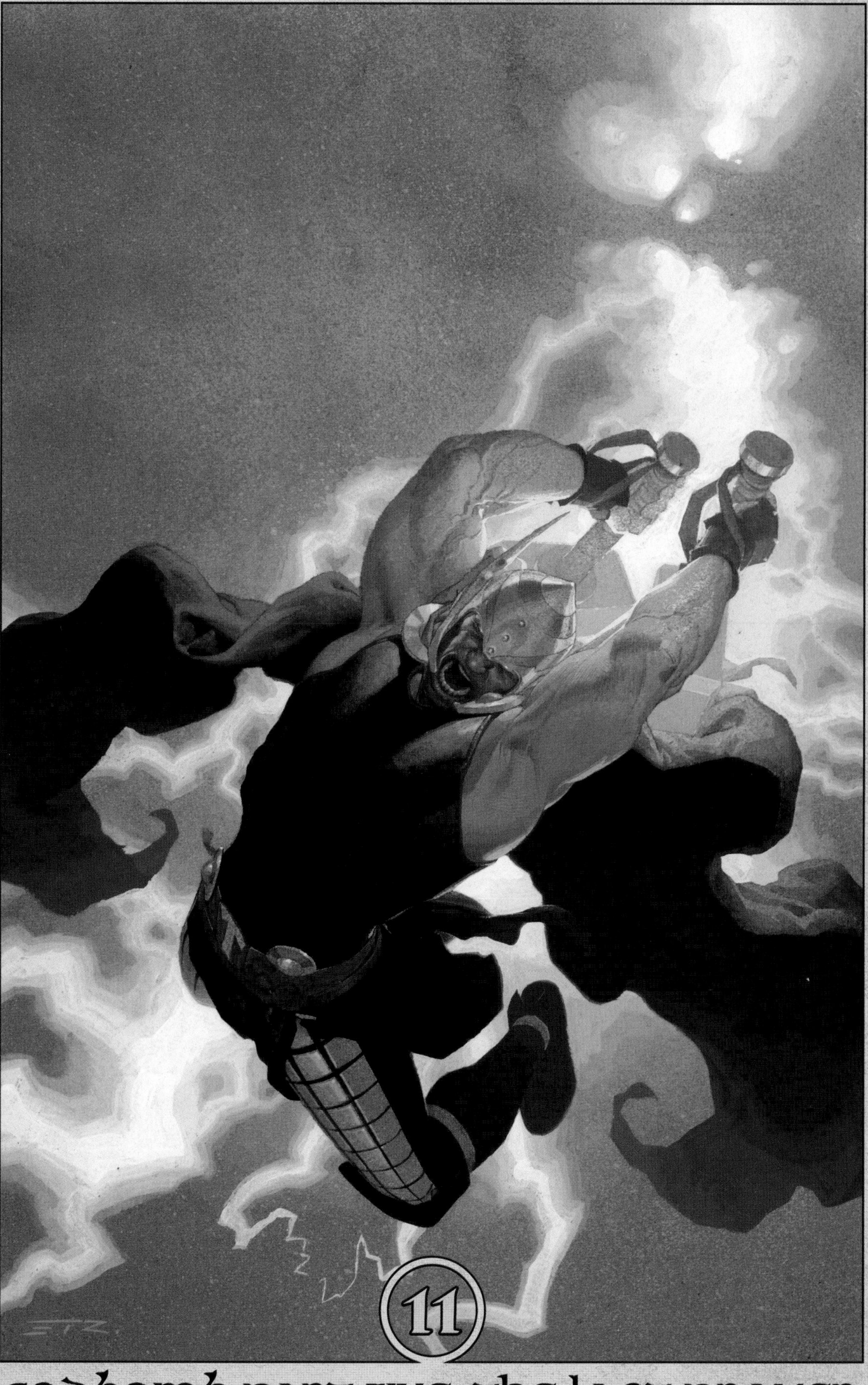
11

GODBOMB PART FIVE: THE LAST PRAYER

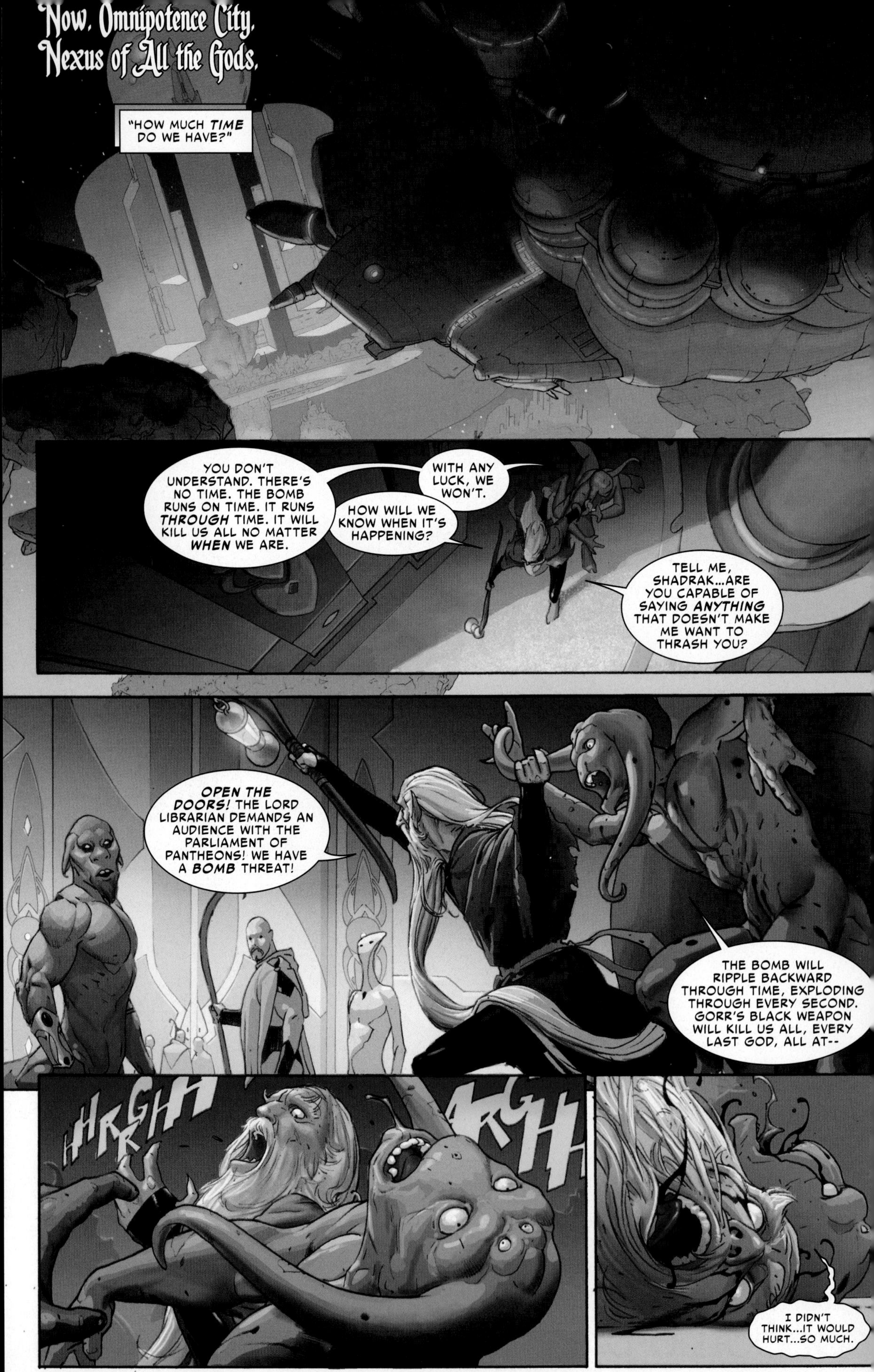
Now, Omnipotence City, Nexus of All the Gods.
"HOW MUCH TIME DO WE HAVE?"
YOU DON'T UNDERSTAND. THERE'S NO TIME. THE BOMB RUNS ON TIME. IT RUNS THROUGH TIME. IT WILL KILL US ALL NO MATTER WHEN WE ARE.
WITH ANY LUCK, WE WON'T.
HOW WILL WE KNOW WHEN IT'S HAPPENING?
TELL ME, SHADRAK...ARE YOU CAPABLE OF SAYING ANYTHING THAT DOESN'T MAKE ME WANT TO THRASH YOU?
OPEN THE DOORS! THE LORD LIBRARIAN DEMANDS AN AUDIENCE WITH THE PARLIAMENT OF PANTHEONS! WE HAVE A BOMB THREAT!
THE BOMB WILL RIPPLE BACKWARD THROUGH TIME, EXPLODING THROUGH EVERY SECOND. GORR'S BLACK WEAPON WILL KILL US ALL, EVERY LAST GOD, ALL AT--
HRRGHH
ARGHH
I DIDN'T THINK...IT WOULD HURT...SO MUCH.

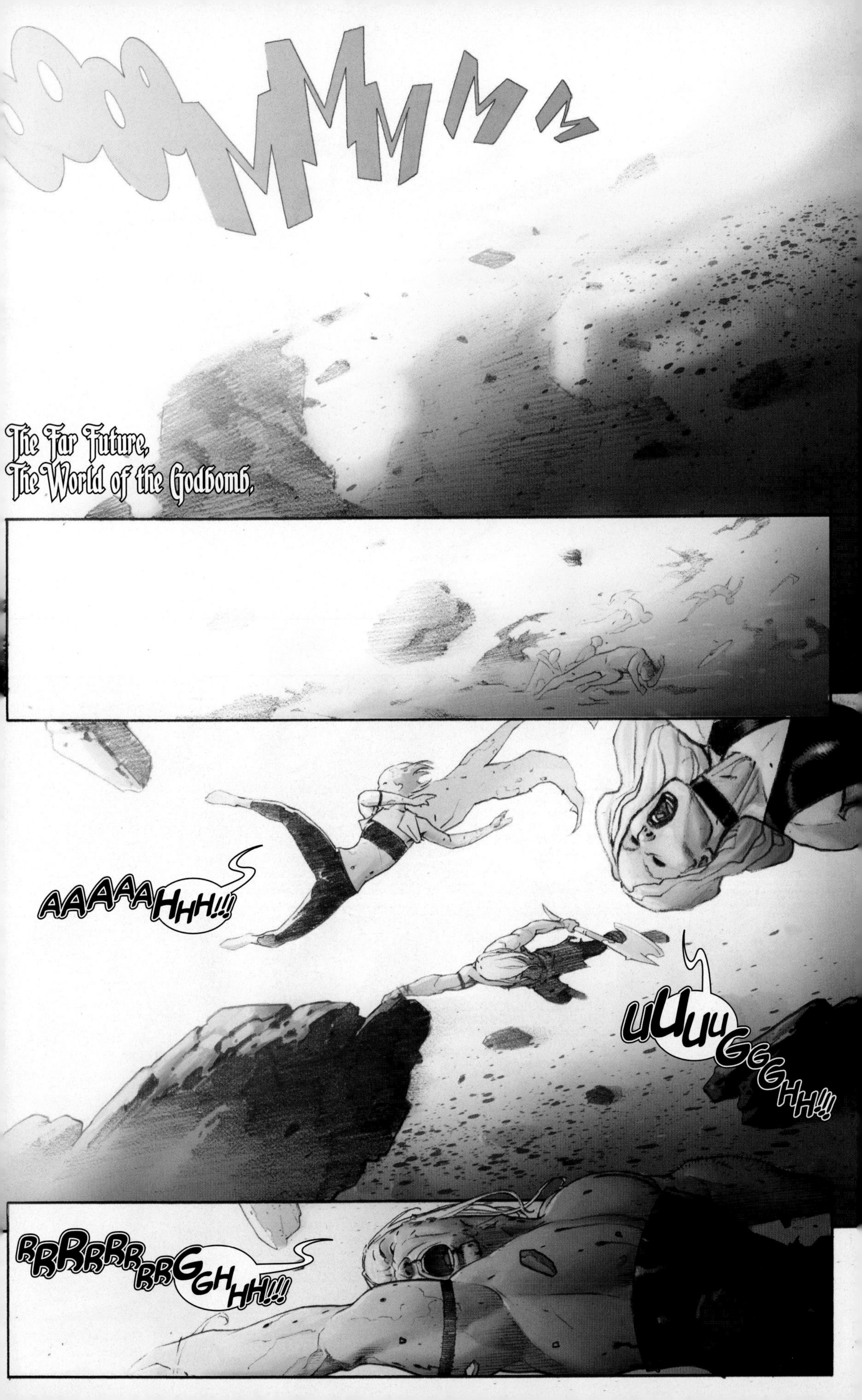

BOOOOOMMMMMM
The Far Future,
The World of the Godbomb.
AAAAAAHHH!!!
UUUUGGGHH!!!
RRRRRRRRRGGHHH!!!

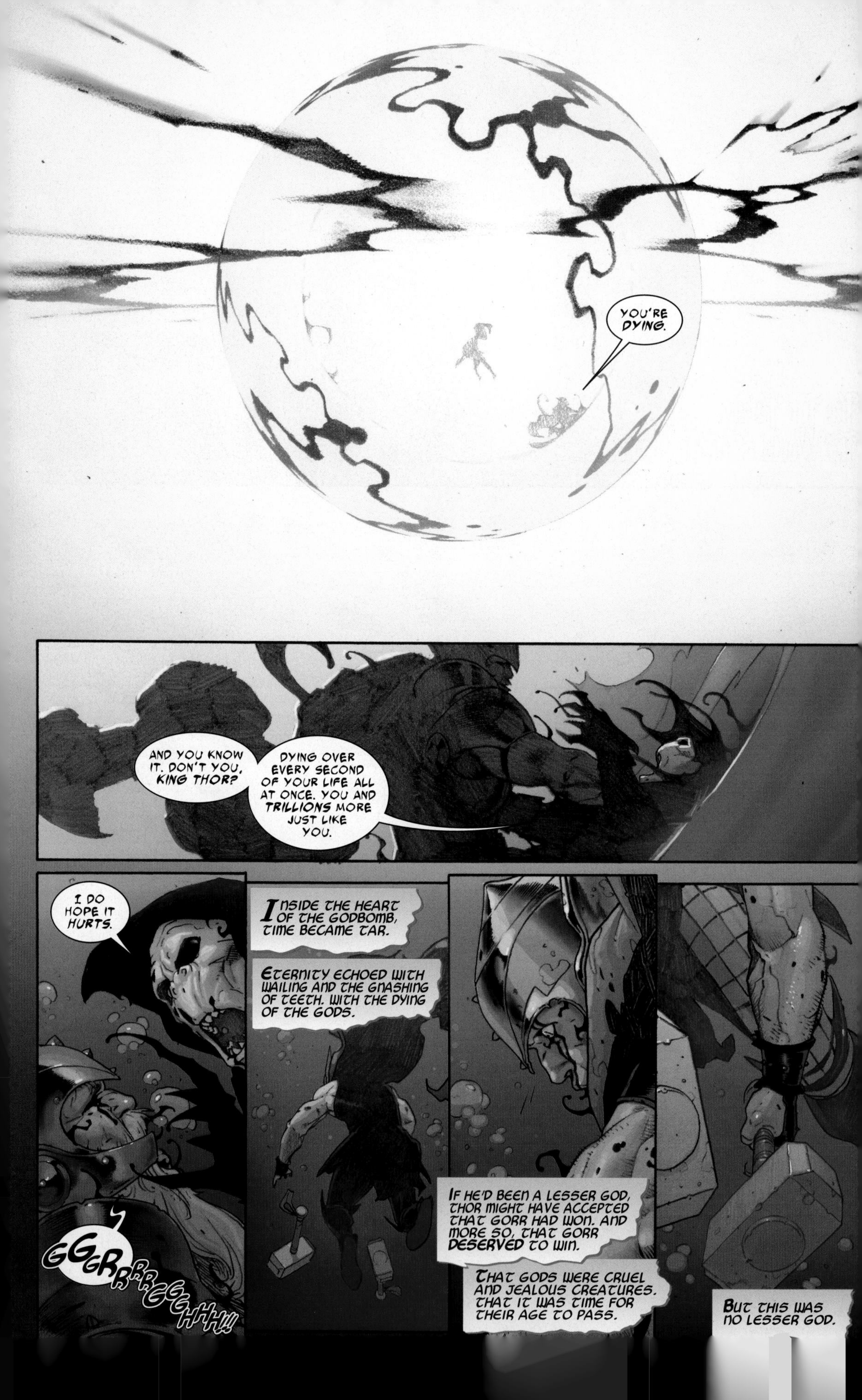

YOU'RE DYING.
AND YOU KNOW IT. DON'T YOU, KING THOR?
DYING OVER EVERY SECOND OF YOUR LIFE ALL AT ONCE. YOU AND TRILLIONS MORE JUST LIKE YOU.
I DO HOPE IT HURTS.
GGGRRRRRGGGHHH!!
INSIDE THE HEART OF THE GODBOMB, TIME BECAME TAR.
ETERNITY ECHOED WITH WAILING AND THE GNASHING OF TEETH. WITH THE DYING OF THE GODS.
IF HE'D BEEN A LESSER GOD, THOR MIGHT HAVE ACCEPTED THAT GORR HAD WON. AND MORE SO, THAT GORR DESERVED TO WIN.
THAT GODS WERE CRUEL AND JEALOUS CREATURES. THAT IT WAS TIME FOR THEIR AGE TO PASS.
BUT THIS WAS NO LESSER GOD.

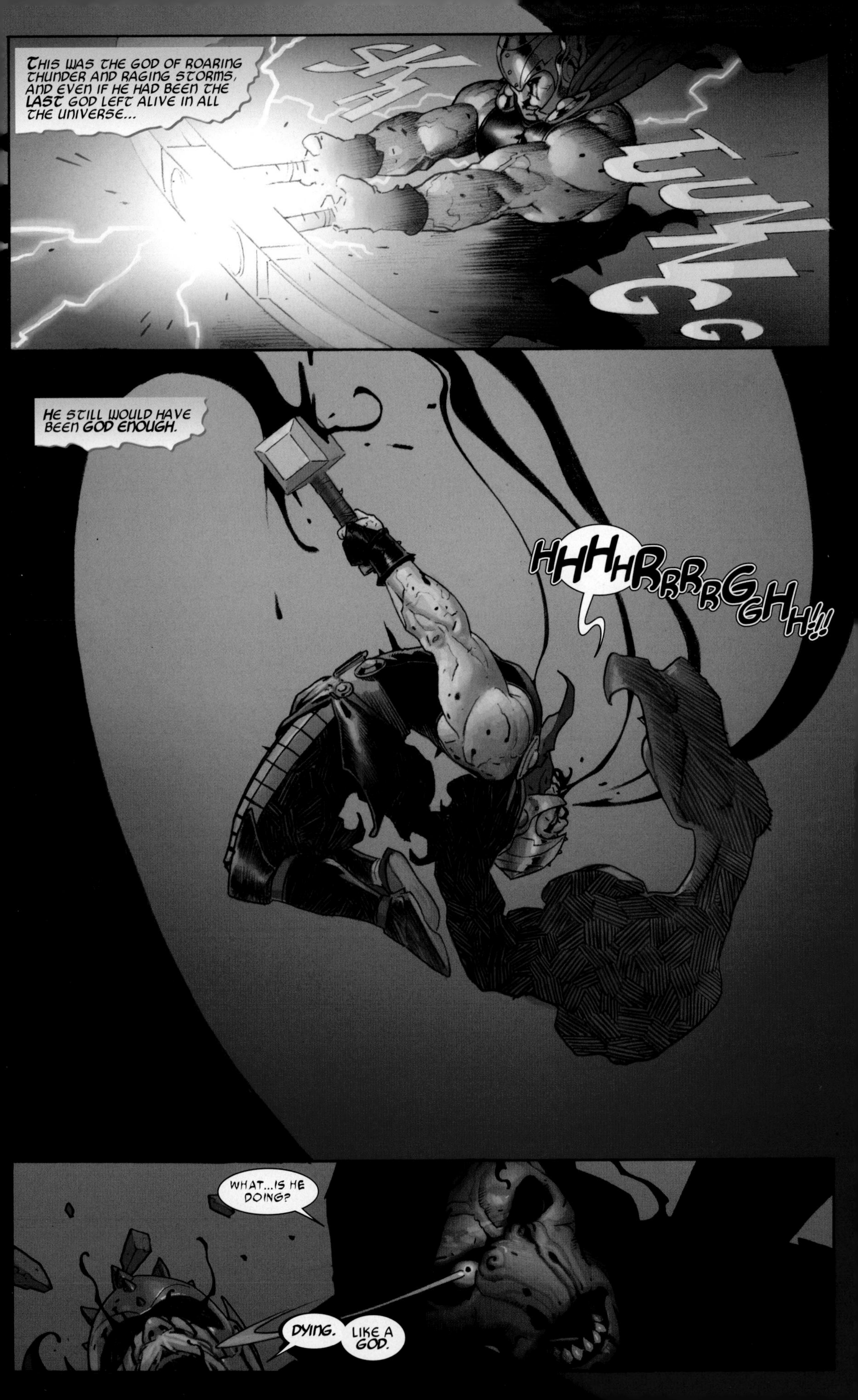
THIS WAS THE GOD OF ROARING THUNDER AND RAGING STORMS, AND EVEN IF HE HAD BEEN THE LAST GOD LEFT ALIVE IN ALL THE UNIVERSE...
SKA
TUNNG
HE STILL WOULD HAVE BEEN GOD ENOUGH.
HHHHRRRRGHH!!!
WHAT...IS HE DOING?
DYING.
LIKE A GOD.

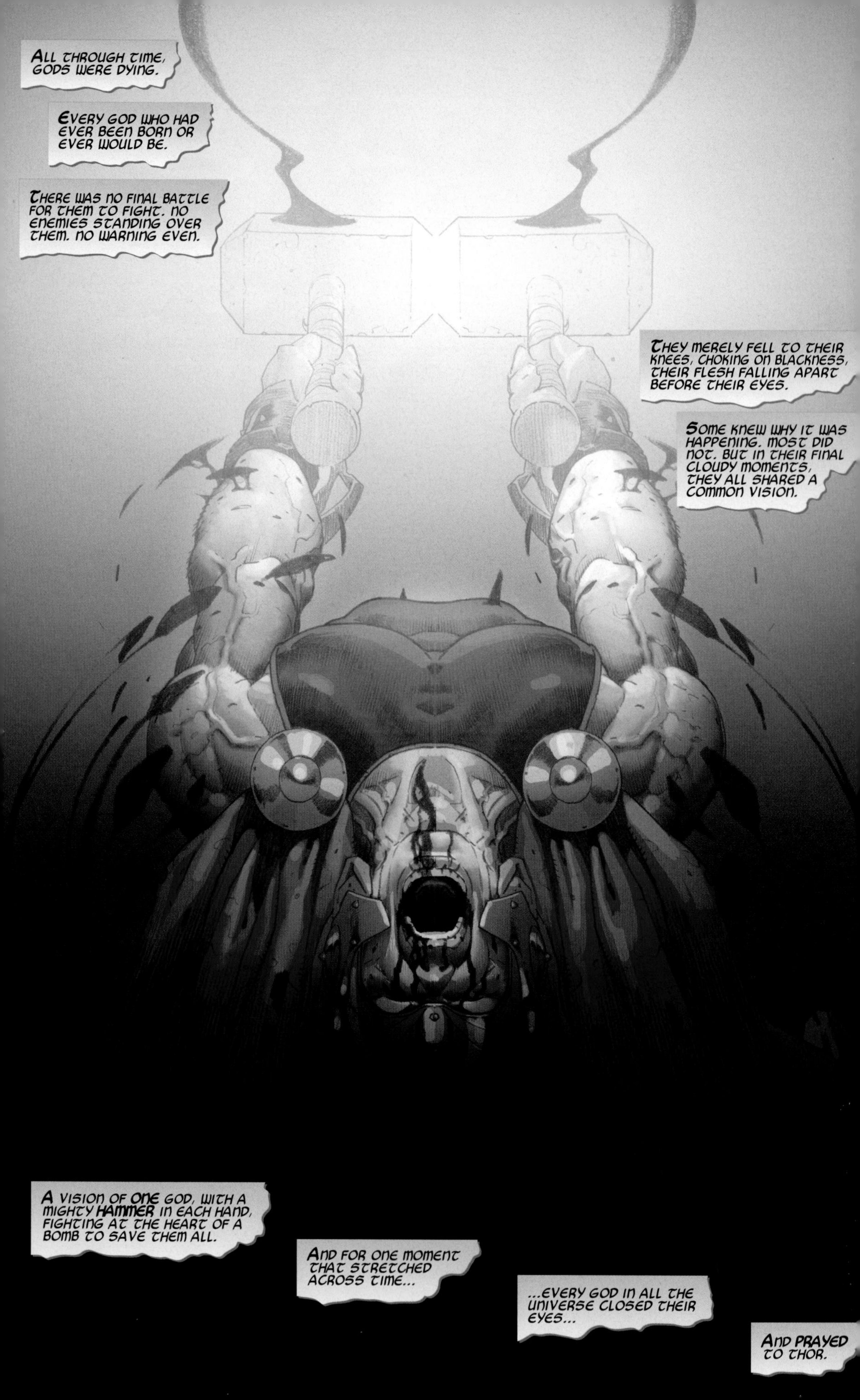

ALL THROUGH TIME, GODS WERE DYING.
EVERY GOD WHO HAD EVER BEEN BORN OR EVER WOULD BE.
THERE WAS NO FINAL BATTLE FOR THEM TO FIGHT. NO ENEMIES STANDING OVER THEM. NO WARNING EVEN.
THEY MERELY FELL TO THEIR KNEES, CHOKING ON BLACKNESS, THEIR FLESH FALLING APART BEFORE THEIR EYES.
SOME KNEW WHY IT WAS HAPPENING. MOST DID NOT. BUT IN THEIR FINAL CLOUDY MOMENTS, THEY ALL SHARED A COMMON VISION.
A VISION OF ONE GOD, WITH A MIGHTY HAMMER IN EACH HAND, FIGHTING AT THE HEART OF A BOMB TO SAVE THEM ALL.
AND FOR ONE MOMENT THAT STRETCHED ACROSS TIME...
...EVERY GOD IN ALL THE UNIVERSE CLOSED THEIR EYES...
AND PRAYED TO THOR.

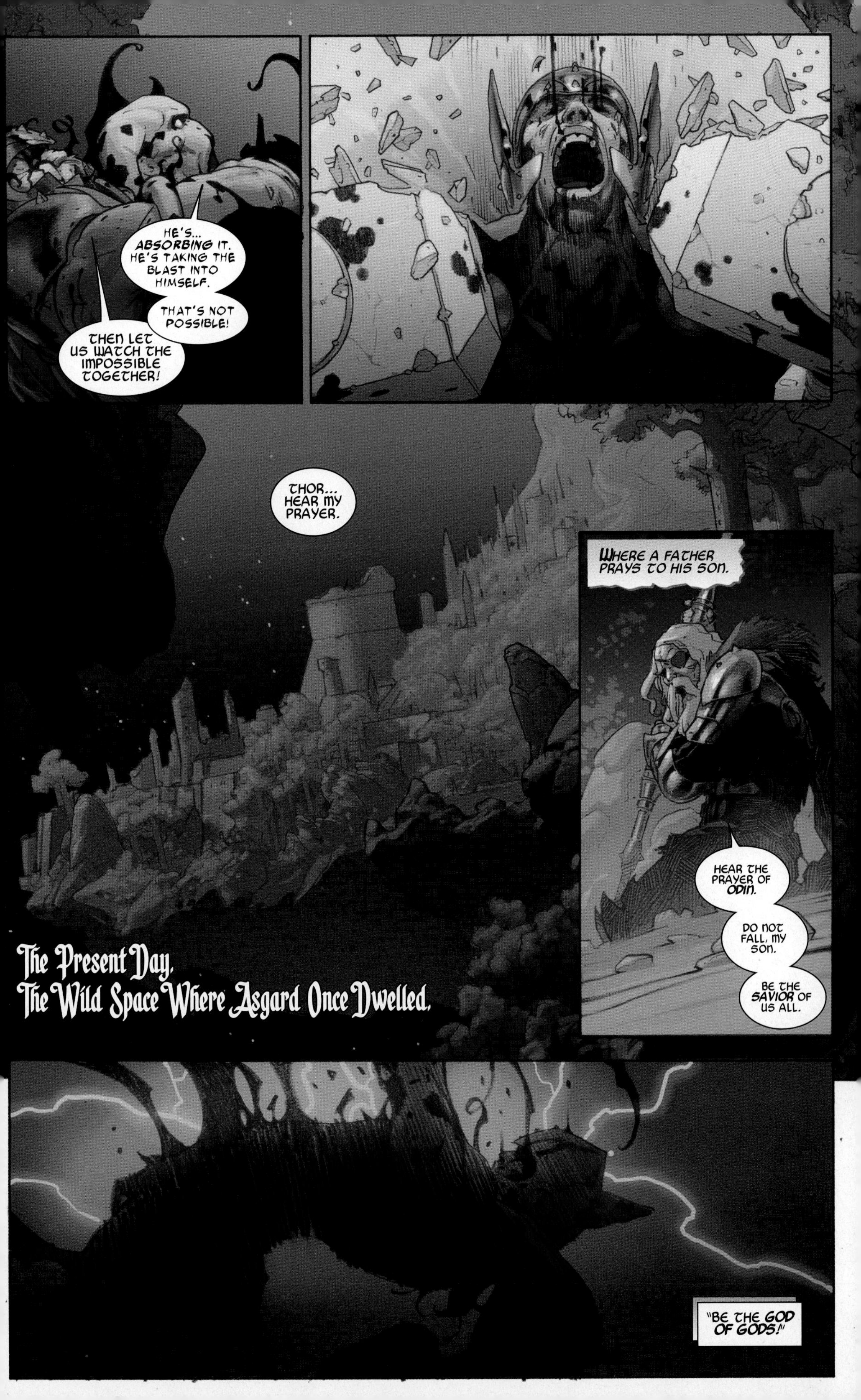
HE'S... ABSORBING IT. HE'S TAKING THE BLAST INTO HIMSELF.
THAT'S NOT POSSIBLE!
THEN LET US WATCH THE IMPOSSIBLE TOGETHER!
THOR... HEAR MY PRAYER.
The Present Day.
The Wild Space Where Asgard Once Dwelled.
WHERE A FATHER PRAYS TO HIS SON.
HEAR THE PRAYER OF ODIN.
DO NOT FALL, MY SON.
BE THE SAVIOR OF US ALL.
"BE THE GOD OF GODS!"

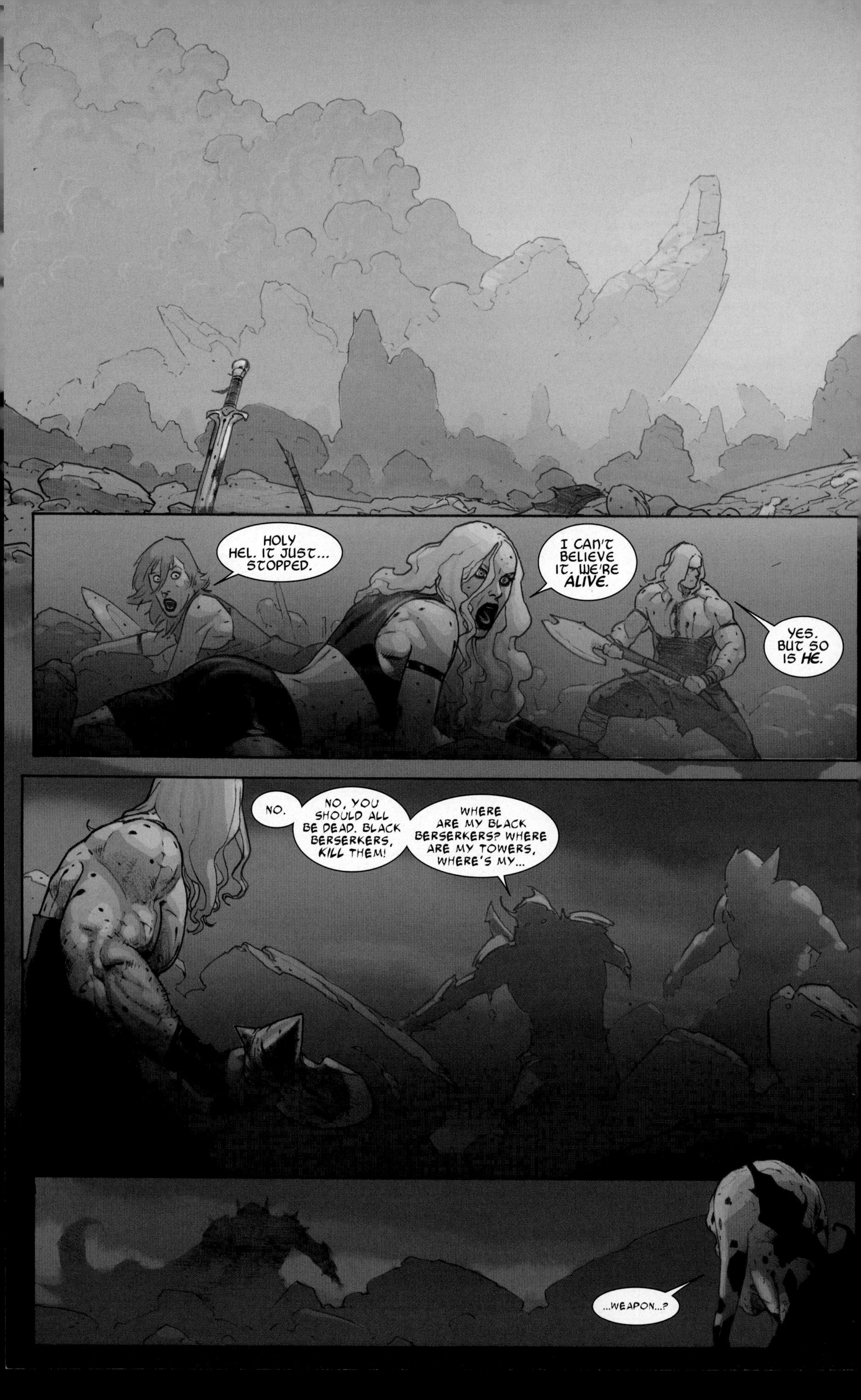
HOLY HEL. IT JUST... STOPPED.
I CAN'T BELIEVE IT. WE'RE ALIVE.
YES. BUT SO IS HE.
NO.
NO, YOU SHOULD ALL BE DEAD. BLACK BERSERKERS, KILL THEM!
WHERE ARE MY BLACK BERSERKERS? WHERE ARE MY TOWERS, WHERE'S MY...
...WEAPON...?

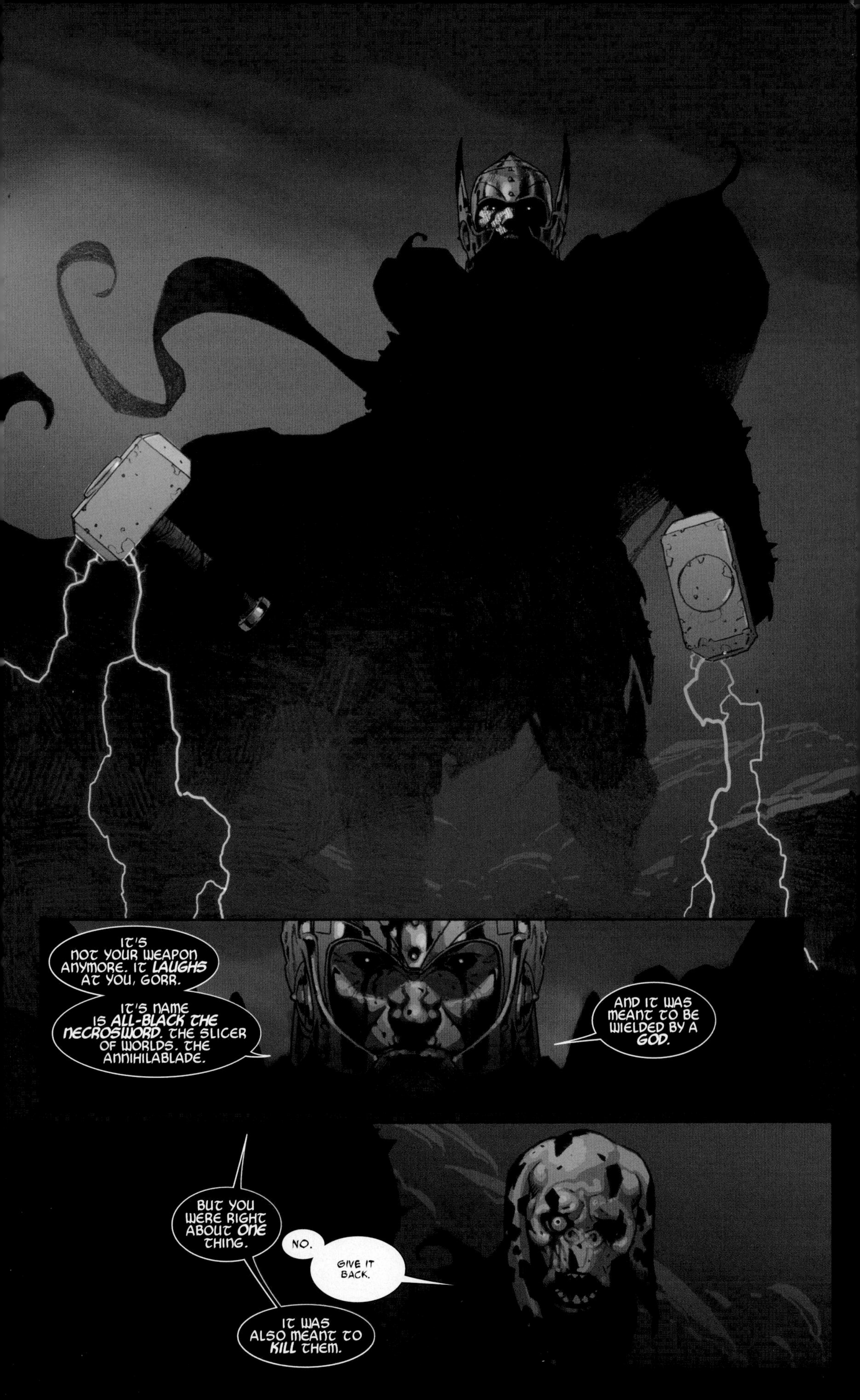
IT'S NOT YOUR WEAPON ANYMORE. IT LAUGHS AT YOU, GORR.
IT'S NAME IS ALL-BLACK THE NECROSWORD. THE SLICER OF WORLDS. THE ANNIHILABLADE.
AND IT WAS MEANT TO BE WIELDED BY A GOD.
BUT YOU WERE RIGHT ABOUT ONE THING.
NO.
GIVE IT BACK.
IT WAS ALSO MEANT TO KILL THEM.

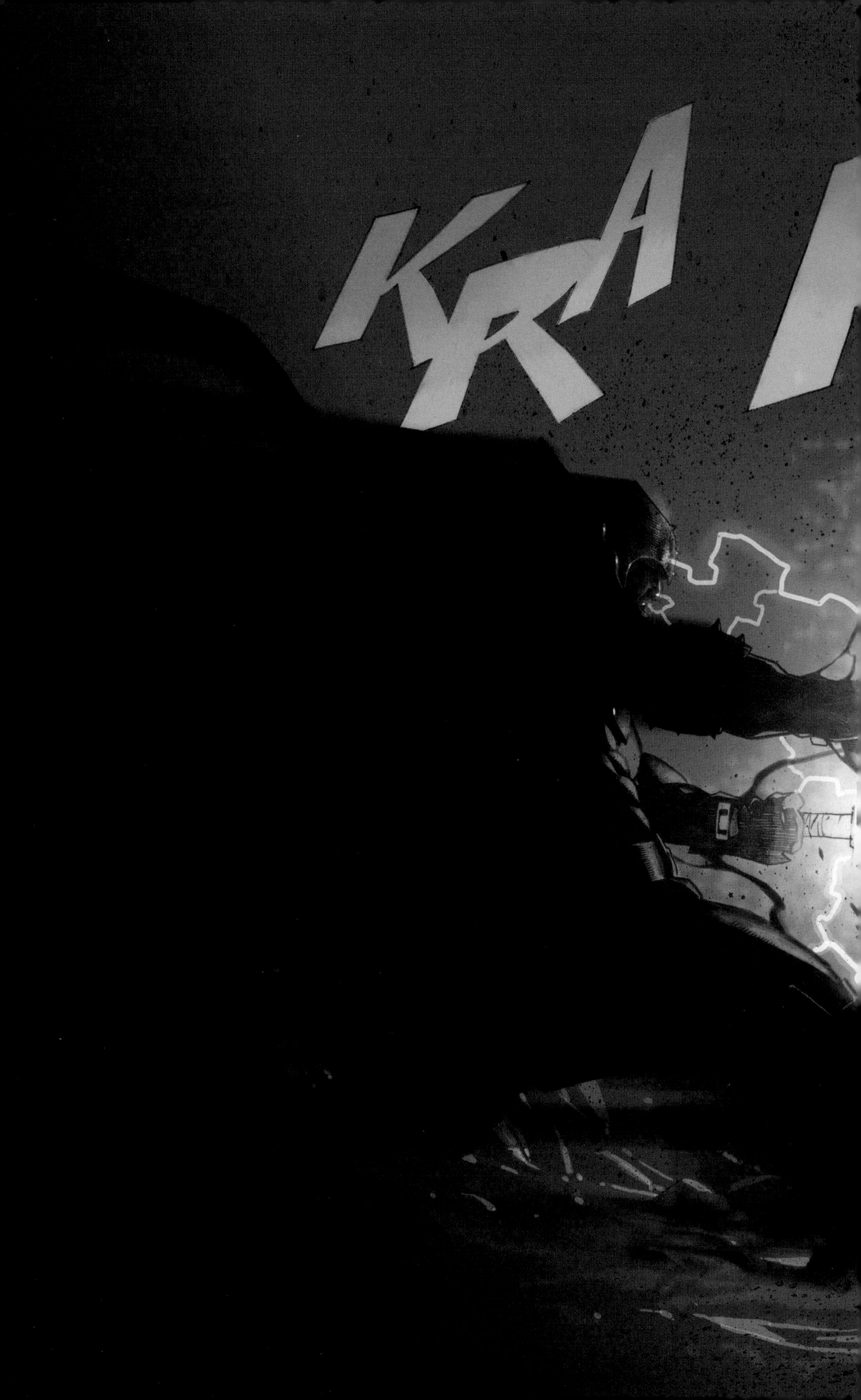
KRA

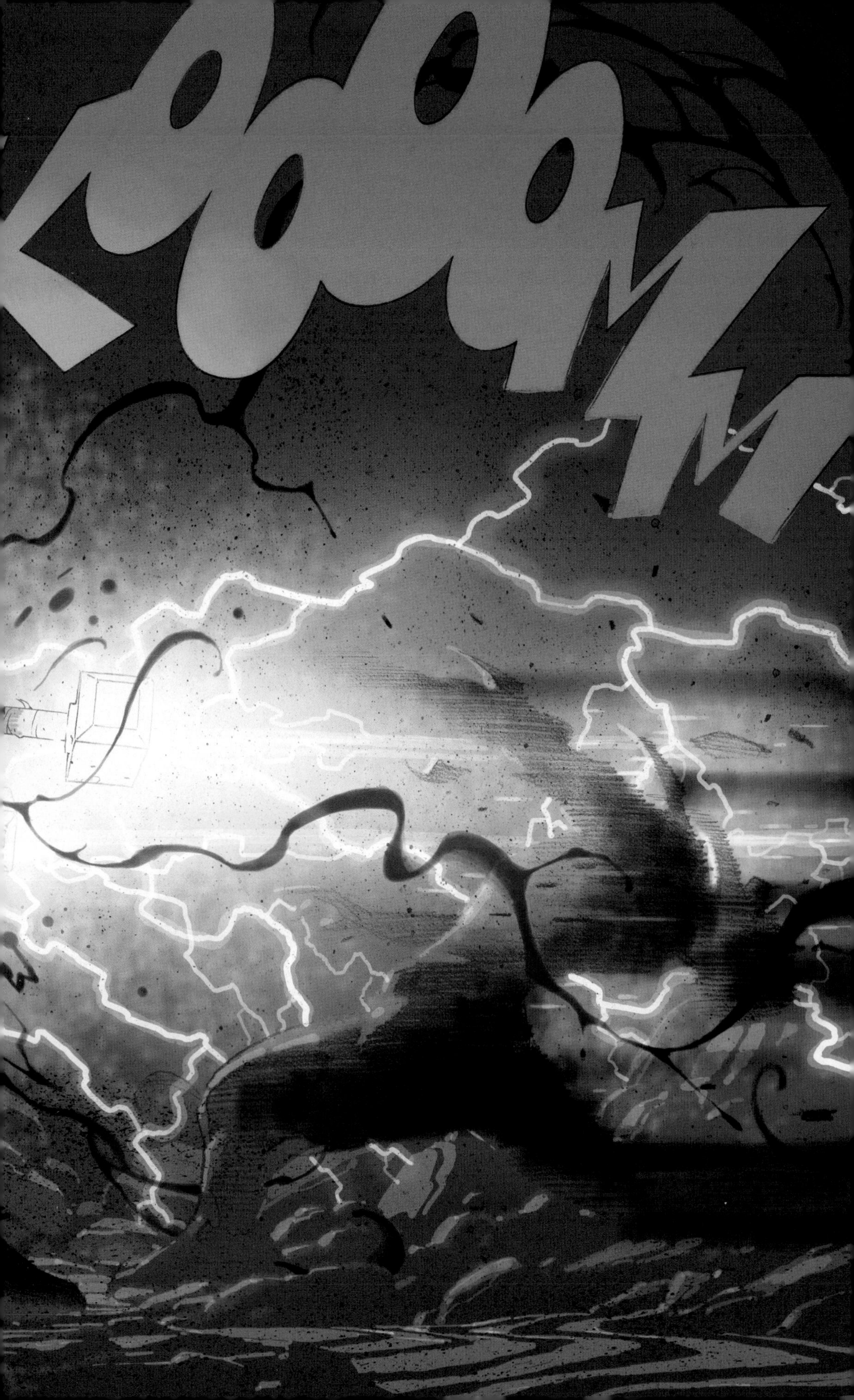

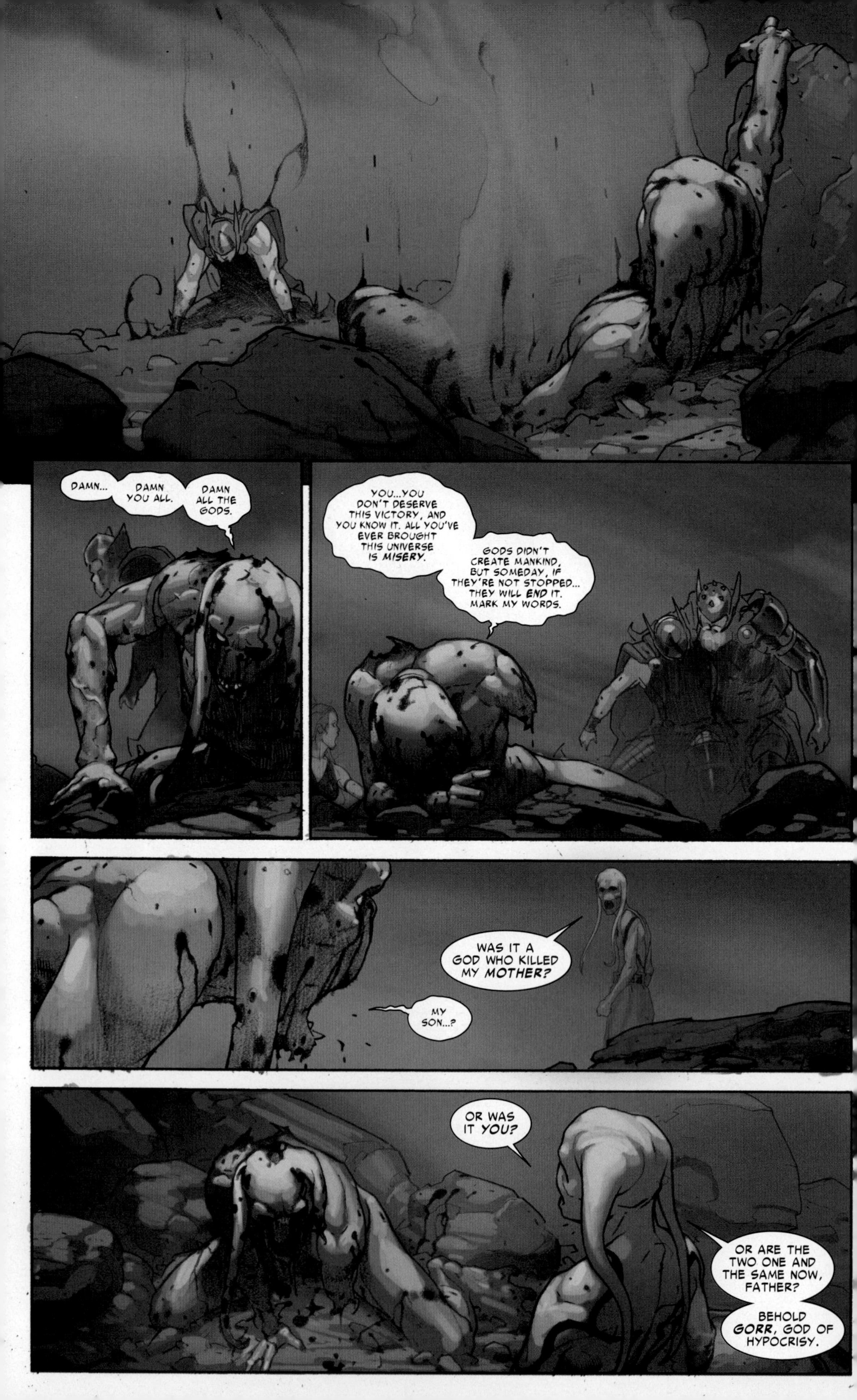
DAMN...
DAMN YOU ALL.
DAMN ALL THE GODS.
YOU...YOU DON'T DESERVE THIS VICTORY, AND YOU KNOW IT. ALL YOU'VE EVER BROUGHT THIS UNIVERSE IS MISERY.
GODS DIDN'T CREATE MANKIND, BUT SOMEDAY, IF THEY'RE NOT STOPPED... THEY WILL END IT. MARK MY WORDS.
WAS IT A GOD WHO KILLED MY MOTHER?
MY SON...?
OR WAS IT YOU?
OR ARE THE TWO ONE AND THE SAME NOW, FATHER?
BEHOLD GORR, GOD OF HYPOCRISY.

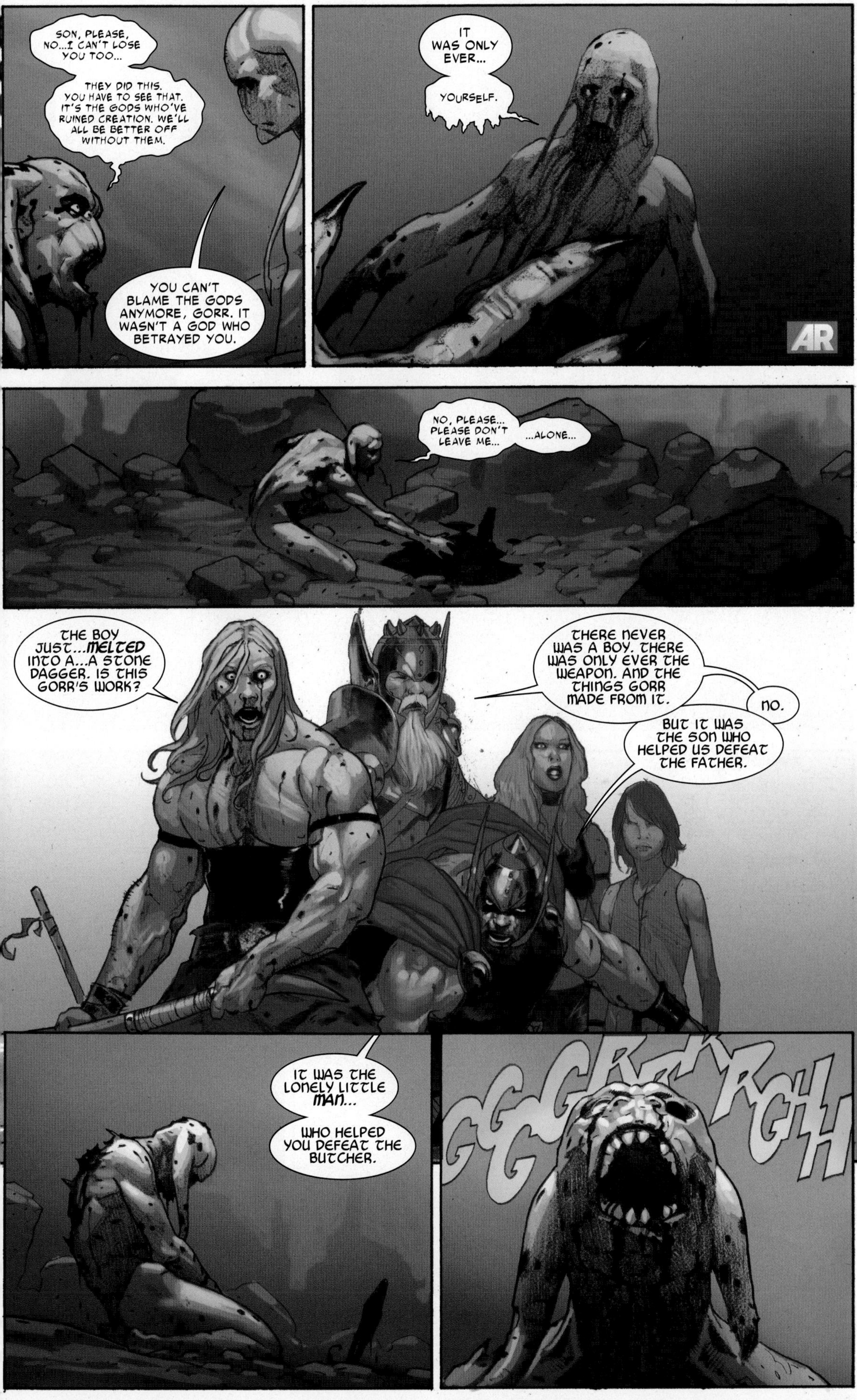
SON, PLEASE, NO...I CAN'T LOSE YOU TOO...
THEY DID THIS. YOU HAVE TO SEE THAT. IT'S THE GODS WHO'VE RUINED CREATION. WE'LL ALL BE BETTER OFF WITHOUT THEM.
YOU CAN'T BLAME THE GODS ANYMORE, GORR. IT WASN'T A GOD WHO BETRAYED YOU.
IT WAS ONLY EVER...
YOURSELF.
NO, PLEASE... PLEASE DON'T LEAVE ME...
...ALONE...
THE BOY JUST...MELTED INTO A...A STONE DAGGER. IS THIS GORR'S WORK?
THERE NEVER WAS A BOY. THERE WAS ONLY EVER THE WEAPON. AND THE THINGS GORR MADE FROM IT.
NO.
BUT IT WAS THE SON WHO HELPED US DEFEAT THE FATHER.
IT WAS THE LONELY LITTLE MAN...
WHO HELPED YOU DEFEAT THE BUTCHER.

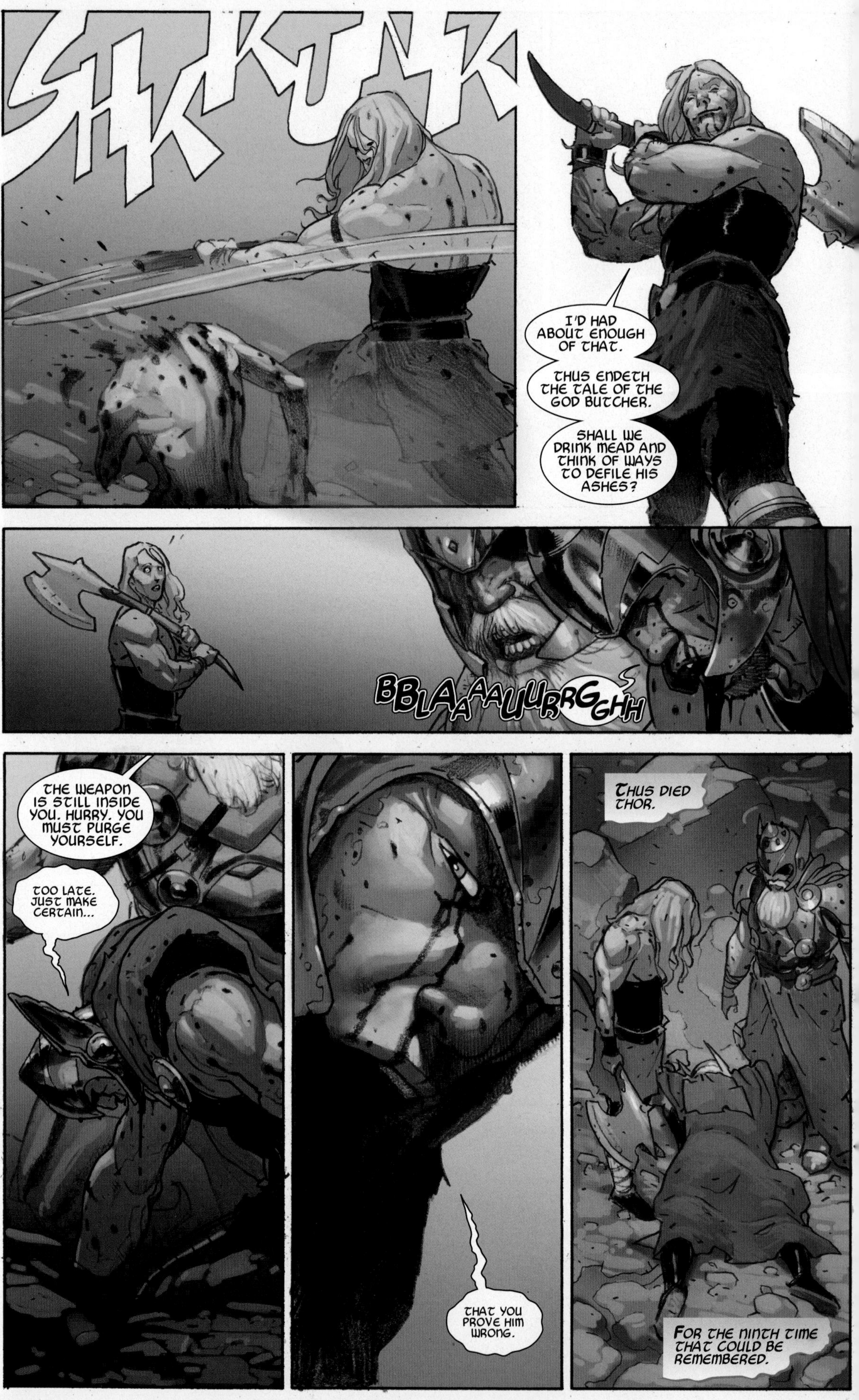
SHKKTUNK
I'D HAD ABOUT ENOUGH OF THAT.
THUS ENDETH THE TALE OF THE GOD BUTCHER.
SHALL WE DRINK MEAD AND THINK OF WAYS TO DEFILE HIS ASHES?
BBLAAAAAUURRGGHH
THE WEAPON IS STILL INSIDE YOU. HURRY. YOU MUST PURGE YOURSELF.
TOO LATE. JUST MAKE CERTAIN...
THAT YOU PROVE HIM WRONG.
THUS DIED THOR.
FOR THE NINTH TIME THAT COULD BE REMEMBERED.

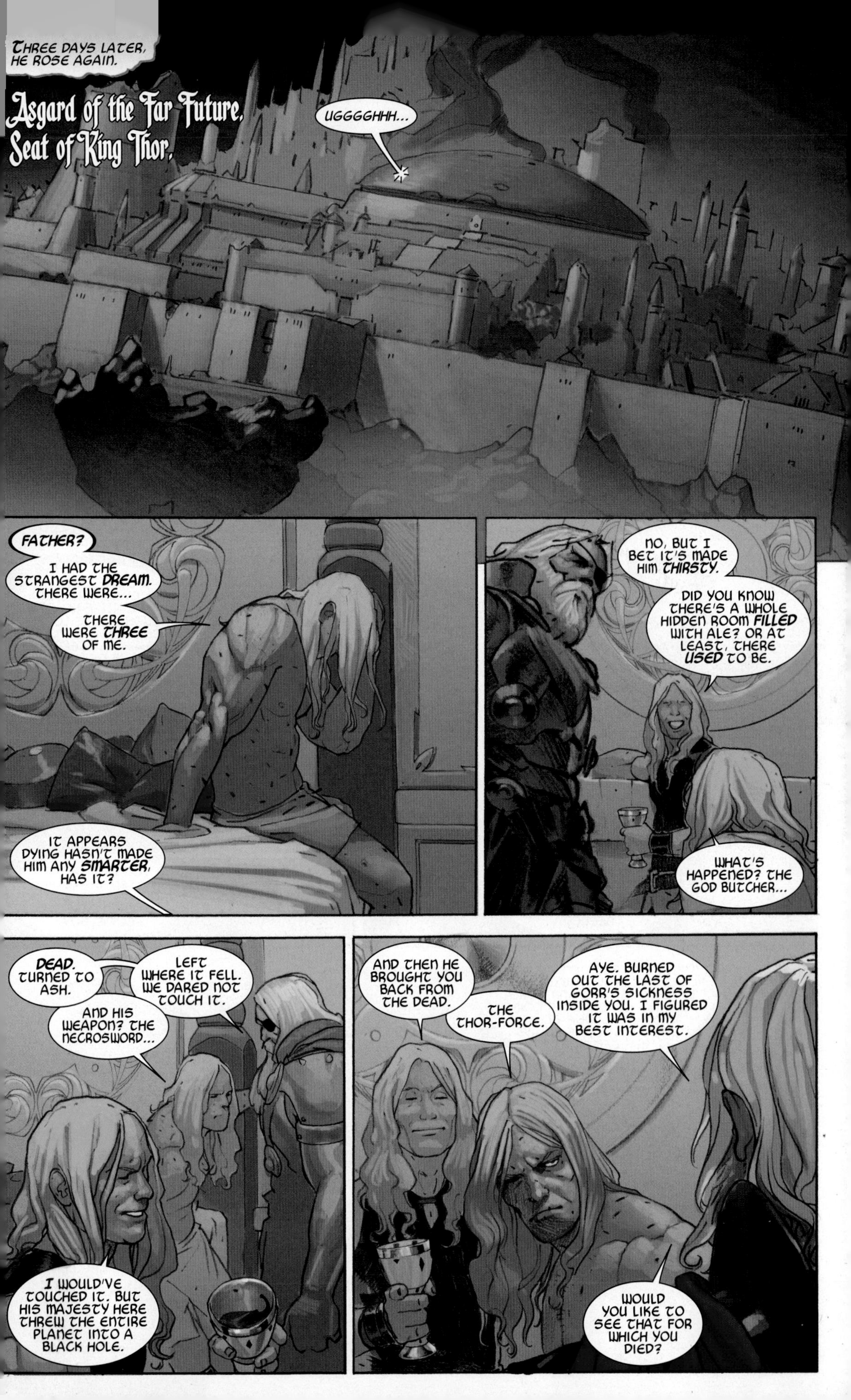
THREE DAYS LATER, HE ROSE AGAIN.
Asgard of the Far Future, Seat of King Thor.
UGGGGHHH...
FATHER?
I HAD THE STRANGEST DREAM. THERE WERE...
THERE WERE THREE OF ME.
IT APPEARS DYING HASN'T MADE HIM ANY SMARTER, HAS IT?
NO, BUT I BET IT'S MADE HIM THIRSTY.
DID YOU KNOW THERE'S A WHOLE HIDDEN ROOM FILLED WITH ALE? OR AT LEAST, THERE USED TO BE.
WHAT'S HAPPENED? THE GOD BUTCHER...
DEAD. TURNED TO ASH.
LEFT WHERE IT FELL. WE DARED NOT TOUCH IT.
AND HIS WEAPON? THE NECROSWORD...
I WOULD'VE TOUCHED IT. BUT HIS MAJESTY HERE THREW THE ENTIRE PLANET INTO A BLACK HOLE.
AND THEN HE BROUGHT YOU BACK FROM THE DEAD.
THE THOR-FORCE.
AYE. BURNED OUT THE LAST OF GORR'S SICKNESS INSIDE YOU. I FIGURED IT WAS IN MY BEST INTEREST.
WOULD YOU LIKE TO SEE THAT FOR WHICH YOU DIED?

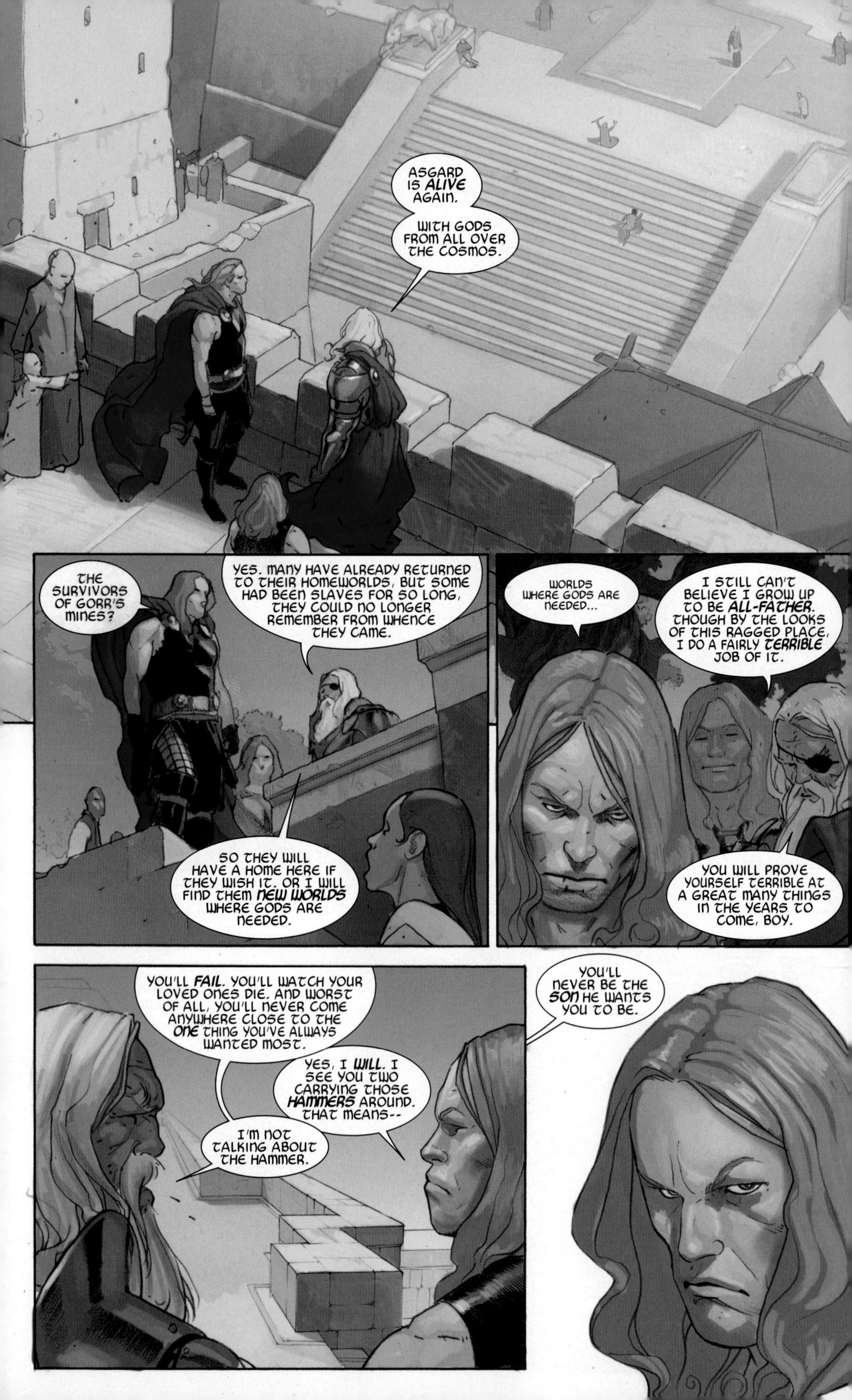
ASGARD IS ALIVE AGAIN.
WITH GODS FROM ALL OVER THE COSMOS.
THE SURVIVORS OF GORR'S MINES?
YES. MANY HAVE ALREADY RETURNED TO THEIR HOMEWORLDS, BUT SOME HAD BEEN SLAVES FOR SO LONG, THEY COULD NO LONGER REMEMBER FROM WHENCE THEY CAME.
SO THEY WILL HAVE A HOME HERE IF THEY WISH IT. OR I WILL FIND THEM NEW WORLDS WHERE GODS ARE NEEDED.
WORLDS WHERE GODS ARE NEEDED...
I STILL CAN'T BELIEVE I GROW UP TO BE ALL-FATHER. THOUGH BY THE LOOKS OF THIS RAGGED PLACE, I DO A FAIRLY TERRIBLE JOB OF IT.
YOU WILL PROVE YOURSELF TERRIBLE AT A GREAT MANY THINGS IN THE YEARS TO COME, BOY.
YOU'LL FAIL. YOU'LL WATCH YOUR LOVED ONES DIE. AND WORST OF ALL, YOU'LL NEVER COME ANYWHERE CLOSE TO THE ONE THING YOU'VE ALWAYS WANTED MOST.
YES, I WILL. I SEE YOU TWO CARRYING THOSE HAMMERS AROUND. THAT MEANS--
I'M NOT TALKING ABOUT THE HAMMER.
YOU'LL NEVER BE THE SON HE WANTS YOU TO BE.

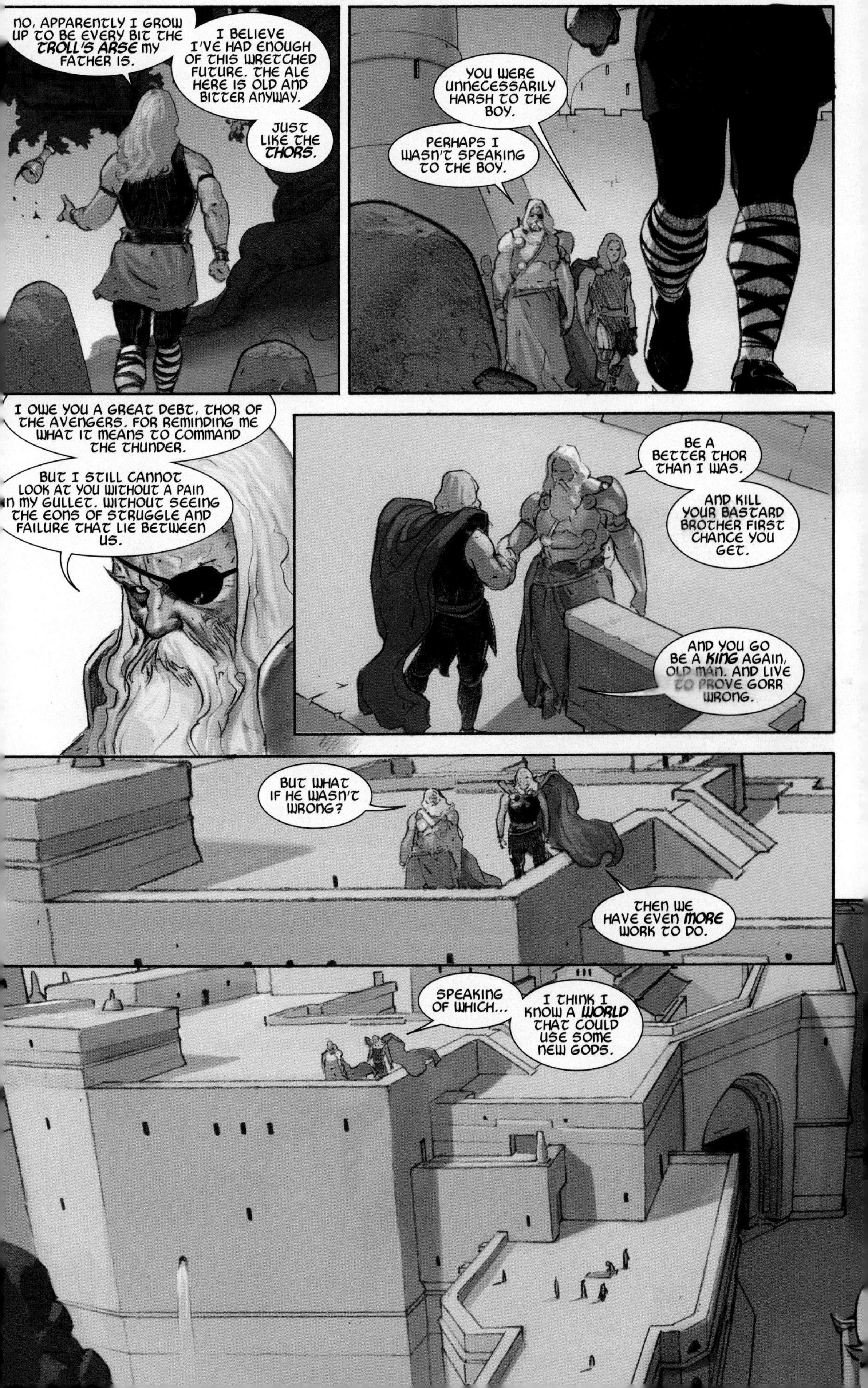
NO, APPARENTLY I GROW UP TO BE EVERY BIT THE TROLL'S ARSE MY FATHER IS.
I BELIEVE I'VE HAD ENOUGH OF THIS WRETCHED FUTURE. THE ALE HERE IS OLD AND BITTER ANYWAY.
JUST LIKE THE THORS.
YOU WERE UNNECESSARILY HARSH TO THE BOY.
PERHAPS I WASN'T SPEAKING TO THE BOY.
I OWE YOU A GREAT DEBT, THOR OF THE AVENGERS. FOR REMINDING ME WHAT IT MEANS TO COMMAND THE THUNDER.
BUT I STILL CANNOT LOOK AT YOU WITHOUT A PAIN IN MY GULLET. WITHOUT SEEING THE EONS OF STRUGGLE AND FAILURE THAT LIE BETWEEN US.
BE A BETTER THOR THAN I WAS.
AND KILL YOUR BASTARD BROTHER FIRST CHANCE YOU GET.
AND YOU GO BE A KING AGAIN, OLD MAN. AND LIVE TO PROVE GORR WRONG.
BUT WHAT IF HE WASN'T WRONG?
THEN WE HAVE EVEN MORE WORK TO DO.
SPEAKING OF WHICH...
I THINK I KNOW A WORLD THAT COULD USE SOME NEW GODS.

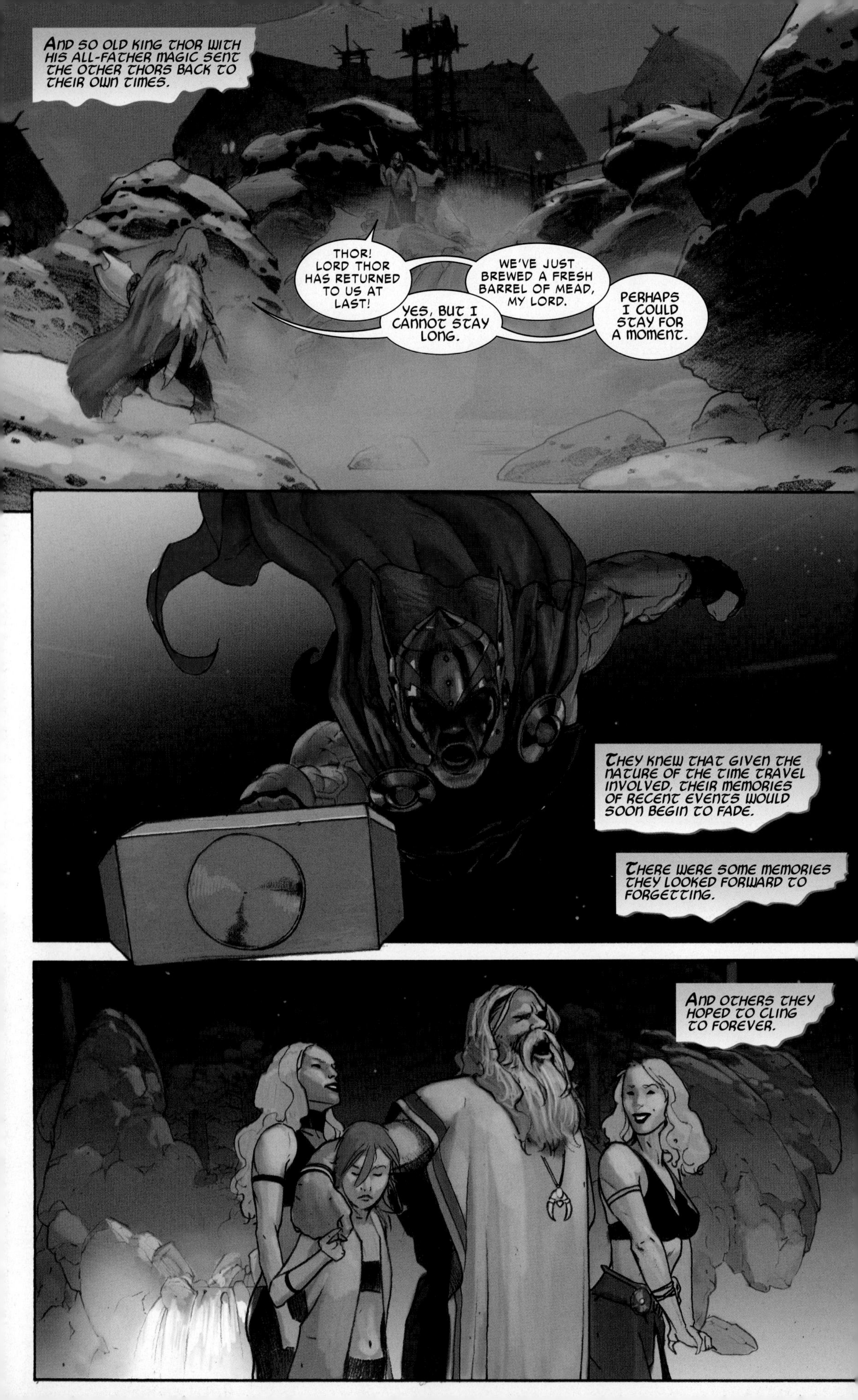
AND SO OLD KING THOR WITH HIS ALL-FATHER MAGIC SENT THE OTHER THORS BACK TO THEIR OWN TIMES.
THOR! LORD THOR HAS RETURNED TO US AT LAST!
YES, BUT I CANNOT STAY LONG.
WE'VE JUST BREWED A FRESH BARREL OF MEAD, MY LORD.
PERHAPS I COULD STAY FOR A MOMENT.
THEY KNEW THAT GIVEN THE NATURE OF THE TIME TRAVEL INVOLVED, THEIR MEMORIES OF RECENT EVENTS WOULD SOON BEGIN TO FADE.
THERE WERE SOME MEMORIES THEY LOOKED FORWARD TO FORGETTING.
AND OTHERS THEY HOPED TO CLING TO FOREVER.

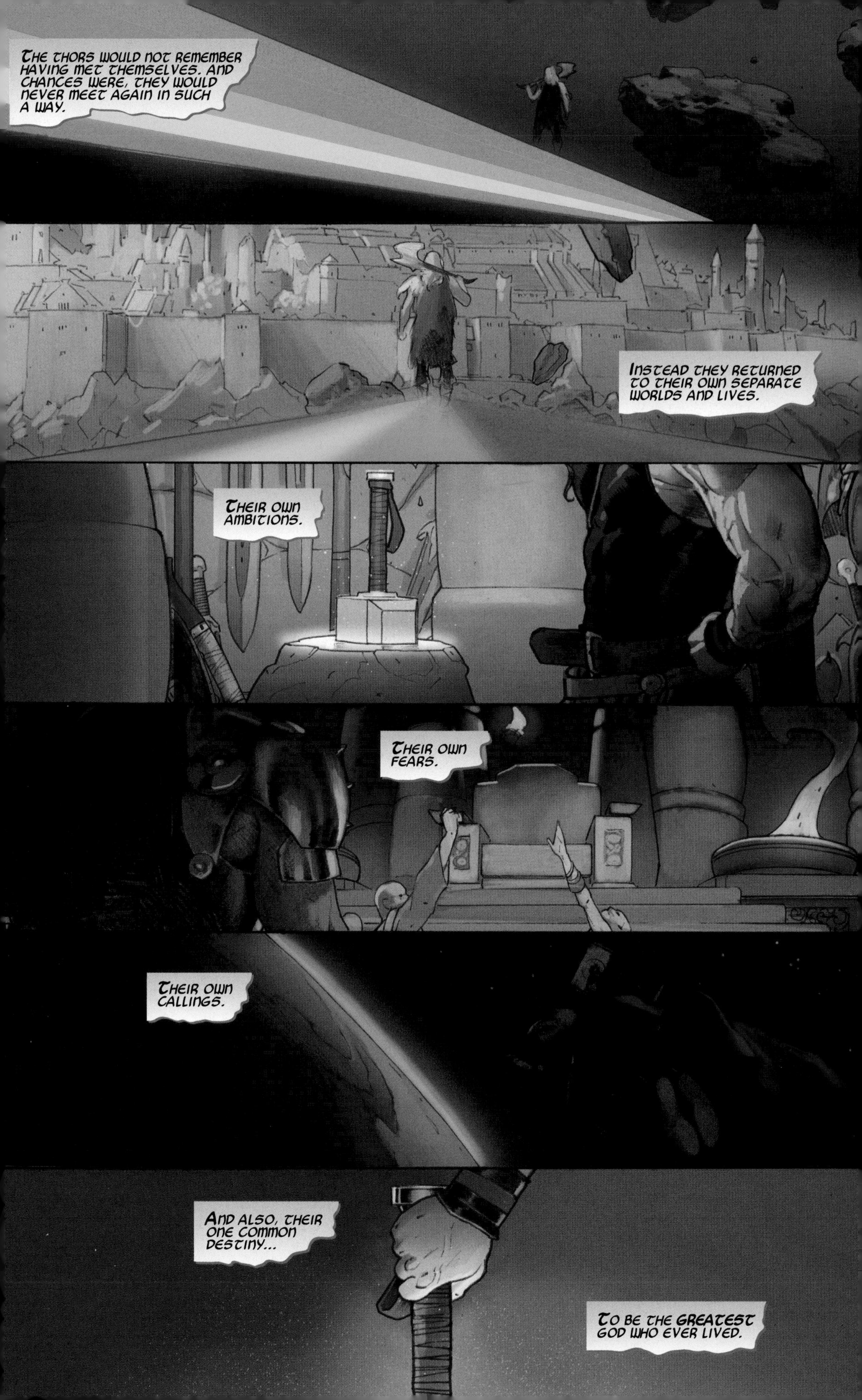
THE THORS WOULD NOT REMEMBER HAVING MET THEMSELVES. AND CHANCES WERE, THEY WOULD NEVER MEET AGAIN IN SUCH A WAY.
INSTEAD THEY RETURNED TO THEIR OWN SEPARATE WORLDS AND LIVES.
THEIR OWN AMBITIONS.
THEIR OWN FEARS.
THEIR OWN CALLINGS.
AND ALSO, THEIR ONE COMMON DESTINY...
TO BE THE GREATEST GOD WHO EVER LIVED.

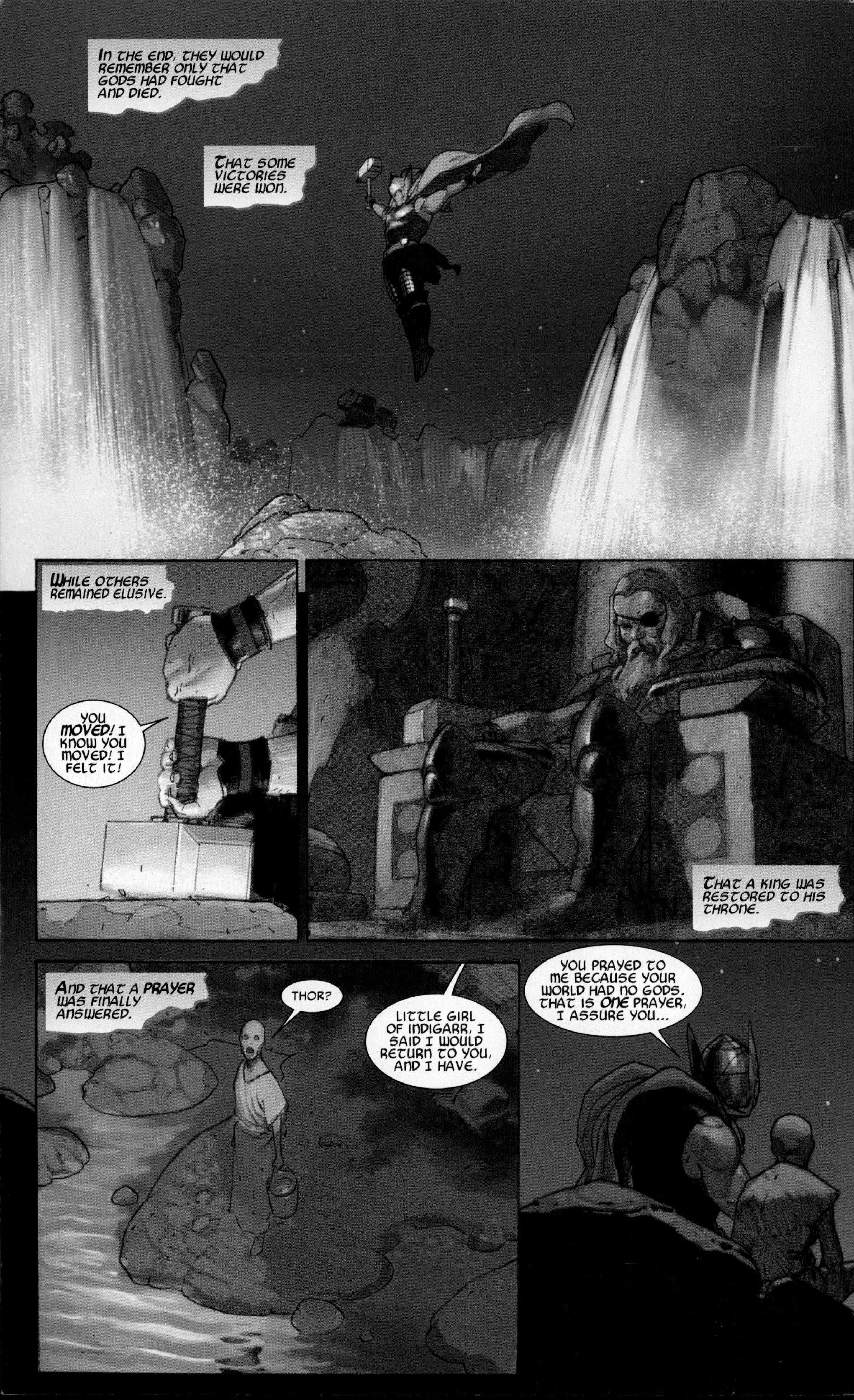
In the end, they would remember only that gods had fought and died.
That some victories were won.
While others remained elusive.
You moved! I know you moved! I felt it!
That a king was restored to his throne.
And that a prayer was finally answered.
Thor?
Little girl of Indigarr, I said I would return to you, and I have.
You prayed to me because your world had no gods. That is one prayer, I assure you...

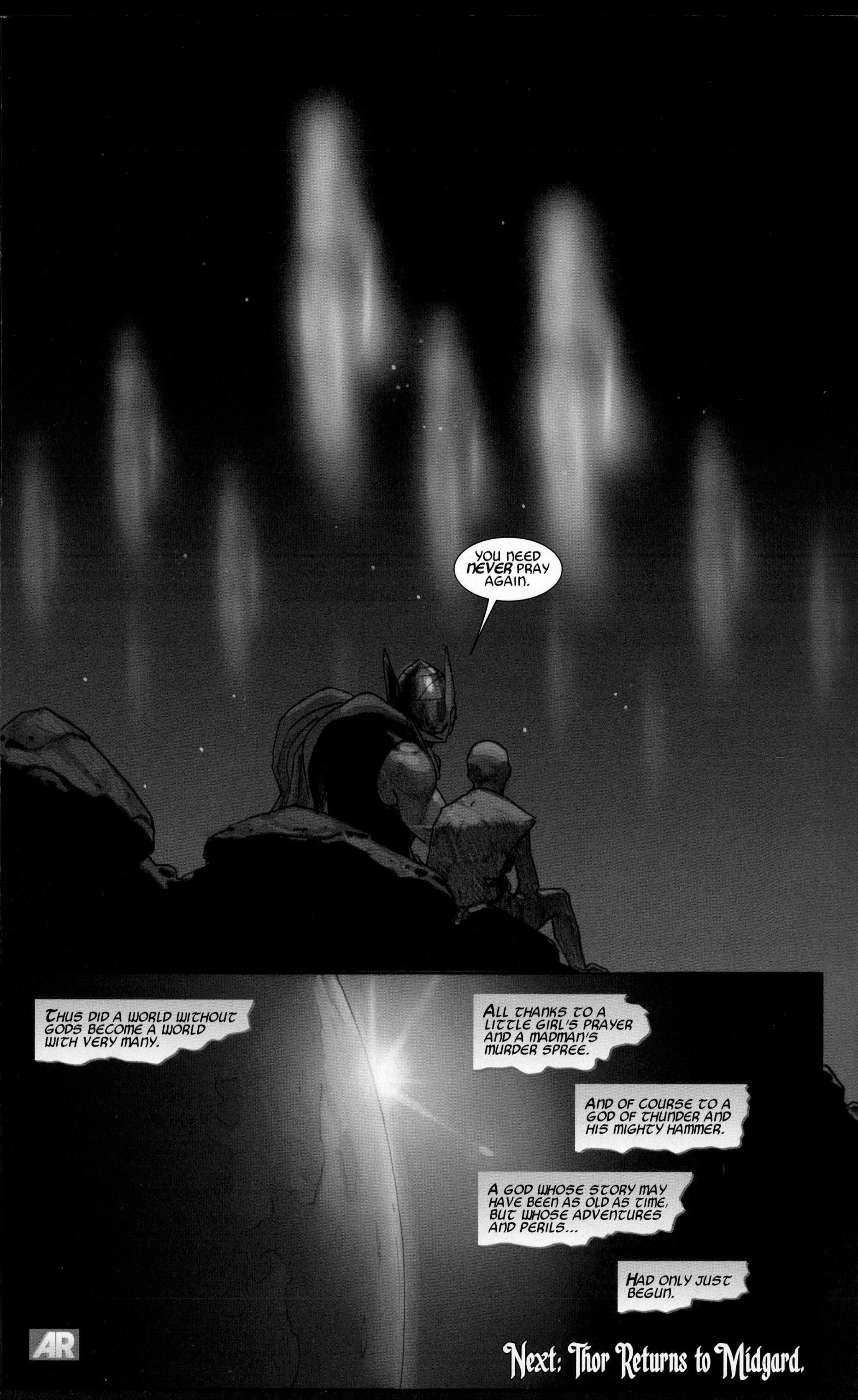
YOU NEED NEVER PRAY AGAIN.
THUS DID A WORLD WITHOUT GODS BECOME A WORLD WITH VERY MANY.
ALL THANKS TO A LITTLE GIRL'S PRAYER AND A MADMAN'S MURDER SPREE.
AND OF COURSE TO A GOD OF THUNDER AND HIS MIGHTY HAMMER.
A GOD WHOSE STORY MAY HAVE BEEN AS OLD AS TIME, BUT WHOSE ADVENTURES AND PERILS...
HAD ONLY JUST BEGUN.
Next: Thor Returns to Midgard.

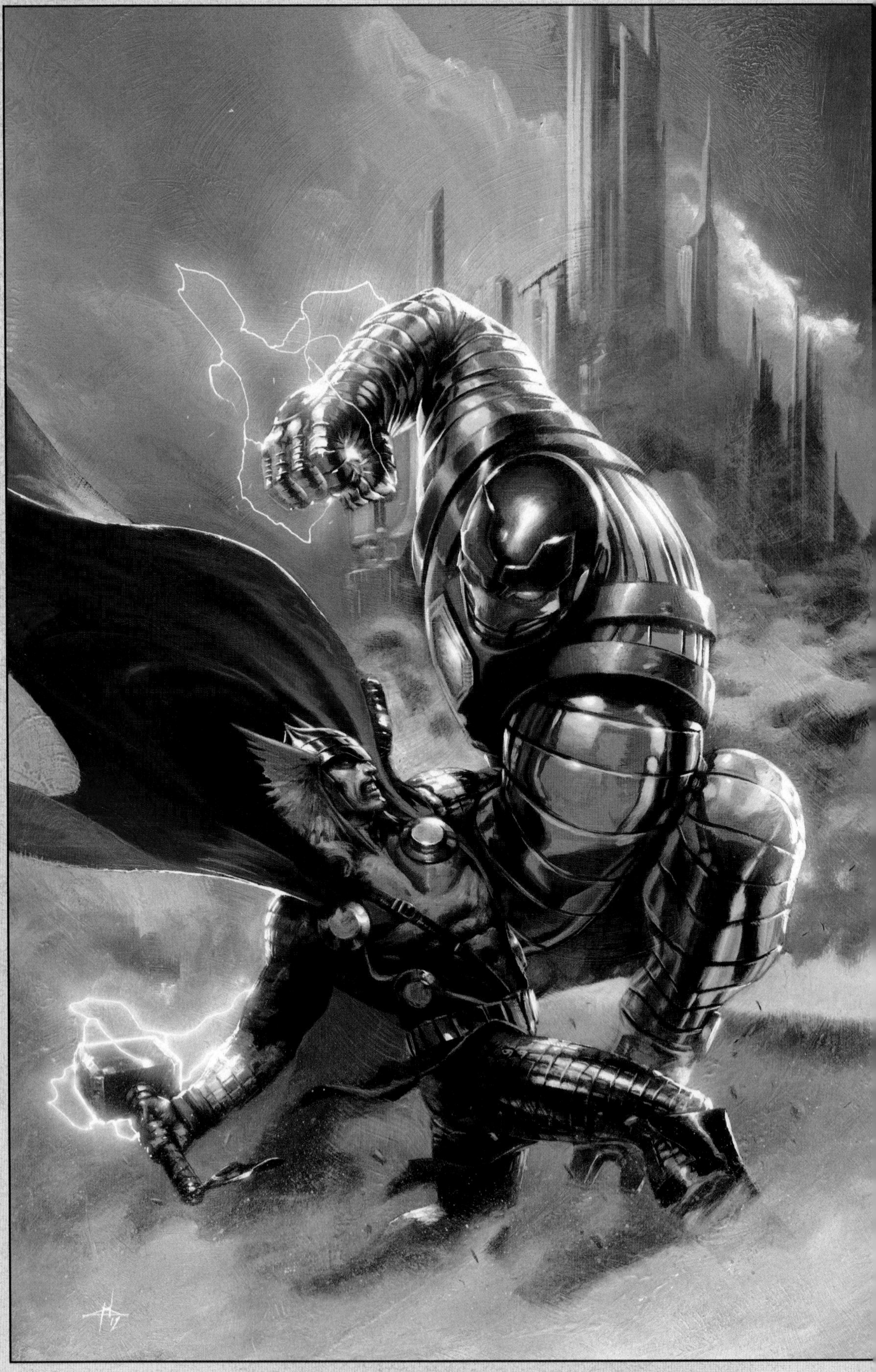

#7 MANY ARMORS OF IRON MAN VARIANT
BY GABRIELE DELL'OTTO

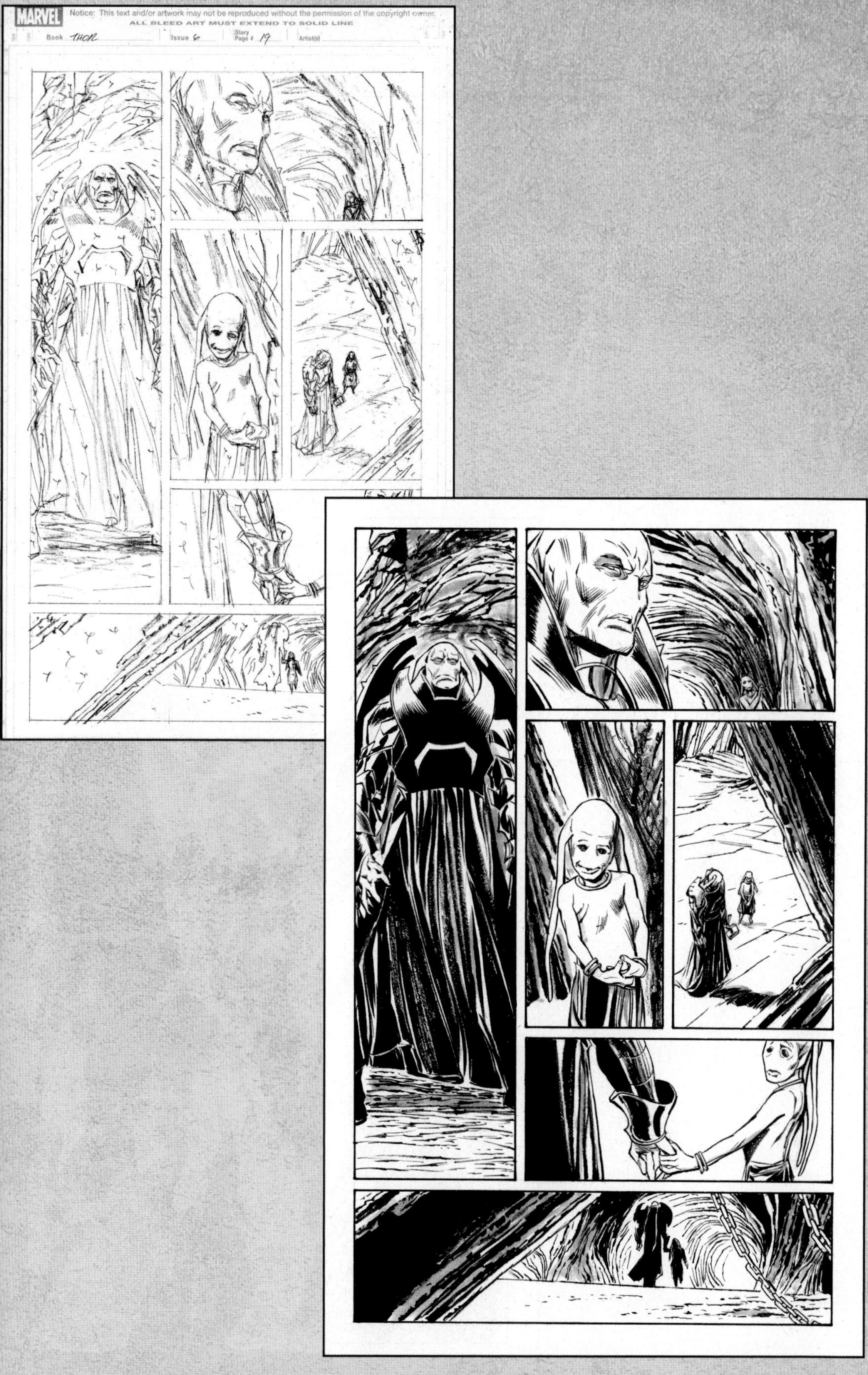
MARVEL
Notice: This text and/or artwork may not be reproduced without the permission of the copyright owner.
ALL BLEED ART MUST EXTEND TO SOLID LINE
Book THOR
Issue 6
Story Page # 19
Artist(s)

#6, PAGE 19 PENCILS & INKS
BY BUTCH GUICE & TOM PALMER

#6, PAGE 20 PENCILS & INKS
BY BUTCH GUICE & TOM PALMER

MARVEL AR AUGMENTED REALITY

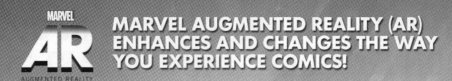

MARVEL AUGMENTED REALITY (AR) ENHANCES AND CHANGES THE WAY YOU EXPERIENCE COMICS!

TO ACCESS THE FREE MARVEL AR CONTENT IN THIS BOOK*:

1. Locate the AR logo within the comic.
2. Go to Marvel.com/AR in your web browser.
3. Search by series title to find the corresponding AR.
4. Enjoy Marvel AR!

*All AR content that appears in this book has been archived and will be available only at Marvel.com/AR – no longer in the Marvel AR App. Content subject to change and availability.

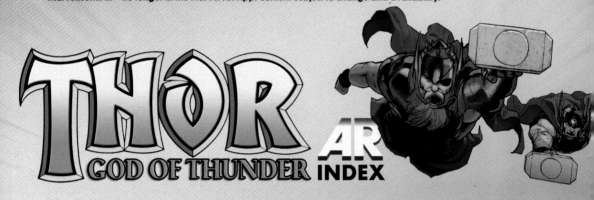

THOR GOD OF THUNDER AR INDEX